theories of mass communication

theories of mass communi-cation

4th edition

Melvin L. De Fleur *Miami University*

Sandra J. Ball-Rokeach *Washington State University*

Longman
New York & London

Theories of Mass Communication

Longman Inc., 19 West 44th Street, New York, N.Y. 10036
Associated companies, branches, and representatives
throughout the world.

Developmental Editor: Gordon T.R. Anderson
Editorial and Design Supervisor: Diane Perlmuth
Interior Design: Diana Hrisinko
Manufacturing and Production Supervisor: Anne Musso
Composition: A&S Graphics
Printing and Binding: Fairfield Graphics

Library of Congress Cataloging in Publication Data

De Fleur, Melvin Lawrence, 1923–
    Theories of mass communication.

    Includes index.
    1. Mass media—Social aspect—History. 2. Mass
media—Social aspects—United States—History.
I. Ball-Rokeach, Sandra J. II. Title.
HM258.D3 1982   302.2′3   81-8215
ISBN 0-582-28278-0   AACR2
ISBN 0-582-28277-2 (pbk.)

Manufactured in the United States of America

9 8 7 6 5 4 3 2 1

contents

In the ever-changing field of communication and media studies it is not surprising that there are few books that can seriously be called "classics," that is, works having widely recognized and enduring value. *Theories of Mass Communication* is one of those rare exceptions. Although it was originally written with the rather modest aim of providing a coherent

foreword

text for undergraduate students in an experimental course called The Sociology of Mass Communication, the book quickly won acclaim as a sound organizing framework for the study of the field. Undergraduates read the book with interest, but it soon became an essential volume in the library of nearly every graduate student in mass communication, journalism, media sociology, speech communication, and other related fields. With the book now translated into several languages, including Chinese, it is having a worldwide impact.

If the simply stated title of this book suggested a rather lifeless inventory of existing systematic scholarship, a look beyond the title page dispelled any assumption. From the first through the fourth editions, *Theories of Mass Communication* has, in the clearest terms, articulated a world view of mass communication study while creatively integrating the fragmented work of many scholars into a cohesive and understandable pattern. This book did what others had generally failed to do: It blended the explanations of human communication at its most basic level with the development of societal media systems and the process of mass communication. To understand one necessitates knowledge of the other, and that is what *Theories of Mass Communication* set out to do. Professor De Fleur (who was joined in the third and fourth editions by Professor Ball-Rokeach) did this with unusual and creative integration of material. These authors were interdisciplinary, drawing on theoretical constructs and research findings from diverse fields, but doing so in a more inclusive and open-minded manner than had heretofore been the case. While some admirable works of communication scholarship had been interdisciplinary, few had related the field of social science studies, using the tools of scientific research, with the insights and observations of historians who had blocked out their view of communication study in a quite different fashion. Looking at communication as an essential organizing feature of human society, Professors De Fleur and Ball-Rokeach take their readers through various intellectual paradigms to explain how different kinds of scholars with different assumptions and methods have attempted to assess and evaluate the field. And blessedly, they have done so with an easily grasped framework of their own vivid, highly readable prose. The book, therefore, has great value not simply for its substantive content but also for its organization and its lively delivery of information. It is a model of both substance and form.

For those of us who are the consumers of *Theories of Mass Communication*, whether as students, teachers, researchers, media professionals, or general readers, the book is an old and valued friend. It is like that special kind of friend who has important qualities and lasting values that we like and respect, but who also has the capacity for change. Perhaps because

viii

this book was in advance of others in its willingness to seek answers from many sources rather than cling narrowly to a single theory or method, it has not needed sweeping transformation, but instead, incremental change. This, I believe, helps explain the book's great influence and success. It is not the kind of work one reads, digests and forgets about. Instead, if one is to be conversant with the field, it is necessary to come back to each new edition and to study carefully its extensions of ideas, new contours of thinking, and clarifications of earlier discussions. This is, of course, the central reason why the book is so highly regarded, widely quoted, and recognized as the starting point for so much subsequent research by various scholars.

From the book we know something of the dimensions of the field of mass communication theory. This provides context and gives us a fix (as scholars or simply as readers) on where we are in our own understanding. It gives us the classical formulations of scholarly enterprise while accounting for new and sometimes trendy research directions in the field. And finally, it presents us with new theoretical directions that are worthy of probing discussion and debate as well as scientific testing. In the third edition of *Theories of Mass Communication,* for example, the authors offered an "integrated model of media effects," which became known as the De Fleur/Ball-Rokeach "dependency theory." Graduate students and their teachers rapidly grasped the importance of dependency theory as a construct for understanding the impact and effects of mass communication. The result was a variety of studies by scholars that probed into and elaborated on these ideas.

Now comes the fourth edition, not to be outdone by the third. It too brings new and stimulating perspectives. Especially notable is Chapter 1, which takes a cue from the historian and philosopher of science Thomas Kuhn and offers a broad and inclusive discussion of paradigms of general and communication scholarship that helps us plot our own intellectual history. Again, as in earlier editions, the most basic act of communication is thoughtfully related to the larger-scale activities of mass communication industries. The unpretentious originality of this set of his material gives the reader an ever-widening backdrop both for the familiar discussion that follows in succeeding chapters and for the new presentation that appears in Chapter 6.

With little fanfare, Chapter 6 launches matter-of-factly into what the authors call a "biosocial theory of human communication." Here they set forth a strikingly original product of hard thought and make it seem easy and obvious. Clearly, it is neither. *Theories of Mass Communication* presents here for the first time in published form a "trace" theory of communication that is not based on the integrated findings of the social sciences as much as on recent advances in the physical and biological sciences that have unveiled vital new information about the functioning of the human brain and the processes of memory. Because research in neuropsychiatry and other related fields has profoundly enlarged and extended our knowledge of the workings of the human brain, the authors of *Theories of Mass Communication* rightly feel that we should reassess our view of communication theory by taking into account this essential information.

The whole field of mass communication clearly benefits from the continued dedication of Professors De Fleur and Ball-Rokeach to the maintenance and development of *Theories of Mass Communication*. The book has been and continues to be intellectually satisfying in itself while serving as a scout for scholars looking for new perspectives and a master teacher for students seeking a comprehensive view of advanced conceptualization in mass communication. Because of this, it is truly worthy of the designation "classic."

Everette E. Dennis

The fourth edition of *Theories of Mass Communication* is considerably changed from earlier editions. In part these changes take into account recent advances in theory and research published in the communication literature. Perhaps more important, many changes introduce completely new material.

preface

The most significant change is the addition of new material in Chapter 6, "The Nature and Consequences of Human Communication." This chapter presents a biosocial theory of human communication and discusses the consequences of viewing the process in this manner. The basic ideas of the chapter, developed jointly by Melvin L. De Fleur and Timothy G. Plax, were first presented to communication scholars at the 1980 meetings of the International Communication Association in Acapulco, Mexico. As a result of the interest generated by that presentation, and on the basis of generous input from a number of communication theorists, we decided to include the theory and a discussion of its implications as part of the present work.

Another noteworthy addition appears in Chapter 1. It is the discussion of general theoretical paradigms that provide the basic analytical and interpretive frameworks of the social and behavioral sciences for the study of human society and human individuality. These paradigms provide the foundations for more specific conceptualizations concerning social structure, conformity, deviance, change, and process. They also provide foundations for developing specific theories about psychic organization and the psychodynamics of individual behavior. They are presented here in greatly simplified form in the hope that communication students and scholars will understand the intellectual and theoretical roots of their interdisciplinary area more fully.

These paradigms from the past are important for the present. They underlie efforts to build theories concerning a host of specific communication issues including the study of agenda-setting, needs and gratifications among media audiences, cultivation analysis regarding fear of crime, the process of persuasion, and many others. The concepts and assumptions concerning human nature and the social order used in all such attempts at theory construction are ultimately derived from these more general paradigms. Arguments can easily be generated about whether the paradigms outlined briefly in Chapter 1 are the appropriate ones, whether they are adequately summarized, or whether they need substantial revision. This is to be expected when basic paradigms remain topics of strong debate in the social and behavioral sciences in which they were formulated. But the main point for our present purposes is that these fundamental sets of competing assumptions must be made more visible to communication students and scholars if we are to increase the level of sophistication of theory development in the field.

A number of the existing chapters are improved substantially. Sandra Ball-Rokeach modernized Chapter 5, "Emerging Media Systems," and completely reworked and extended Chapter 10, "Theories of the Effects of Media Violence." In addition, she has substantially improved, brought up to date, and extended both Chapter 8, "Encountering the Media," and Chapter 11, "Basic Models of Persuasion Via the Mass Media." More important, in Chapter 12, "Toward An Integrated Model of Media Effects," she develops further a number of her original ideas concerning the Media System Dependency Theory. She shows how individuals' media system dependencies can be traced back to the structure of interdependent relations between the media and other social systems in our society. In this way, the discussion of the origins of media system dependency is flesh-out and made more specific with regard to the societal as well as the psychological determinants of individuals' dependency on the media system. It is hoped that these revisions will contribute to the theory and research efforts of those who have utilized the dependency framework in recent investigations of media and mass media effects.

Overall, the guiding principle in preparing the fourth edition has been to preserve or improve those features of *Theories of Mass Communication* that brought such favorable responses to earlier editions from communication students, faculty, researchers, scholars, and other users. The principle has led to the inclusion of new ideas and perspectives that we hope will provide additional tools for studying and thinking about mass communication.

Melvin L. De Fleur and Sandra J. Ball-Rokeach

Ancient people regarded the process of communication with reverence and awe. Such phrases as "In the beginning was the word" and "It is written" testify to the power and authority associated with oral and written language

1 media and society

in the Judeo-Christian and Islamic traditions. Similar attitudes characterized the early Chinese and the literate civilizations of the New World. Today, by contrast, reading and writing are so taken for granted that the general public voices only minor concern as communication skills decline among the nation's youth.

One reason why oral and written modes seem less important in modern life may be because we now have other forms of communication that are far more exciting to experience and that permit a more passive role on the part of the receiver. Radio, television, and the movies—at least as these operate in many countries—make limited intellectual demands on their audiences. One need not know how to speak eloquently or write coherently to participate in their communication systems. At an earlier time, the survival of one's cultural heritage depended on oral communication skills. Later, the complexities of the first written languages, and the power that could be exercised through their use, commanded deep respect for the skills of literacy.

Even though the ability to use our modern media does not provoke profound respect, mass communication is a truly significant process in modern society. The media do more than entertain us. They provide us with a flow of information that is central to our political system, our economic institution, the day-to-day life styles of each of us, and even our forms of religious expression. Because of the deep dependency of contemporary societies on their mass media, they are worthy objects of intense scholarly scrutiny. It may be far more important for us to know about the influences of mass communication on our individual and collective lives than to develop knowledge on many other issues studied by various sciences. It matters little to most of us, for example, whether the universe originated in a "big bang," how many rings there are on Saturn, when the first human forms emerged on the planet, or exactly what animals lived during the Pleistocene period. It matters a great deal whether our daily behavior is shaped by what we read or see on television. For this reason, the major goal of this book is to trace the development of the mass media of communication and set forth theoretical frameworks for the interpretation of their role in a modern society and in the lives of individuals. To do this, an appropriate beginning is to look first at societies in earlier stages of development to see the process of *cultural accumulation* by which human beings acquired increasingly effective techniques and technologies that were capable of extending their messages beyond the range of the human voice in terms of both distance and time. These events, in turn, need to be interpreted against broader perspectives of social and cultural changes that both influenced and were influenced by developments in communication.

The present chapter, therefore, looks first at societies in the oral tradition. It then discusses briefly the emergence of increasingly sophisticated procedures and media for communicating—writing, printing, mass media, and the far more complex media of the twentieth century. These events can be viewed as successive "communication revolutions" that had profound influences on the societies in which they occurred. Finally, the chapter sets forth a number of broad theoretical frameworks, drawn from the social sciences, that are used by communication scientists as sources for conceptualizing their analyses.

COMMUNICATION WITHOUT MEDIA

The origins of human speech are lost in the mists of prehistory, but our most informed guesses suggest that our remote ancestors were communicating animals living in small bands millions of years ago. At some point, they began to use simple tools and evolve a primitive division of labor based on specialization of tasks. Even then we assume that communication played a key part in defining the roles people were expected to play in that pattern of social organization and in transmitting the accumulating lore of the group of the next generation. Early human beings, in other words, were probably as dependent on communication to maintain their social structure and socialize their young as we are today.

Languages developed into increasingly complex systems of symbols during succeeding eons, with few fundamental innovations other than slow changes in general structure, grammatical complexity, and vocabulary size. During this purely oral period, the communication process was limited to the face-to-face situation. Accuracy in transmitting to large numbers was limited to the ability of human beings to remember details correctly. A single person might address a multitude, but only if that multitude was collected together in an acoustically favorable location. Aside from this, such individuals could neither extend their ideas effectively across space nor preserve them accurately through time.

It was not until writing appeared, less than 250 generations ago, that the concept of communication media could even be defined. Societies in the oral stage had no media—unless one would wish to include the air through which sound waves passed from mouth to ear. Perhaps one could say that such forms as animal representations painted on cave walls, pottery decoration, or even tattoos on the human body represented communication with "media." But if such phenomena are included as examples of communication media, then one would also have to make a place for representational dances and stylized rituals. Human beings, in other words, have been using the graphic and plastic arts for symbolic and representational purposes since they acquired speech. But such premedia, and such pictorial or stylized art forms, need to be distinguished from the kinds of symbols that are used for what we would classify as writing—substitutes for words, phrases, and ideas.

WRITING AND SOCIAL DEVELOPMENT

The development of writing, which occurred independently and at different times in several areas of the world, brought those who were able to use it two significant forms of power: It gave mankind increasing power over nature, and it provided power over people. At first, these powers were limited. As writing, the ability to use it, and media to bring messages to larger numbers of people spread, however, the two forms of power grew in significance.

Writing as Power Over Nature

One of the first uses of symbols to represent ideas in a highly systematic way was related to discoveries in astronomy. For example, the early Egyptians were faced with the need to predict the behavior of the Nile River. The valley of the Nile was the only arable land they could use for agriculture. The Nile overflowed its banks every year, flooding the agricultural plain with rich new soil. The Egyptians discovered that certain star movements tended to coincide with the period of the flood. Eventually they developed a calendar that reconciled lunar months with the solar year. Symbols and rules for using them to make calculations were devised in order to make calendrical predictions. These became a source of royal and religious power and authority.

The same was true at a later time in Central America when the Maya began to discover elaborate relationships between the growing seasons and movements of the sun, the moon, and the stars. Over a long period of time, they made astronomical observations and began to be able to predict the arrival of the rainy season and the best times for planting, harvesting, and other events. They symbolized the months and days in an elaborate code, and this provided the first step toward the development of written language. At first, pictographic symbols were used mainly to decorate tombs, temples, and monuments. These depicted the great power and authority of mighty people or gods. Once established, however, the pictorial writing method was extended, simplified, and stylized. Out of this came hieroglyphic writing.

Writing as Power Over People

From about 4000 B.C., Egyptians were recording the names of kings, accounts of wars, political events, and religious doctrines. These were still mainly carvings or decorations on stone. The Maya, on the other side of the world, independently developed hieroglyphic writing shortly after the birth of Christ. Similar events had taken place in China at an earlier time.

In ancient societies, the knowledge and power implied by the ability to use media—to read and write—was jealously guarded by rulers and high priests. Literacy was a source of great power and prestige. This principle is illustrated well in the accounts of Diego de Landa, the great missionary and sixteenth-century scholar of the Maya.

> In the high priest was the key of their learning, and it was to these matters that they dedicated themselves. They taught the computation of the years, months, days, the festivals and ceremonies, the administration of the sacraments, the fateful days and seasons, their methods of divination and their prophesies, their events and the cures for disease, and their antiquities and how to read and write with the letters and characters . . . along with the drawings which illustrate the meaning of the writings.[1]

Much the same situation prevailed in other places where writing was invented. Ordinary people could not read; they did not know how to calculate time nor how to interpret the almanacs. Such skills were reserved for the elite.

The Significance of Portable Media

The earliest forms of writing beyond mere pictorial representation of words and ideas were in the form of elaborate glyphs. As we have noted, in its beginnings such writing was generally restricted to stone carvings on temples and other monuments. The great problem here was that these "documents" were not very portable. Stone as a medium had the capacity to endure through time, but could not be transported readily across space. As ancient societies became more sophisticated, they sought media by which writing could be transported more easily.

About twenty-five hundred years before Christ, the Egyptians discovered a method of making a kind of durable paper from papyrus. Compared to stone, papyrus was extremely light. Moreover, it was much easier to write on papyrus with brush and ink than it was to chisel glyphs laboriously on stone. Papyrus is found only in the Nile Delta. Fresh green stems of the reed are cut and stripped, sliced into thick strips, laid next to one another, and pounded until they weld into a single mass, which is then pressed out and dried. Long rolls of considerable length can be prepared by joining one sheet to another. The scribe used two types of ink (black and red) and a brush made from another kind of plant. The glyphs began to be simplified as scribes required smoother, easier forms for faster writing.

Among the Maya, a similar transformation of media took place. They had discovered that long strips of light-colored bark could be pulled from the ficus tree. Long, clean strips of this inner bark, six to eight inches wide and as long as twenty feet, were removed from the trees. The strip was soaked in water and beaten to make it both uniform in thickness and pliable. The bark was then folded into a long, pleated, and very neatly trimmed book with wooden end pages to enclose it like an accordion. Hieroglyphic writing was painted on both sides and often beautifully decorated. The conquistadors were astonished to find people in the New World who lived in elaborate stone dwellings complete with libraries and books. During the conquest, thousands of these books were burned by the Spanish military in an effort to reduce the power of the priests and leaders over their people. Only a few examples remain.

The most important point in this change from heavy stone to light and portable media is that it opened the possibility for a significant change in the social organization and culture of society. The acquisition of a communication technology based upon a light and portable medium, plus a system of written symbols that could be produced quickly and read by scribes, provided necessary conditions for great social and cultural changes.[2] The whole institutional structure was influenced. For example, in Egypt by 2000 B.C., papyrus was widely used to transmit written orders and record information of various kinds. The central administration employed an army of scribes. Literacy was a valuable skill, providing a door-opener to prosperity and social rank. Scribes became a privileged class under the control of the elite. Great changes in political and religious institutions took place as a result of the ability to write and record. Libraries opened. Religious doctrines and scriptures were recorded. Schools were established to teach scribes. Even the arts and sciences began to develop. Successful treatments for diseases could be written down. Observations of numerous features of nature and their interpretations could be recorded. The human mind was freed from the burdensome task of having to remember entire cultures and reproduce them in the minds and memories of every new generation. Ideas could be stored, accumulated, and drawn upon by subsequent generations. This was the great step forward provided by the ancient communication revolutions.

THE SOCIAL MEANING OF PRINTING

Aside from writing, one of the greatest human accomplishments of all time was the development of printing. Prior to the fifteenth century, books were reproduced in Europe by preparing *manu scripti*, copies of existing books laboriously printed by hand. While it is true that many were beautiful works of art, the process often introduced errors. More important, the number of books available was severely restricted and could be purchased only by persons of considerable means. Printing brought a fantastic change. Hundreds or even thousands of copies of a particular book could be reproduced with great precision. It was a fabulous invention that astounded the literate world of the time.

The critical point in the eventual emergence of print in the Western world was when paper began to replace parchment in the Islamic world during the eighth century. (Paper originated much earlier, in China.) From there it slowly diffused to Christian Europe, particularly when the Moors occupied Spain. Not until the invention of the printing press in the fifteenth century, however, did priests, political elites, scholars, and scribes begin to lose their monopoly on reading and writing. As literacy spread, few could foresee that it would profoundly affect the directions of human history.

The Spread of Literacy

As the sixteenth century began, presses with movable type were turning out thousands of copies of books printed on paper. They were being published in all the European languages. Thus, they could be read by anyone who was literate in his or her own language. The availability of these books spurred broader interest in learning to read.

For the first time in Germany, for example, the Scriptures were available—from the press of Johannes Gutenberg—in a language other than Latin. No longer could the Roman Church carefully guard the holy writings through the use of an ancient language. The availability of the Scriptures to ordinary people in their own languages eventually led to challenges of the authority and interpretations of Rome. A new medium of communication, then, opened the way for protesting the existing religious and social structure. The rise of Protestantism led to further profound changes that have had their impact on Western society right up to the present day.

The basic idea of a newspaper developed quite early on the European continent, in England, and in the New World. The American colonial press was established for some years before the United States was formed as a new nation. The colonial press distributed small papers and pamphlets to the educated elite. Their content was, as we shall see in Chapter 2 in more detail, at a level of sophistication and taste beyond the capacities of the common citizen.[3] Nevertheless, they provided the basic form around which to develop a new kind of newspaper aimed at the broad base of artisans, mechanics, and merchants who constituted the growing middle and working classes of the emerging urban-industrial society. When a means was found to finance a cheap paper for wide distribution, and the techniques were devised for rapid printing and distribution, the first true *mass* medium was born in the form of the penny press. These events occurred in the mid-1830s in New York City. The mass newspaper was a great success, and within a very few years it spread to many parts of the world. The third decade of the nineteenth century, then, saw the technology of rapid printing and the basic idea of a newspaper combined into the first true mass medium of communication.

Two points are important in these events. First, the mass newspaper, like the other media that followed it, was an invention that occurred only after a complex set of cultural elements had appeared and accumulated within the society. Second, like almost all inventions, it represented a combination of these elements in a social setting that permitted the acceptance and widespread adoption of the newspaper as a culture complex. As a technical device, it was consistent with, and perhaps even required by, other cultural institutions of the day. The relevant institutional structure of the society in terms of economic, political, and educational processes, as well as demographic and ecological patterns, provided a setting within which the particular combination of elements represented by the penny press could emerge and flourish.

Print and the Human Condition

By the end of the nineteenth century it was becoming clear to the pioneer social scientists of the time that the new mass media—newspapers, books, and magazines, all of which were widely used in society—were bringing important changes in the human condition. These media represented a new form of communication that not only influenced patterns of interaction in communities and societies but the psychological outlooks of individuals as well. For example, the American sociologist Charles Horton Cooley stated in 1909 that there were four factors that made the new media far more efficient than the communication processes of any earlier society. The new media were more effective, he said, in terms of

Expressiveness, in that they carry a broad range of ideas and feelings
Permanence of record, or the overcoming of time
Swiftness, or the overcoming of space
Diffusion, or access to all classes of men[4]

Cooley pointed out that these features of the (print) media, which had come into existence in the nineteenth century, had forever changed the mental outlooks of those who used them:

> The general character of this change is well expressed by the two words *enlargement* and *animation.* Social contacts are extended in space and quickened in time, and in the same degree the mental unity they imply becomes wider and more alert. The individual is broadened by coming into relation with a larger and more various life, and he is kept stirred up, sometimes to excess, by the multitude of changing suggestions which this life brings to him.[5]

Thus, even before the establishment of still newer media, it was becoming clear that the Age of Mass Communication would erode the barriers of isolation among people in the world and produce significant changes in the organization and functioning of society. Or, as Cooley put it, "the new mass communication represented a revolution in every phase of life; in commerce, in politics, in education, even in mere sociability and gossip. . . ."[6]

THE COMMUNICATION REVOLUTION

With the appearance and acceptance of the mass press, the pace of human communicative activity began to increase sharply. By midcentury the telegraph became a reality. Although not a mass medium of communication, this device was an important element in a technological accumulation that would eventually lead to mass electronic media.[7] A few decades later, experiments were being carried out successfully that were prerequisite to motion pictures and wireless telegraphy. With the dawn of the twentieth century, Western society was about to experience the development of techniques of communication that had been beyond the wildest flights of imagination a century earlier. During the first decade of the new century, motion pictures became a form of family entertainment. This was followed in the 1920s by the development of household radio and in the 1940s by the beginnings of home television. By the early 1950s, radio had reached saturation penetration in American homes, with additional sets widely dispersed in automobiles. There was multiple penetration in the form of bedroom and kitchen radios, and a growing number of transistorized miniature sets. The late 1950s and early '60s saw television beginning to approach such saturation. By the 1970s it was virtually complete in the United States and progressing rapidly elsewhere. Mass communication had become one of the most significant and inescapable facts of modern life.

This brief sketch of major milestones in the ability of people to communicate shows two major facts. First, communication "revolutions" have been occurring throughout human history. Each new medium provided a means by which significant changes could be brought about in the organization of society and the accumulation of culture. Second, the rise of mass media—the most recent communication revolution—has in large part occurred very recently. Many of its major events have taken place within the lifetimes of substantial segments of the contemporary populations. Many people alive today can recall a society without household radio. For our oldest generation there were no motion pictures to see on Saturday nights during their youth. Each of these media added to the total daily availability of language-using opportunities for the average person. Thus, the accumulation of these devices within recent history has implied a dramatic increase in the pace of communicative behavior for the majority of people in Western society; a fundamental change, the impact of which remains to be fully assessed.

The entrance of the newspaper, the radio receiver, or the television set into the ordinary citizen's home represents a technological change that has greater significance for ordinary people than our largest accomplishments at the frontiers of science. With satellites and shuttles streaking through space, we may lose sight of the fact that these achievements are remote from the routine daily activities of the majority of us. The television set, however, is a technological device that has an immediate and direct impact. The children of our society spend more than twenty hours a week, on the average, viewing its offerings. The television set and the other media at the least are innovations around which human beings organize their lives in different patterns because of their presence.

ASSESSING THE NATURE AND INFLUENCE OF MASS COMMUNICATION

Although communication research scholars have not reached a full understanding of the impact that mass media are having upon the psychological, moral, economic, political, creative, cultural, and educational aspects of the ordinary individual's life, they have begun to accumulate a base of research findings that will increasingly aid in understanding these issues.

The growth of the social sciences as disciplines employing quantitative procedures and the logic of science, like the development of the mass media themselves, has occurred principally in the present century. Within that brief span, a limited number of sociologists, psychologists, journalists, speech communication scholars, and others have specialized in the dispassionate study of the role of the mass media within our society. As larger numbers of research specialists turn their attentions to this field, we may expect the generalizations growing out of such research to yield a more complete understanding of the relationship between the mass media and the societies within which they operate. In large part, discussions as to that relationship have been carried on in the past within something other than a dispassionate and objective framework. As each of the major media of communication emerged in our society, it became the object of considerable controversy and debate. These debates began when the first issue of the penny press hit the streets of New York in 1834. They continue today with respect to the role of radio, paperback books, television, comic books, magazines, and films in relation to a variety of issues.

One of the major tasks of students of mass communication in assessing this latest communication revolution, and the controversies it has caused, is to accumulate scientific findings concerning the impact of the media on their audiences. We must replace emotional speculation with valid evidence as a basis for public discussion about mass communication. The different media have variously been charged with responsibility for (1) lowering the public's cultural tastes, (2) increasing rates of delinquency, (3) contributing to general moral deterioration, (4) lulling the masses into political superficiality, and (5) suppressing creativity. This is a damning list, and if the apparently innocent devices in our living rooms are actually guilty of such monstrous influences, they should, of course, be viewed with alarm. The problem is that advocates of opposite points of view tell us that our newspapers, radios, television sets, and the like, are not insidious devices for evil but are in fact our faithful servants or even saviors in that they are (1) exposing sin and corruption, (2) acting as guardians of precious free speech, (3) bringing at least some culture to millions, (4) providing harmless daily entertainment for the tired masses of the labor force, (5) informing us of the world's events, and (6) making more bountiful our standard of living by their unrelenting insistence that we purchase and consume products to stimulate our economic institution. If such claims are true, to reject such benefactors or even to suggest that their content is uninspiring seems an act of flagrant ingratitude. Until reliable research findings can present a convincing case that the media either are or are not causally related to the claims of their critics (or champions), these controversies will continue to rage.

A second important task confronting communication scholars is to explain the basic nature of the communicative act. Many promising leads are available from such fields as semantics, cultural anthropology, sociology, and social psychology. These need to be brought together into an adequate description of human communication in general. The place of mass communication, using complex media, can then be worked out. A tentative version of such a theory of human communication is presented in this book. It explains human communication as a biosocial process that is dependent not only upon human memory but upon such factors as perception, symbolic interaction, and the cultural conventions of specific languages. The way in which mass communication is dependent upon these basic processes is also discussed. This tentative theory will need to be tested thoroughly in many research settings before it can be regarded as a valid explanation of the nature of human communication.

Another major task for those who specialize in the scientific study of the media is to provide adequate data with which to evaluate the consequences of operating mass communication systems under varying conditions of ownership or control. That is, within differing political structures, economic systems, and historical-cultural settings, the structure of the mass media themselves can be expected to take different forms. The production, distribution, and consumption of mass media content is sharply influenced by questions such as whether the society is a free-enterprise democracy, an outright totalitarian dictatorship, or something in between. Societies where mass communication systems operate under conditions of ownership and control quite different from those of the United States can provide a basis for comparative research. Similarly, studies of the historical development of inducing generalizations about the way in which the various forms of the mass media have developed under different sociocultural conditions.

The Central Questions

The task of assessing the nature and influence of mass communication is obviously one with a host of important dimensions. It clearly includes more than simply trying to discover the ways in which message content disseminated by print, film, or broadcast media influences the beliefs, attitudes, or behaviors of audiences. The task includes systematic inquiries into the nature of the historical events and the value systems that have shaped the media in a given society and have led them to produce their particular pattern of content. It includes a systematic probing into the very nature of human communication at the interpersonal level to see if the introduction of media alters the process in some critical way. And finally, that task includes the study of the ways in which mass communication can reshape social and cultural arrangements—the rules and codes of society, its language, and the role expectations that its people have of one another.

Stated more succinctly, the assessment of the nature and influence of mass communication focuses on three critical questions:

1. *What is the impact of a society on its mass media?* That is, what have been the political, economic, and cultural conditions that have led the mass media to operate in their present form?
2. *How does mass communication take place?* In other words, does it differ in principle or only in detail from more direct interpersonal communication?
3. *What does exposure to mass communication do to people?* That is, how does it influence them psychologically, socially, and culturally?

For several reasons, it is to the third question that the majority of mass communication research has in the past been addressed. The first question, although of central significance, has not captured much of the attention of research specialists and scholars. To some degree, the same is true of the second question. It appears likely, since the storm of criticism and controversy surrounding the media has been phrased largely in terms of the third of these fundamental questions, that communication researchers have been guided in their investigations less by theoretical significance than by the dictates of popular interest. Whatever the reasons for this lack of balance between these three issues, the first and second questions have received considerably less scholarly attention than the third. In several of the chapters that follow, special attention is given to discussions of ways in which the social and cultural conditions in the United States have had a role in shaping our mass media. An attempt is also made to pull together what we now know about the nature of the communicative act. In addition, considerable attention is given to the third question.

General Theoretical Paradigms

Relationships between media, society, and individuals, as posed in the three central questions above, cannot be studied in a theoretical vacuum. Research on the processes and effects of mass communication must be guided by some set of basic assumptions about the nature of society, of the human individual, and of the relationship between the two. The term *paradigm* is sometimes used to label a set of such basic assumptions. It is an old term that comes to us from the Latin word *paradigma*. In early times, before the development of modern science, it referred to any sort of "model" that could be copied, or against which something could be compared. For example, an account of the life of a virtuous man was a kind of paradigm. It could serve as a model or example of good behavior against which one's own life might be compared.

In communication science today, the term paradigm combines the idea of a model for comparison with the more complex idea of a set of fundamental assumptions of the nature of some aspect of social or psychological reality. For example, the Freudian account of the human psyche can be thought of as a paradigm. Freud's basic assumptions about our psychological realities describe conditions and relationships that supposedly underlie the psychological functioning of the human being. While not widely used in communication research, at least some investigators have used this paradigm as a broad theoretical framework to guide investigations that study consumer decisions related to advertising and the like.

The assumptions that make up a paradigm are actually *postulates*. That is, they are assumptions that provide a beginning point for deriving theoretical explanations of more specific aspects of the social or psychological phenomena whose nature is set forth in the paradigm. Such postulates are themselves not open to testing; one cannot gather empirical data that can be used to accept or reject postulated assumptions. Instead, they are taken as "givens." This is not in the sense that they are regarded as eternal verities, but only in the sense of *suppositions*. In other words, postulates are statements that specify relationships and conditions that one may choose to regard as true "for the sake of argument"—for the sake of seeing where they logically lead. Postulating a given relationship or condition is like saying "suppose it were true that" (the relationship or condition set forth does indeed accurately describe reality). What then would be the implications for some specific process or effect under study? Those implications are called by various names—corollaries, theorems, or simply derived propositions. It is these implications that serve as *hypotheses* to be tested against data gathered in research projects. Generally, then, paradigms are broad theoretical formulations. They set forth sets of postulates—assumptions that one can choose to regard as descriptions of reality, not because they forever reveal "truth," but for the purpose of obtaining derived hypotheses. Such hypotheses can then guide research on specific processes and effects.

The most important paradigms available to the communication scientist include sets of assumptions drawn mainly from psychology, social psychology, and sociology. Within these fields many sets of postulates have been formulated concerning the nature of society and human nature. From sociology, the three that are of the greatest significance to the study of relationships between the media, society, and the process of mass communications are those that give a central role to (1) the processes by which a society maintains social *stability*, (2) the processes by which it *changes* over time, (3) the nature and significance of social *conflict*, or (4) the forms of interpersonal interaction by which human beings share *meanings*. The more technical terms associated with these distinctive paradigms are *structural functionalism*, *social evolution*, the *social conflict model*, and *symbolic interactionism*. If the focus of communication research is at the level of individual behavior, such as selecting, perceiving, and being influenced by media messages, then one of the psychological paradigms is generally used. There are many to choose from. They range from behavioristic learning theories to psychoanalytic formulations. For the most part, however, the psychological paradigm that has been most widely used in communication research is the *cognitive orientation*, which stresses such concepts as attitudes, beliefs, perception, needs, and gratifications. In the sections that follow, the main postulates of these sociological and psychological paradigms are summarized very briefly.[8] Their significance to the study of mass communication will be made abundantly clear in remaining chapters of the book.

Structural Functionalism   The idea that the organization or structure of a society provides the source of its stability is as old as social philosophy. In his *Republic*, Plato posed the analogy between society and an organism, a system of related parts in dynamic equilibrium. In the ideal society he described, each category of participants in the social structure performed activities that contributed to the overall attainment of social harmony.[9] This general idea was passed on in Western thought and became the central framework for the analysis of societies by the early sociologists. Auguste Comte made the organic analogy central to his conceptions of society. Herbert Spencer organized his entire social philosophy around the idea.[10] The early modern sociologists, such as Emile Durkheim, developed the orientation further at the end of the nineteenth century. The idea of a society as a dynamic system of repetitive activities also became important in the analyses of primitive societies by such anthropologists as Bronislaw Malinowski, and (later) A. R. Radcliffe-Brown.[11] In recent times, the set of assumptions involved in structural functionalism continues to play a significant role in the development and debates of modern sociology through the writings of Robert Merton, Talcott Parsons, and many others.

The term *structure*, of course, refers to the manner in which the repetitive activities of a society are organized. Family behavior, economic activity, political activities, religion and magic, and many other forms of societal activities are highly organized from a behavioral point of view. The term *function* refers to the contribution a particular form of repetitive activity makes in terms of maintaining the stability or equilibrium of the society. Many versions of this general theoretical orientation for studying social processes have been advanced. These versions each list somewhat different sets of assumptions and include many debates over which are most useful. Contemporary anthropologists and sociologists are still thrashing out which is the best version and what are the advantages and disadvantages of structural functionalism in all its forms.

Perhaps the clearest statement of the assumptions of classic structural functionalism remains that set forth by Robert Merton in 1957.[12] He reviewed the many existing versions and consolidated them into a brief but succinct statement. While Merton himself had serious criticisms of this classic orientation, he summarized the postulates of structural functionalism concerning the nature of society as follows:

1. A society can best be thought of as a system of interrelated parts; it is an organization of interconnected, repetitive, and patterned activities.
2. Such a society naturally tends toward a state of dynamic equilibrium; if disharmony occurs, forces will arise tending to restore stability.
3. All of the repetitive activities in a society make some contribution toward its state of equilibrium; in other words, all persisting forms of patterned action play a part in maintaining the stability of the system.
4. At least some of the patterned and repetitive actions in a society are indispensable to its continued existence; that is, there are functional prerequisites that fill critical needs of the system without which it would not survive.

But what does such a set of assumptions have to do with the study of mass communication? The media and the process of mass communication are patterned and repetitive actions in the social system of the society in which they operate. The structural dependencies that exist between the media and other social systems not only affect the everyday workings of our society, but also, as discussed in Chapter 12, influence the way in which individuals use the media in everyday life. They make some contribution to the social equilibrium of that society. In other words, they have consequences for the society as a whole. Indeed, a good case could be made that mass communication could be listed among those indispensable components of the social structure without which contemporary society, as we know it, could not continue. On the other hand, mass communication may be *dysfunctional*, contributing to disharmony rather than stability, if it has the effect of stirring people to various forms of deviant behavior. A number of such issues are addressed in later chapters.

The Evolutionary Perspective   One of the difficulties with the structural functional paradigm is that it stresses stability and equilibrium in society when it is obvious to even the most casual observer that urban industrial societies undergo constant change. One of the oldest sets of assumptions about the basic nature of society is one that focuses centrally on change. The *evolutionary* paradigm was formulated during the founding years of sociology. It also has played a part in the theoretical development of anthropology, economics, and social philosophy. This paradigm rests heavily on the so-called organic analogy—at least in its classic form. The idea here is that society is both organized like and develops like a biological organism. This is not to imply that either classical or contemporary evolutionists maintain that society *is* a biological organism; rather, the idea is that it *resembles* such an organism in its structure and processes of change. Depending upon which version of the evolutionary paradigm one refers to, other assumptions are also made. In its classical form (as advanced by Herbert Spencer) this paradigm was the basis for advocating a *laissez-faire* political policy that maintained it was foolish to try to change a society through legislation, welfare programs, and the like, because the immutable laws of social evolution would inevitably lead the society to a more perfect condition.[13] Most of the ideas of the evolutionary paradigm were formulated before Darwin advanced his famous hypothesis about the origins of species. Nevertheless, because of the similarity between the two sets of ideas, it is often referred to as "social Darwinism."

Today, there are many variations of the earlier paradigm.[14] Essentially they represent an attempt to account for societal change within some set of natural laws (as opposed to attributing such change to divine intervention, random happenstance, and so forth). The social mechanisms of change that appear most often in evolutionary paradigms are natural selection, survival of the fittest, and the inheritance of acquired characteristics. These sound very biological and do appear in strictly biological accounts of evolution. Nevertheless, they have social counterparts in that they can be used to think about the incorporation of new standardized forms of behavior into a society and the disappearance of earlier forms from the culture passed on from one generation to the next. As is perfectly obvious, modern societies constantly incorporate new social forms, ranging from domestic practices (e.g., live-in lovers) to new kinds of business organizations (e.g., multinational corporations). Such innovations are adopted and become accepted because they permit at least some people to achieve goals that they value more effectively than the behavior forms that were previously available. Therefore, some process of natural selection, survival of the fittest, and passing on of the new social form underlies the constant unfolding of society into increasingly differentiated and specialized behavioral patterns. At the risk of considerable oversimplification we can summarize the evolutionary paradigm as including such assumptions as the following:

1. Society can best be thought of as a set of interrelated parts; it is an organization of interconnected, repetitive, and patterned activities.
2. Such a society constantly undergoes change, with its social forms becoming increasingly differentiated and more specialized.
3. New social forms are invented or borrowed from other societies by individuals seeking more effective ways to reach goals that they regard as important.
4. Those social forms that do in fact help people achieve their goals more effectively, and that do not clash with existing values, are adopted, retained and become stable parts of the developing society; conversely, less effective forms are abandoned.

Specifically, how are such assumptions about societal development significant in the study of mass communication? Their importance becomes clear when one examines the history of the media. During that history, many people saw the need for communication systems that were swifter and that could reach larger audiences. To reach these goals, many new social forms were tried as means for making use of developing technologies. Some of these were abandoned. Others were selected, survived, and passed on to later generations. In other words, the development of mass communication has been an evolutionary process, both in terms of its mechanical and scientific technology and the social forms necessary for making effective societal use of that technology to meet goals regarded as important by those in decision-making roles.

The Social Conflict Model   A third paradigm widely used by social scientists assumes that conflict rather than stability or evolution is the most important social process. The idea that a society consists of social elements in conflict is at least as old as the belief that social arrangements are the basis of social stability. The notion that social conflict is the master process in society is another attractive alternative to a commitment to the position that equilibrium is basic. Like the evolutionary paradigm, it is attractive because of the obvious fact of social change, which is very difficult to deal with within a structural functional orientation.

To ancient philosophers it was apparent that many kinds of change were brought about as a result of opposing forces. Much of their thinking was in terms of such concepts as true and false, good and evil; but in the world of ideas they saw new forms emerging from the interplay of antagonistic forces. This conception, of resolving conflict to attain something new, came to be called a *dialectic* process. Plato used a dialectic format in his discussions of various issues in the *Republic*. For centuries the idea continued to be a part of the study of logic, to describe the way in which knowledge could be obtained through a process of debate and examination of opposing views.

Social conflict as a basic human process also has played a key role in social philosophy. Hobbes made it central to his analysis of the origins of sovereign power in his *Leviathan*.[15] It became the central thesis of the social contract theorists. However, it was from the writings of G. W. Hegel, Karl Marx, and Frederick Engels that the ideas of social conflict and the dialectic process were brought together into an analysis of societal change.[16] Marx is generally thought of by contemporary social scientists as the father of the conflict model of society and social change. Indeed, his sociopolitical theories provide well-known analyses of the way that new societal forms supposedly arise from struggles between the "haves" and "have nots." But one does not have to be committed to Marxian ideologies to assume that social conflict can be a significant source of social change.

One of the clearest statements of the social conflict model is that made by Ralph Dahrendorf in 1958.[17] He reviewed the issues and debates and posed a model of society that incorporates conflict and change as the central issues. In more recent times debates continue as to how such a model can best be formulated and used to derive hypotheses and theories about more specific social processes, including analyses of communication. Essentially, however, the contemporary conflict model can be simplified into the following basic assumptions:

1. A society can best be thought of as consisting of categories and groups of people whose interests differ sharply from one another.
2. All these components of society attempt to pursue their own interests in competition with others or to preserve their interests by resisting the competitive efforts of others.
3. A society so organized constantly experiences conflict as its components try to attain new gains or to preserve their interests; conflict, in other words, is ubiquitous.
4. Out of the dialectic process of competing and conflicting interests

comes an ongoing process of change; societies are not in a state of equilibrium but are ever-changing.

Why is such a paradigm important in the study of mass communication? The mass media in America are competitive enterprises devoted to making a profit. They compete with one another and pursue their interests in a complex web of restraints placed on them by the courts, federal regulative agencies, the moral codes of society, their own organizational structures, and the advertisers who support them. In addition, the press and government have a long history as adversaries. There are other arenas of conflict as well. These include controversies concerning the rights of the press versus the rights of citizens to privacy; the rights of government to protect its secrets in times of national emergency; the rights of citizens to a fair trial; the rights of consumers to be protected from false claims in advertising; and so on. Through legal battles over the interpretation of the First Amendment, and other forms of conflict, the process and patterns of mass communication in American society are constantly being reshaped. They are not now and have never been in a total state of stability. In other words, the social conflict model offers a fruitful theoretical paradigm for conceptualizing and studying significant issues concerning our changing system of mass communication.

Symbolic Interactionism   Still another way of viewing the social order is to place an emphasis on the critical role of language in both the development and maintenance of society and in shaping the mental activities of the individual. This is a more social-psychological approach. It emphasizes the relationships between individual mental activities and the social process of communicating. Although it has ancient sources, this approach has been developed in modern times mainly by social psychologists whose training has been in sociology. Writing in the late 1600s, John Locke in his *Essays on Human Understanding* described the relationship between words, their internal meanings among individuals, and the bonds between people that form society. Language, he said, is "the great Instrument, and common Tye of Society."[19] During the eighteenth century, such writers as Immanuel Kant developed the theme that human beings react not to the world as it exists in the sense of objective reality but to the world they construct in their minds. This distinction between the world outside and the constructions in our heads was further refined at the end of the nineteenth and in the early twentieth centuries in the writings of the American pragmatists, such as John Dewey, William James, and Charles Pierce.[20] They held the view that people collectively shape ideas about the environments with which they cope. One of their basic assumptions was that the significance of objects or situations resides not in their objective nature but in the behavior of people toward them.

In the present century, two writers stand out as the founders of contemporary symbolic interactionism, the sociologist Charles Horton Cooley and the philosopher George Herbert Mead.[21] Cooley was one of the most significant scholars in finally resolving the ancient "nature-nurture" debate. He developed an impressive case for the contemporary view that people acquire their human nature rather than inherit it in their genes. His ideas about the subjective nature of social life and the processes by which people develop beliefs about themselves and others as guides to social behavior were instrumental in reversing thinking about the role of instincts in human behavior. George Herbert Mead developed an elaborate analysis of the central nature of language symbols in individual and collective human life. Today the paradigm continues to be elaborated, debated, and refined. Many of the modern versions of what should be the proper assumptions of symbolic interactionism can be found in the anthology developed by Jerome G. Manis and Bernard N. Meltzer.[22] At the risk of vast simplification, however, the central assumptions of this paradigm can be set forth as follows:

1. Society can best be thought of as a system of meanings. For individuals, participation in the shared meanings linked to the symbols of a language is the interpersonal activity from which emerges stable and commonly understood expectations that guide behavior into predictable patterns.
2. From a behavioral point of view, both social and physical realities are labeled constructions of meanings; as a consequence of people individually and collectively participating in symbolic interaction, their interpretations of reality are both socially conventionalized and individually internalized.
3. The bonds that unite people, the ideas that they have of others, and their beliefs about themselves are personal constructions of meanings emerging from symbolic interaction; thus, the subjective beliefs people have of one another and themselves are the most significant facts of social life.
4. Individual conduct in a given action situation is guided by the labels and meanings people associate with that situation; thus, behavior is not an automatic response to stimuli of external origin but is a product of subjective constructions about self, others, and the social requirements of the situations.

How are such matters related to the study of mass communication? Clearly, the media are a central part of the communication processes of modern societies. They provide in their portrayals and accounts interpretations of reality that their audiences internalize. People can develop subjective and shared constructions of reality from what they read, hear, or view. Thus, their personal and social behavior can be shaped in part by media-provided interpretations of social events and issues concerning which people have few alternative sources of information. This is one of the most complex, but most important, paradigms used in communication research. It is essential in understanding long-range indirect influences of mass communication on individuals and society.

Psychological Frameworks From the complex discipline of psychology comes a number of competing paradigms formulated to describe and explain the patterning of individual human behavior. Psychological paradigms are useful primarily with respect to individualistic aspects of central question number 3 that we listed earlier (i.e., What does exposure to mass communication do to people?). They are important in conceptualizing possible explanations about the relationship between mass media messages and such phenomena as attitudes, patterns of perception, imitating the behavior of models, decision making, and overt behaviors like voting and buying. Psychological paradigms are of less significance in studying such social issues as the historical development of the media, their bureaucratic organization, day-to-day operations, conflicts with other institutions in society, or processes of change. Nevertheless, insofar as mass media messages can stimulate responses in individuals, psychological paradigms offer basic assumptions about the psychological nature of the human being that help in understanding why a given stimulus is likely to elicit a particular form of response. Several of these paradigms are listed below to show the richness of psychology as a field that has developed numerous models for the interpretation of individual behavior patterns.

A continuing focus of some psychologists is on the *neurobiological* approach. This paradigm identifies the brain and other nerve systems as the most significant bases from which to seek explanations of human conduct.[23] This approach is closely related to the *comparative* perspective. This view of human nature stresses the continuity between *homo sapiens* and other forms of animal life. Psychologists working within the comparative perspective feel that patterns of behavior found in animals are likely to have counterparts in human beings, and vice versa.[24] The implication is that these similarities arise from the principles of biology shared by all

THEORIES OF MASS COMMUNICATION

living creatures. Such paradigms are not central to the study of mass communication effects.

At the heart of much contemporary psychology is the *behavioral* approach. There are several versions.[25] Here the focus is on externally observable phenomena as opposed to "mental" processes. Behaviorists distrust explanations that require assumptions about thought, belief structures, or other unobservable inner activities or processes. Behaviorism is a stimulus-response (S-R) psychology. It studies the stimuli that elicit particular forms of response—in the sense of clearly observable action. It attempts to understand the patterns of rewards and punishments that maintain these responses, and the modifications in behavior that occur when changes take place in reward/punishment sequences. Behaviorism incorporates many of the basic assumptions of the comparative perspective and is generally compatible with the neurobiological approach.

In contrast to behaviorism stressing overt and observable actions is the *psychoanalytic* paradigm, which comes in several variations.[26] Generally, these give a central place to individual mental activities, but they stress unconscious processes. The human psychological system is seen as a set of components (e.g., id, ego, superego) in conflict for the control of behavior; in this paradigm, overt conduct and communication behavior are less important in their own right than is their significance as data for making inferences about the unconscious aspects of personality that shape the behavior of the individual. The psychoanalytic paradigms were originally devised as aids in therapeutic treatment for people with neuroses or other mental problems. While they have been expanded and advanced as general models of the psychological structure and functioning of human individuals, they remain controversial. Again, neither classic behaviorism nor psychoanalytic paradigms have been particularly useful in media studies.

More significant to the study of communication is a paradigm that openly gives a central place to the mental activities of normal human beings in shaping their conduct. There are several versions, but collectively they can be called the *cognitive orientation*.[27] This view of human nature has been developed mainly in the present century by social psychologists whose training is in psychology rather than sociology. Many of its concepts have emerged from impressive experimental research. Unlike symbolic interactionism, however, the cognitive approach does not place its strongest emphasis on language and meanings. It stresses a variety of concepts and processes that are said to be part of the personality structure of all human beings. A major question is how these operate in balance or conflict to shape behavioral responses. The assumptions of the cognitive approach are said to be helpful in understanding many aspects of the communication process. Its basic postulates can be summarized as follows:

1. Individual members of a society can best be thought of as active receivers of sensory input, whose behavioral responses to such stimuli are shaped by inner mental (cognitive) processes.
2. Cognitive processes enable individuals to transform sensory input in various ways: code it, store it, interpret it selectively, distort it, and retrieve it for later use in decisions about behavior.
3. The cognitive processes that play key parts in shaping an individual's behavior include perception, imagery, belief systems, attitudes, values, tendencies toward balance in such factors, plus remembering, thinking, and numerous other mental activities.
4. The cognitive components of a given individual's mental organization are products of his or her prior learning experiences, which may have been either deliberate, accidental, social, or solitary.

The cognitive approach has wide uses in the study of the effects of communication on individuals, particularly in attempting to understand how messages are perceived; how patterns of action are learned from media portrayals; and how attitudes, knowledge, values, and behavioral probabilities can be altered through persuasion. Contemporary research efforts to understand what needs are met by mass communication content and the gratifications provided for media audiences also represent the use of this paradigm.

The existence of such a large number of theoretical paradigms from which to choose offers great advantages for the communication scientist. Each provides a set of basic assumptions about the human condition, either at the individual or the social level. They provide broad descriptions of the organization, functioning, or processes of change in society, or about the underlying psychological factors that shape individual human conduct. The fact that there may be several competing paradigms that purport to explain the same thing (e.g., evolution vs. conflict theory to explain social change, or behaviorism vs. cognitive orientations to explain individual behavior) should not be regarded as a source of confusion. One need not decide which is "really true." In a sense they are all "true"; or any given one can be supposed true to provide a convenient set of theoretical tools from which more specific approaches to understanding and explaining particular communication phenomena can be derived and formulated. For example, in Chapter 7 the functionalist approach is used to derive an explanation of the persistence of low intellectual levels in media content, in spite of intense efforts by critics to get the media to raise their standards. In Chapter 5 the symbolic interactionist paradigm provides the basis, along with other theoretical frameworks, for developing a detailed and specific theory of the nature of human communication. In the analysis of the history of the media, both the evolutionary and conflict paradigms provide frameworks for understanding. Chapter 12 integrates the structural functional, conflict, symbolic interactionist, and cognitive paradigms around the phenomenon of media effects.

In the past, many communication scholars and researchers failed to raise the question as to what theoretical paradigm they are assuming in formulating their hypotheses and designing their investigations. As the field has matured, however, it has become increasingly important to clarify the underlying theoretical assumptions that explicitly or implicitly guide one's investigation. There are a number of reasons why this is so critical. Some researchers simply plunge ahead in data gathering, making use of a mixed bag of concepts drawn unsystematically from several theoretical paradigms. Such a naive procedure does little to build an accumulation of well-tested hypotheses that can explain the phenomena under study as special cases of more general propositions. Even worse are the "devotees." These are researchers who adopt a given paradigm as the True Faith and naively assume that it provides the only legitimate guide to significant research hypotheses and problems. Often, they are unaware that alternative paradigms even exist. Still others make use of theoretical formulations that are themselves derived from underlying paradigms that are not well understood by the researcher. The result is that some specific formulation, such as "cognitive dissonance theory," is dragged into a research problem by the scruff of the neck, often in an arena for which the formulation was never intended. A far better procedure would be to begin designing a research strategy from the base of a particular paradigm or combination of paradigms relevant to the issues that will be studied and then formulate a lower-level theory intended from the outset to describe and explain the issues to be investigated.

Generally, then, communication research can be made more theoretically sophisticated by developing clear relationships between the particular study at hand and the kinds of paradigms that have been discussed. There is always the additional possibility, of course, that completely new paradigms will emerge from the efforts of communication scholars, just as they have from the work of social and behavioral scientists in the past.

NOTES

1. Frey Diego de Landa, *Relacion de las Cosas de Yucatan*, ed. with notes by A. M. Tozzer, *Papers of the Peabody Museum*, vol. 18 (Cambridge, Mass., 1941). Original written in 1566.
2. An excellent discussion of media and change in ancient societies is found in Harold A. Innis, *Empire and Communications* (Toronto: University of Toronto Press, 1972). See esp. p. 14.
3. Edwin Emery, *The Press and America* (Englewood Cliffs, N.J.: Prentice-Hall, 1972).
4. Charles Horton Cooley, *Social Organization* (Boston: Charles Scribner's Sons, 1909) p. 63.
5. Ibid., p. 64.
6. Ibid., p. 65.
7. For detailed definitions and discussions of the distinctions between *media, mass media, human communication* and *mass communication,* see Melvin L. De Fleur and Everette E. Dennis, *Understanding Mass Communication* (Boston: Houghton Mifflin, 1981), pp. 6–23.
8. These brief summaries do little more than sketch the central ideas of each paradigm in an introductory manner. Each is, in fact, a complex set of propositions that has generated wide controversy. The references cited in connection with each provide entry points for exploring the substantial literature associated with each paradigm.
9. *The Republic of Plato,* trans. Frances M. Cornford (London: Oxford University Press, 1954).
10. Auguste Comte, *The Positive Philosophy*, trans. Harriet Martineau (London: George Bell and Sons, 1915); see vol. 2, Herbert Spencer, *The Principles of Sociology* (New York: D. Appleton, 1898).
11. Bronslaw Malinowski, "Anthropology" *Encyclopedia Britannica*, First Supplementary Volume (London and New York, 1926), pp. 132–33; A. R. Radcliffe-Brown, *Structure and Function in Primitive Society* (Glencoe, Ill.: Free Press, 1956).
12. Robert K. Merton, *Social Theory and Social Structure* (Glencoe, Ill.: Free Press, 1949), Chap. 1, pp. 19–84.
13. Herbert Spencer, *The Principles of Sociology* (New York: D. Appleton, 1898).
14. J. D. Y. Peel, "Spencer and the Neo-Evolutionists," *Sociology,* May 1969, pp. 173–91; reprinted in R. Serge Penisoff et al., *Theories and Paradigms in Contemporary Sociology* (Itasca, Ill.: F. E. Peacock, 1974), pp. 188–209.
15. Thomas Hobbes, *Leviathan* (Oxford: James Thornton, 1881). First printed in 1651.
16. Karl Marx and Frederick Engels, *The German Ideology* (New York: International Publishers, 1947); Herbert Marcuse, *Reason and Revolution: Hegel and the Rise of Social Theory* (Boston: Beacon Press, 1960).
17. Ralph Dahrendorf "Toward a Theory of Social Conflict," *Journal of Conflict Resolution*, 2, no. 2 (June 1958); 170–83.
18. Jürgen Habermas, trans. Thomas McCarthy (Boston: Beacon Press, 1975).

19. John Locke, *An Essay Concerning Human Understanding*, ed. Peter Nidditch (Oxford: Clarendon Press, 1975), p. 402. First published in 1690.
20. "Intellectual Antecedents and Basic Propositions of Symbolic Interactionism" in Jerome G. Manis and Bernard N. Meltzer, *Symbolic Interactions: A Reader in Social Psychology* (Boston: Allyn and Bacon, 1978), pp. 1–9.
21. Cooley, *Social Organization*; George Herbert Mead, *Mind, Self, and Society*, ed. and with an Introduction by Charles W. Morris (Chicago: University of Chicago Press, 1934).
22. Manis and Meltzer, *Symbolic Interaction*.
23. For example, see H. J. Eysenck, *The Biological Basis of Personality* (Springfield, Ill.: Charles C. Thomas, 1967); and M. D. Schwartz, *Physiological Psychology* (Englewood Cliffs, N.J.: Prentice-Hall, 1973).
24. One of the classics is Wolfgang Köhler, *The Mentality of Apes* (New York: Harcourt Brace Jovanovich, 1925). A provocative treatment is R. Audrey, *The Territorial Imperative* (New York: Atheneum, 1966); more typical of contemporary works is D. N. Daniels, M. F. Gilula, and F. M. Ochberg, *Violence and the Struggle for Existence* (Boston: Little, Brown, 1970).
25. The classics include John B. Watson, *Psychology from the Standpoint of a Behaviorist* (2nd ed.; Philadelphia: Lippincott, 1919); Ivan P. Pavlov, *Conditioned Reflexes* (New York: Oxford University Press, 1927); and B. F. Skinner, *Behavior of Organisms* (New York: Appleton-Century-Crofts, 1938). More contemporary are H. Rachlin, *Introduction to Modern Behaviorism* (San Francisco: Freedman, 1970); Albert Bandura, *Principles of Behavior Modification* (New York: Holt, Rinehart and Winston, 1969); and a work more significant for students of communication: Albert Bandura, *Social Learning Theory* (Englewood Cliffs, N.J.: Prentice-Hall, 1977).
26. The classic source is Sigmund Freud, *Outline of Psychoanalysis* (standard ed.; London: Hogarth Press, 1940). More contemporary are G. S. Blum, *Psychodynamics: The Science of Unconscious Mental Forces* (Belmont, Calif.: Wadsworth, 1966); and K. Menninger and P. S. Holzman, *Theory of Psychoanalytic Technique* (2nd ed.; New York: Basic Books, 1973).
27. The cognitive orientation is an outgrowth of the gestalt psychology of the 1920s, field theories advanced during the 1930s, and a large contemporary literature in experimental social psychology. Among the more significant works of later decades are Leon Festinger, *A Theory of Cognitive Dissonance* (Stanford, Calif.: Stanford University Press, 1957); J. W. Brehm and A. R. Cohen, *Explorations in Cognitive Dissonance* (New York: Wiley, 1962), R. P. Abelson et al., (eds.), *Theories of Cognitive Consistency: A Sourcebook* (Chicago: Rand McNally, 1968); D. J. Bem, *Beliefs, Attitudes, and Human Affairs* (Belmont, Calif.: Brookes-Cole, 1970); and L. Berkowitz, ed., *Advances in Experimental Social Psychology* (New York: Academic Press, 1974).

The first of the central questions posed for analysis in the previous chapter is the most logical starting point for a contemporary assessment of the current communication revolution. We may begin, then, by asking what

2

society and the mass press

has been the impact of the American society as a social and cultural system on the development of its mass media of communication? To understand the relationships between the society and its media, both the evolutionary perspective and the conflict model provide valuable interpretive frameworks. These two paradigms give perspectives on both the broad changes in society that occurred and on specific changes in technology and social organization that took place as the media developed.

The mass media as they exist today in our particular society have a somewhat unique structure of control, a particular set of institutionalized norms relating them to their audiences and readers, and characteristic forms of content. They have worked out specific types of financial support and clearly defined relationships to other important social institutions such as government. They have all experienced in greater or lesser degree a somewhat repetitive set of problems associated with conflicts between their goals and the goals, aspirations, and hopes of those whose cultural tastes and educational backgrounds are substantially higher than those of the common citizen. Finally, their developmental patterns, in terms of their quantitative spread as innovations through the society and in terms of general problems encountered during their institutionalization as culture complexes, have been rather similar from one medium to another.

Each of the media was, from the point of view of the ordinary family, a new device that could be adopted or rejected as a form of technology within the home or at least as an innovation requiring the family to adopt new modes of behavior. The evolutionary principles governing the adoption of innovation by individuals and families are becoming increasingly understood. While the mass media today are intimately involved in the stimulation of innovative behavior, they can also be viewed as innovations themselves. A study of their adoption patterns as well as the social and cultural variables related to their spread can reveal some of the ways in which a society can significantly influence and shape its mass media.

We need not go far back in history to talk about a society without mass media. For more than half a century after the original thirteen colonies had declared their independence from England, there was no true mass press to bring news to the average person. There were limited-circulation newspapers, to be sure, but these tended to differ sharply in their content, cost, audience, method of distribution, and size of circulation from the later mass readership papers. Motion pictures and broadcasting (both radio and television) have long technical histories; but as devices playing a part in the communication behavior of the average family, they are innovations of the present century.

A full understanding of how our various media came into being at the particular times they did requires considerably more than a mere listing of inventions of technical apparatus along with a few dates and names. The historical study of the mass media within any societal context, for the purpose of establishing recurrent patterns that have appeared during their growth, requires that attention be focused upon three important questions:

1. What technological elements or other cultural traits accumulated in what pattern to be combined into new culture complexes such as the mass newspaper, film, radio, or television industry?
2. What were the social and cultural conditions of the society within which this accumulation took place and how did these conditions create a climate favorable for the emergence and widespread adoption of the innovation?
3. What have been the patterns of diffusion of the innovations through the society, and what sociological conditions have been related to their rates and patterns of growth?

Obviously, all complex questions of this kind cannot adequately be answered within two or three chapters of one small book. Such issues require the extended attention of investigators with different perspectives, using various paradigms from the several social sciences, and scholars devoted to the study of each particular communication medium as well. Our task, then, is to sketch briefly the highlights of these historical developments in an attempt to illustrate, within the context of the American society, the impact a society can have in shaping its mass media. We will summarize very briefly some of the major events and social forces that have been associated with the development of each of the larger media of communication within the United States. Beginning with the press, newspapers, motion pictures, radio, and television will be discussed within the framework of the three questions noted above.

THE MASS PRESS

The basic culture traits later to be combined into a mass newspaper extend far back into history. The modern newspaper is a combination of elements from many societies and from many periods of time. Even before the birth of Christ the Romans posted newssheets called *acta diurna* in public places. The Chinese and Koreans were using movable type and paper for printing several centuries before these appeared in Europe. In the sixteenth century, well after printing had come to Europe, the Venetian government printed a small newssheet which could be purchased for a *gazeta* (a small coin). The use of the word "gazette" to refer to newspapers has survived to this day. Something closer to our modern idea of a newspaper appeared in the early 1600s in Germany. Scholars of the history of journalism suggest that many features of the modern newspaper, such as the editorial, sports articles, illustrations, political columns, and even comics, were used in one place or another long before the true mass press came into being.

Forerunners of the Newspaper

Printing was introduced to England in the late 1400s, but it was not until 1621, nearly a century and a half later, that early forerunners of the newspaper began to appear. These were called *corantos*. Their content focused on foreign intelligence, and they were not published regularly (as were the actual newspapers that came later). From the beginning, the publication of corantos was strongly regulated by the government. The seventeenth century in general was one of close regulation, or attempted close regulation, of all forms of printing. One of the interesting patterns discernible in the history of the press is that in societies with strong central governments, an unregulated press tended to grow very slowly. Where centralized authority was weak, the press tended to develop under less control and to advance more rapidly. In a general way the greater the extent to which a form of government is actually dependent upon favorable public opinion, the more likely it is to support a free press. When the common people play significant roles in the determination of their own political destiny, the distribution of news and political opinions is an important process. Strong monarchies, or societies with other forms of highly centralized power, do not require active public discussion of issues about which every citizen must reach an informed decision.

The long struggle to establish the important principle of freedom of the press was fought during a period when the older feudal monarchies were beginning to decline, and new concepts of political democracy were on the rise. Such considerations immediately suggest that one of the most significant changes in Western society, favoring the development of some form of mass communication, was the changing political institution that eventually vested voting power in the majority of citizens. This long and complex change established traditions of journalism which from the beginning made the newspaper an arena of public debate, partisan protest, and political comment. By the time the other major media emerged, this political transformation had been substantially achieved and neither motion pictures nor the broadcast media, in the United States at least, have developed the deep interest in politics that has long characterized the press. These variables and factors have obviously been related in different patterns in other countries.

During the period before the seeds of the American and French revolutions began germinating, the whole fabric of Western society was undergoing change. The Dark Ages had given way to the Renaissance, and the ancient feudal society with its rigid stratification pattern was slowly being replaced by a new social structure within which a strong middle class would be a key element. These changes were inseparable from the growth of commercialism that eventually culminated in the industrial revolution. This commercialism was to be dependent upon improvement in the availability of various kinds of communication media. Techniques were sorely needed to coordinate manufacturing, shipping, production of raw materials, financial transactions, and the exploitation of markets.

Newspapers in the American Colonies

Rapid, long-distance media would be slow in coming. Meanwhile, the rising middle class itself began to constitute an *audience*, not only for the latest information about commercial transactions, but also for political expression, essays, and popular literary fare. In England these needs were met by such skilled writers and journalists as Addison, Steele, Samuel Johnson, and Daniel Defoe. In the American colonies a middle class with commercial interests developed rapidly. New England was a land of ships, seaports, and trade of all kinds. During the first part of the eighteenth century a number of small newspapers were published. Many were financial failures, but some survived over a period of years. Their circulations were never large, usually well under a thousand. By the time the Declaration of Independence was written, there were about thirty-five of these small and crudely printed newspapers in the thirteen colonies. For the most part, their publishers eked out a precarious existence by selling their newspapers on a subscription basis (they were relatively expensive) and by carrying a few commercial announcements. If the publisher happened to be a postmaster, or could land a government printing contract to help out, the financial risk was not so great.

The colonial press, as these papers are collectively called, was edited and published by people who were not great literary figures with the exception of notable American colonial journalists such as the remarkable Benjamin Franklin. They were still using basically the same printing technology used by Gutenberg three centuries earlier. They did not have a mass audience with widespread reading skills. There were no large con-

THEORIES OF MASS COMMUNICATION

centrated urban centers that could serve as markets, and they lacked an adequate basis upon which to finance a mass press. However, a complex array of culture traits had accumulated in the society, including elementary printing technology, private ownership of newspapers, and, as was mentioned, the principle of freedom of the press.

Newspapers for Everyone

Before a true mass press could develop, a series of sweeping social changes was necessary in Western society. The changing political roles of the common citizen have already been mentioned. Also noted was the growth of commercialism, which led to changing patterns of social stratification and the rise of the middle class. To these can be added the necessary development of printing and paper technology, which increased its tempo with the mechanical advances of the early industrial revolution. Finally, when mass public education became a reality with the establishment of the first statewide public school system (in Massachusetts) during the 1830s, the stage was set for a combination of these many elements into a newspaper for the comon people.

A number of printers and publishers had experimented with the idea of a cheap newspaper that could be sold not by yearly subscription but by the single copy to the urban masses. Various approaches to this problem were tried both in England and in the United States, but without success. It remained for an obscure New York printer, Benjamin H. Day, to find a successful formula. His little paper, the *New York Sun*, began modestly enough on September 3, 1833, with the motto "It shines for ALL." As subsequent events proved, it did indeed shine for all. Day had begun a new era in journalism that within a few years would revolutionize newspaper publishing.

The *Sun* emphasized local news, human interest stories, and even sensational reports of shocking events. For example, to add spice to the content, Day hired a reporter who wrote articles in a humorous style concerning the cases brought daily before the local police court. This titillating content found a ready audience among the newly literate working classes. It also found many critics among more traditional people in the city. The paper was sold in single copies for a penny in the streets by enterprising newsboys. These boys soon established regular routes of customers; and daily circulation rose to 2000 in only two months. The breezy style and vigorous promotion of the paper shot this figure up to 5000 in four months and to 8000 in six months. The astonishing success of this controversial paper had the rest of the newspaper publishers in an uproar. By this time the steam engine had been coupled to the new rotary press. The famous Hoe cylinder press was available in the United States, along with abundant supplies of cheap wood-pulp newsprint. The technical problems of producing and distributing huge numbers of newspapers on a daily basis had largely been solved, and the emergence of the mass press was an accomplished fact.

The *Sun* attracted its impressive circulation primarily by appealing to new readers who had not previously been reached by a newspaper. One of the most important features of Day's penny paper, and of those that followed it, was the redefinition of "news" to fit the tastes, interests, and reading skills of this less-educated level of society. Up to that time, "news" generally meant reports on social or political events of genuine importance, or of other happenings that were of widespread significance. Benjamin Day, however, filled his paper with news of another sort— accounts of crimes, stories of sin, catastrophe, and disaster—news the people in the street found exciting, entertaining, or amusing. His staff even invented an elaborate hoax, concerning new "scientific discoveries" of life on the moon. When the hoax was exposed by another paper, his readers took it in good humor because it had been fun to read about. The paper was vulgar, cheap, and sensational; it was aimed directly at the newly literate masses who were beginning to participate in the spreading industrial revolution. There was some serious material in the paper to be sure, but its editorials and reports of political and economic complexities were much more superficial than in the earlier partisan papers written for more politically sophisticated readers. By 1837, the *Sun* was distributing 30,000 copies daily, more than the combined total of all New York daily papers when the penny paper was first brought out.

Imitators of Day had started rival papers almost immediately. The penny press was a financial success because it had great appeal for advertisers. In fact, advertising revenue was its only real support; the penny for which it was sold could scarcely pay for the raw newsprint. But goods and services for mass consumption could be successfully advertised through the penny press. These advertisements reached huge numbers of potential customers much more successfully than those appearing in the preceding limited-circulation newspapers. Patent medicines, "for man and beast," were one such mass-use product that played a prominent part in supporting the new penny papers. Early department stores also took readily to the newspaper as a means for publicizing their wares.

For such advertisers, size of circulation was thought to be a good index of the amount of profit one could anticipate. The newspaper that could place an advertising message before tens of thousands attracted the advertising dollar. This simple principle set into motion rugged competition between rival papers for new readers. This had important implications for the development of the popular press during the latter half of the nineteenth century, and indeed had implications for mass media that would not even be invented until a full century later! The foundations of an important institutionalized pattern of social relationships, which linked advertiser, media operators, and audience into a functional system for the production of particular types of mass communicated content, were worked out in the early years of the development of the mass press.

Meanwhile, Benjamin Day's most colorful and successful competitor was James Gordon Bennett, who founded a newspaper empire on only $500 in a barren office in a cellar. Bennett, a shrewd and tough Scot, started the *Herald* in New York. He flouted the conservative moral norms of the time and published flaming news accounts of murder trials, rape, sin, and depravity. At the same time, he reported effectively on politics, financial matters, and even on the social affairs of high society. This variety of content gave his *Herald* a wide appeal and made it a strong financial success. Bennett himself made many enemies with his forceful and often scandalous newspaper articles. For example, in 1836 he wrote:

> Books have had their day—the theatres have had their day—the temple of religion has had its day. A newspaper can be made to take the lead in all of these in the great movements of human thought and of human civilization. A newspaper can send more souls to Heaven, and save more from Hell, than all the churches or chapels in New York—besides making money at the same time.[1]

Although Bennett's startling prediction did not come true, the newspaper was about to begin its spread through the American society and to start playing an increasingly important part in its daily affairs.

THE PERIOD OF RAPID DIFFUSION

Although the mass newspaper arrived in the 1830s, it was still limited in terms of news gathering, printing technology, and distribution. Before it could diffuse widely into the homes of every American city, a number of important problems remained to be solved. The decades just preceding the Civil War were filled with important mechanical, scientific, and technical developments that were to make it possible for the infant mass newspaper to grow into a giant. Railroads were built between the principal cities in the eastern part of the nation. The steamboat arrived as a major transportation link after about 1840. The telegraph grew increasingly useful as a means for rapid transmission of news from the scenes of important events to editorial offices. These developments substantially increased the newspaper's appeal to its readers and increased the number of people to whom newspapers could be distributed.

The Evolution of Social and Mechanical Technology

More and more, newspapers began to seek out the news. The role of reporter grew more complex and specialized as papers added foreign correspondents and special news gatherers of various kinds. Reporters were sent to the scenes of battles; others were permanently stationed in Washington, D.C., to cover political events. The "surveillance" function of the press became well established.[2]

The rising demand for fresh news was met by newly formed cooperative news-gathering agencies, which made use of the telegraph wires. These agencies sent stories to papers in many parts of the country with which they had contractual arrangements. Through such agreements, the staff of a paper near an event could cover the story for many papers elsewhere, thereby greatly reducing the cost of news gathering. These advances brought the newspaper to the smaller cities and towns and even to the newly established cities in the West.

Printing technology was making rapid strides, moving toward ever-increasing automation. Revolving presses, with print cast in a solid lead stereotype, became capable of rolling out ten and even twenty thousand sheets an hour.

The Civil War brought maturity of a sort to the newspaper as it reinforced the concept that the paper's principal function is to gather, edit, and report the news. The older concept of the paper as primarily an organ of partisan political opinion had faded considerably. The post–Civil War papers increasingly clarified their roles as locators, assemblers, and purveyors of the news. This is not to suggest that newspapers become either uninterested or nonpartisan with respect to politics—quite the opposite. Individual editors and publishers often used their newspapers to champion causes of one kind or another and to wage "crusades" against political opponents. But at the same time, they were all heavily involved in straightforward reporting of the news.

The Peak of Newspaper Popularity

Papers continued to gain in popularity. In 1850 there were about two copies of a daily newspaper purchased in the United States for every ten families. The rate of growth of newspaper circulations increased steadily, but not spectacularly, until the 1880s. During the two decades 1890–1910, however, the rate of newspaper circulation per household rose sharply. This rapid growth actually continued until about the time of World War I and then tended to level off during the 1920s. But the last decade of the nineteenth century is one of special significance in the growth of the press because it was the beginning of a new kind of journalism. While this new journalism did not become permanently established, it left its mark on the American newspaper. Let us look in greater detail at this development because it is of importance for understanding patterns in the development of later mass media as well.

THE NEWSPAPER AND SOCIETAL CHANGE

While the newspaper was growing up, the second half of the nineteenth century was for American society a period of rapid change, upheaval, and transition. It was an era characterized simultaneously by an expanding frontier, a devastating Civil War and its aftermath, the arrival of wave after wave of immigrants, a pronounced rural to urban movement, and an increasingly rapid transition to an industrial society. Any one of these changes could have fundamentally altered the basic social organization of the society. Their combined effect was even more deeply felt. New norms replaced old; firmly established mores were cast aside; a traditional way of life gave way to a new social order. If ever a society was in a state of cultural upheaval and transition, it was American society during the five-decade period of the last half of the nineteenth century.

Yellow Journalism

The social context within which the mass press spread and matured was one characterized by cultural conflict and anomie. The new medium had to devise and institutionalize the basic codes that would regulate its responsibilities to the public it served, and would place limits upon the kind of content it contained. With the normative structure of the society itself in a state of turmoil, it is not surprising that the mass press was able to work out its "canons of journalism" only after a rather stormy period of adolescence.

One of the most dramatic episodes in the development of the press was the period of "yellow journalism." By the 1880s, the newspaper had achieved wide adoption by American households, and further astronomical increases in circulation were increasingly difficult to stimulate. At the same time, the press was firmly established financially as long as the number of newspapers sold could be kept at a maximum. Within this competitive context, brutal struggles for additional readers developed between the leaders of giant rival papers. In New York, in particular, William Randolph Hearst and Joseph Pulitzer fought by any means available to expand their circulation figures. These were, of course, the key to increased advertising revenue and profits. Various features, devices, gimmicks, styles, and experiments were tried by each side to make its paper more appealing to the mass of readers. Newspapers today contain many of the devices that were actually products of the rivalries of the 1890s. (One of these was color comics. An early comic character was called the "Yellow Kid," from which "yellow journalism" is said to derive its name.)

As the competition intensified into open conflict, the papers turned more and more to any sensationalistic device that would attract additional readers, no matter how shallow and blatant. In the early 1890s yellow journalism burst full blown upon the American public:

> . . . the yellow journalists . . . choked up the news channels upon which the common man depended, with a callous disregard for journalistic ethics and responsibility. Theirs was a shrieking, gaudy, sensation-loving, devil-may-care kind of journalism which lured the reader by any possible means. It seized upon the techniques of writing, illustrating and printing which were the prides of the new journalism and turned them to perverted uses. It made the high drama of life a cheap melodrama, and it twisted the facts of each day into whatever form seemed best suited to produce sales for the howling newsboy. Worst of all, instead of giving its readers effective leadership, it offered a palliative of sin, sex and violence.[3]

Yellow journalism offended a sufficient number of groups and individuals so that a storm of criticism gradually made clear to the operators of the mass press that they had exceeded the limits which the society, and particularly representatives of the norm-bearing institutions, would tolerate. Intellectuals in general and the literati in particular were deeply wounded. The great new means of communication, which held forth the tantalizing potential of mass cultural and moral uplift, had in their eyes turned out to be a monstrous influence for societal degeneration.

Emerging Systems of Social Control

Leaders in religion, education, law, and government increasingly voiced strong protests. The press lords were faced with the threat of losing public confidence, and the even more chilling possibility of regulation imposed from without. These considerations led a number of major publishers to begin to put their own houses in order. Gradually, the press became less sensational and more responsible. A set of codes and norms defining its limits and responsibilities gradually became increasingly clear. Professional associations of editors and publishers established canons of journalism intended to guide their members. While the mass press today varies substantially in its degree of adherence to such codes, the excesses of yellow journalism appear to be a thing of the past. Out of these experiences of the newspaper came a number of institutionalized principles which in one way or another have helped clarify the roles, responsibilities, and policies of media that followed. The way in which this has been the case will be made clear in later sections.

DIFFUSION PATTERN OF THE MASS PRESS

Data on newspaper circulations are given in Table 1. These figures report both circulations of newspapers and the growth of the number of households for the period 1850–1973. Rates of newspaper circulation *per household* are given in the last column of the table. The pattern these rates form over time is shown in Figure 1. Rates of daily newspaper circulation per household follow an S-shaped "curve of diffusion" that is more or less typical of growth patterns followed by a variety of cultural innovations as these are adopted by a given population.[4] This particular innovation had been accepted by only a small proportion of the population up to about 1870. A number of factors (e.g., limited education, transportation, and printing facilities) played a part in keeping the number of "early adopters" small. Between 1880 and 1890, however, the newspaper swept rapidly through the American population to a point of near saturation by the end of the century. Improved press technology, better transportation, and spreading literacy were significant factors in this sudden change. By 1910, at the eve of World War I, there was more than one newspaper circulated for every household. Thus, during the first decade of the century, newspapers approached their peak in the American society.

Increases in circulation slowed after 1910. The apparent high point in the American newspaper occurred in about 1920, just following World War I. Since that time, the medium has suffered a steady and very noticeable decline. Even further improvements in the technology of news gathering, printing, distribution, and literacy have not slowed this downward trend. Even though more newspapers are sold today in an absolute sense, they have not kept pace with increases in the number of American households.

Table 1 Daily Newspaper Circulation in the United States (1850–1977)

Year	Total Circulation of Daily Newspapers Excluding Sunday (in thousands)	Total Number of Households (in thousands)	Circulation per Household
1850	758	3,598	.21
1860	1,478	5,211	.28
1870	2,602	7,579	.34
1880	3,566	9,946	.36
1890	8,387	12,690	.66
1900	15,102	15,992	.94
1910	24,212	17,806	1.36
1920	27,791	20,697	1.34
1930	39,589	29,905	1.32
1940	41,132	34,855	1.18
1950	53,829	43,468	1.24
1955	56,147	47,788	1.17
1960	58,882	52,610	1.12
1965	60,358	57,251	1.05
1966	61,379	58,092	1.06
1967	61,561	58,845	1.05
1968	62,535	60,444	1.03
1969	62,060	61,805	1.00
1970	62,108	62,875	.99
1971	62,231	64,374	.97
1972	62,510	66,676	.94
1973	63,147	68,251	.93
1974	61,901	69,859	.89
1975	60,655	71,120	.85
1976	60,976	72,867	.84
1977	61,495	74,142	.83

SOURCES: U.S. Bureau of Census, *Historical Statistics of the United States, Colonial Times to 1957* (Washington, D.C., 1960), Series R 176, p. 500; Series R 169, p. 500; Series 255, p. 16; Series A 242–44.

U.S. Bureau of Census, *Historical Statistics of the United States, Continuation to 1962 and Revisions* (Washington, D.C., 1965), Series R 170, p. 69.

U.S. Bureau of Census, *Statistical Abstract of the United States* (Washington, D.C., 1973), p. 53 and p. 503.

U.S. Bureau of Census, *Current Population Reports: Population Characteristics*, Series P 20, no. 166 (4 August 1967), p. 4.

Editor and Publisher International Yearbook (New York: Editor and Publisher, 1979).

NOTE: All figures after 1960 include Alaska and Hawaii. Some figures have been revised from previous editions because of revisions in source materials.

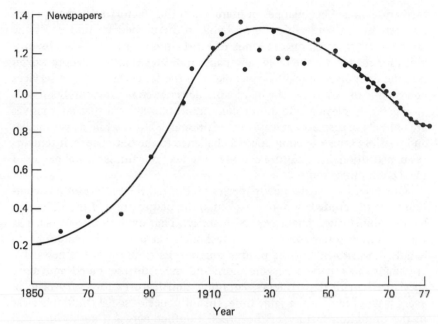

Figure 1. The cumulative diffusion curve for daily newspapers; subscriptions per house-hold in the United States (1850–1977).

What has been the basis of this decline? An adequate theory of the relationship between a society and its mass media should be able to account for such a social change as well as for media growth. In other words, an analysis of the invention, adoption, and institutionalization of a cultural item such as the newspaper, and the organizational complex that produces it, would be incomplete without consideration of variables that can lead to its *obsolescence*. As far as the newspaper is concerned, the factors that have led to its decline are not difficult to suggest. Other media forms, meeting needs in the population similar to those met by newspapers, began to appear in the society during that decade. Shortly afterward (during the 1930s) weekly news magazines began to gain mass acceptance. Even the film played a part. By the late 1940s and during the 1950s, of course, television swept through the American society. To a greater or lesser extent, each of these *functional alternatives* to the newspaper has eaten into the circulation of the daily press. Each, in some sense or other, provides news, information, or entertainment in a way that once was the exclusive province of the newspaper.

What of the newspaper's future? It will probably survive with some further decline. Few changes in literacy or other factors related to potential increases in readership are probable in the immediate future. By the same token, research on the kinds of satisfactions and gratifications provided for readers by the daily newspaper indicates that it is deeply woven into the daily lives of ordinary people. It provides certain unique services and gratifications. When the newspaper does not come, it is sorely missed. It apparently plays a role in our communication system that alternatives are unlikely to displace, at least for the present.[5] Thus, while newer media, and possibly others to come, pose a challenge to the newspaper, it remains as an institutionalized culture complex as one of our fundamental modes of mass communication.

Our brief look at the newspaper has indicated the pattern of its evolution from the crude beginnings, through the penny press of the 1830s, up to the sophisticated chain papers of today. That evolution took place as various innovators proposed new technological and social solutions to handle old problems in the production and distribution of the news. Increasingly, newspapers became more and more differentiated and more specialized, with departments, columns, and features for every taste in every walk of life. At the same time, the influence of social conflict is clear in the unfolding history of the press. Conflict between authorities and printers began early. It shaped the historical background that brought the founding fathers to include a First Amendment in the Constitution. Conflict between press and government continue to shape the nature and destiny of the newspaper as the First Amendment and the courts resolve the dialectical process that takes place between those in power and the Fourth Estate. Similarly, intense competition between newspapers produced such forms as yellow journalism, and eventually, codes of good practice governing publishing in the United States. Finally, conflict and competition between the newspapers and newer media have altered the public's use of the newspaper, and consequently its place in the American system of mass communication.

NOTES

1. Eric Barnouw, *Mass Communication* (New York: Holt, Rinehart, and Winston, 1956), p. 7.
2. For an excellent summary of functions of mass communication today, including "surveillance," see Charles R. Wright, *Mass Communication: A Sociological Perspective* (New York: Random House, 1959), pp. 17–23.
3. Edwin Emery and H. L. Smith, *The Press and America* (Englewood Cliffs, N.J.: Prentice-Hall, 1954), pp. 415–16.

4. See, for example, H. Earl Pemberton, "The Curve of Culture Diffusion Rate," *American Sociological Review* 1, no. 4 (August 1936): 547–56; Stuart C. Dodd, "Diffusion Is Predictable: Testing Probability Models for Laws of Interaction," *American Sociological Review* 20, no. 4 (August 1955): 392–401; Everett M. *Rogers, Diffusion of Innovations* (New York: Free Press of Glencoe, 1962), pp. 152–59.
5. The following two research studies bear directly on this point: Bernard Berelson, "What Missing the Newspaper Means," in *Communication Research, 1948–1949*, ed. P. F. Lazarsfeld and F. N. Stanton (New York: Harper & Brothers, 1949), pp. 111–29; Penn Kimball, "People Without Papers," *Public Opinion Quarterly* 23, no. 3 (Fall 1959): 389–98.

Like the evolution of the newspaper, the history of the motion picture can be interpreted as a process of evolution that has been heavily influenced by social conflict. That evolution has been one whereby technological and

3

sociocultural influences on the development of motion pictures

social forms most suited to the needs of society and to those attending to the medium have been adopted and retained. Conflicts have occurred, not only between various interests attempting to own and control the emerging medium, but between the moral majority in the society and those who sought to increase profits by appealing to less noble gratifications in preparing motion picture content. Such conflicts have played a central role in shaping the nature of the motion picture in America.

The historical antecedents of the motion picture extend backward in time at least as far as those of the mass press. The development of the motion picture's technological base, however, followed different paths and was a result of different social forces than those that characterized the background of the newspaper. The technological culture traits eventually combined in the development of the projected motion picture were invented and refined as by-products of several somewhat unrelated developments in science. The major contributors to the fundamental technology upon which motion pictures depend were for the most part persons of science who made their discoveries or developed their apparatus while searching for solutions to specific problems. There were exceptions, of course, but generally the people who were to become the founders of the motion picture had little interest in the development of a medium by which people could be entertained. They were far more interested in discovering such things as the physical principles of light refraction, the neurological basis of human vision, or the way in which the illusion of motion was perceived. Throughout the long history of invention and development there were also indications of great potential popular interest in a medium of entertainment based upon the projection of shadow images. At least, the nonscientific friends of many of the inventors were continuously fascinated by the strange devices and effects these people produced.

THE INSTITUTIONAL FRAMEWORK

We may contrast sharply the development of the motion picture, as it occurred within the institutional framework of science, with that of the newspaper, which was traced out in rough outline in the previous chapter. We saw that the history of the mass press was very closely related to important developments within the *economic* and *political* institutions of Western society. Commercialism and political partisanship were characteristics clearly associated with early forms of newspapers as well as the more mature press. When a viable financial structure was found for a mass press in the democratic capitalistic societies, this structure was based firmly upon commercial advertising. And, even though the newspaper redefined its relationship to political affairs more than once, the press continued to regard political activities as one of its major areas of responsibility, at least in reporting and analyzing if not in actual proselytizing. The motion picture, on the other hand, has never been more than marginally related to the presentation of commercial advertising content in a direct sense. And, although movies occasionally deal with politically or socially significant themes, they have not often been used (in American society at least) for the open advocacy of political ideologies. A complete understanding of the impact of society upon its communication media requires that we understand why, in the United States, motion pictures became a major communication medium devoted principally to entertainment rather than edification or persuasion, and why paid admissions as opposed to advertising or government subsidy provided their most important means of financial support. The present discussion cannot fully provide answers to these questions. It can show, however, within the context of American society, how political, social, and economic forces played a role in the formation of the motion picture as a system of mass communication. Comparative analyses of other societies, where the structure of the political institution and the functioning of the economic system have followed different patterns, would indicate why the form and content of the entire system of motion pictures varies from country to country.

THE EVOLUTION OF TECHNOLOGY

The early history of the motion picture is more accurately the story of developments related to three scientific-technical problems that required solution before an apparatus for the projection of motion pictures could even be envisioned. We need to consider these three problems and some of the technical devices that eventually led to their solution. The story of these devices and solutions is, however, inseparable from that of the human beings who achieved them, but the accomplishments of these people are intimately related to the social and cultural context within which they achieved their success.

Projection and the Camera Obscura

The first of the major problems referred to above was the development of a means for showing shadow images with the use of an *illuminated projector* that passed light through a transparency to cast an image on a reflecting screen in a darkened room.

The list of elements making up this complex is obviously extensive. Basic to the technology of such projection is some understanding of the principles of optics. The use of mirrors and lenses is involved, including concave mirrors for the focusing of light from an artificial source so as to pass through a lens in suitable intensity. Of these various traits, the lens is probably the oldest. Adequate records exist showing that by the time of the Greeks, the "burning glass" was known by scientists.[1] Archimedes (born 287 B.C.), for example, attempted to construct a large lens, which was purported to have the power to set a ship on fire some distance away by focusing the rays of the sun. Whether this was actually accomplished or not is debatable, but the principle was understood. The field of optics was advanced further by the work of the Arab philosopher and scientist Alhazen (born A.D. 965) who worked out some of the first explanations of refraction and reflection with mirrors and lenses. The pace in invention and cultural accumulation was agonizingly slow in this beginning period. By the time of Roger Bacon (born 1214), scientists and philosophers had done little more than discover various ways to use mirrors in periscopelike devices to reflect images in such ways that the ordinary folk of the time were mystified.

One of the more important elements from this early period of invention and discovery was the *camera obscura* (literally "dark room"). The basic idea is that of the pinhole camera, within which a weak, upside-down, and reversed image of an external scene can be observed on a wall opposite a small hole in a lightproof rectangular chamber.[2] This phenomenon had undoubtedly been observed very early in human experience, but the rules and principles of its operation were not systematically investigated until the time of Leonardo da Vinci (born 1452).[3] Leonardo worked in a small room sealed from light and into which light rays coming from a scene outside were allowed to enter through a hole about the size of a pencil. The image formed on the opposite wall could be clearly recognized as the outside scene in full color, although weak and sometimes blurred. With the suitable addition of a lens for focusing and a mirror to reverse the image, the camera obscura became a useful device for artists concerned with the problems of perspective and color in the painting of landscapes. The camera obscura caught the attention of a number of scientists as well as artists, and it was used to observe eclipses of the sun. This avoided the damage to the eyes that resulted from direct observation, even through darkened glass.

The camera obscura fell into the hands of magicians, charlatans, and others who preyed upon the ignorance of people of the period and who claimed magical powers for themselves on the basis of the effects they were able to produce. Scientists and experimenters were constantly harassed with the problem of magic and witchcraft being associated with their work. Attempts were made from time to time to publicize the "secrets" of these wonders to dispel such charges. This was true not only in the area of optics but in all branches of science. One of the most interesting of the early attempts to popularize science was a book by Giambattista della Porta or Giovanni Battista della Porta (born about 1535). In the seventeenth "book" (chapter) of his famous work, *Natural Magick*, translated and published in English in 1658, della Porta discoursed on the matter "Of Strange Glasses" (lenses and mirrors).[4] After discussing the mechanics of the camera obscura, he went on to describe how the device could be used to present plays and other amusements:

> *How in a Chamber you may see Hunting, Battles of Enemies, and other delusions.*
>
> . . . nothing can be more pleasant for great men, and Scholars, and ingenious persons to behold; That in a dark Chamber by white sheets objected, one may see as clearly and perspicuously, as if they were before his eyes, Huntings, Banquets, Armies of Enemies, Plays and all things else that one desireth. Let there be over against that chamber, where you desire to represent these things, some spacious Plain, where the Sun can freely shine: Upon that you shall set Trees in Order, also Woods, Mountains, Rivers, and Animals that are really so, or are made by Art, of Wood, or some other matter. You must frame little children in them, as we use to bring them in when Comedies are Acted: and you must counterfeit Stags, Bores, Rhinocerets, Elephants, Lions, and what other creatures you please: Then by degrees they must appear, as coming out of their dens, upon the Plain: The Hunter he must come with his hunting Pole, Nets, Arrows, and other necessaries, that may represent hunting: Let there be Horns, Cornets, Trumpets sounded: those that are in the Chamber shall see Trees, Animals, Hunters Faces, and all the rest so plainly that they cannot tell whether they be true or delusions: Swords drawn will glitter at the hole, that they will make people almost afraid. I have often shewed this kind of Spectacle to my friends, who much admired it, and took pleasure to see such a deceit.[5]

Although della Porta was a scientist, it is clear he also had considerable interest in using various devices and effects to astonish his friends. The moving images of the camera obscura were to be a source of delight and amusement for the wealthy and prominent of Europe for some time to come. All through the historical development of the technological devices that were prerequisites to the modern motion picture, we see the continuous fascination and awe with which the projected image was regarded by the nonscientist.

The camera obscura, of course, produced its image from light reflected from objects in bright sunlight. A step of some importance lay in substituting artificial light for the sun and in passing this light through a transparency instead of depending upon reflected light. The illuminated projector that could throw images on a screen, using precisely the principles involved in the modern slide projector, became a reality through the work of Athanasius Kircher (born 1601).[6] Kircher was a German Jesuit whose learning and scientific discoveries earned him a place at the Collegio Romano, where with the encouragement of Pope Urban VIII and other ecclesiastical authorities he pursued mathematical and scientific investigations. Kircher was able to demonstrate in a dramatic showing before a distinguished audience the crude projector he developed and the dim images it produced with the use of hand-painted transparent slides. Kircher became the object of ugly accusations and gossip as a result of his work. He was accused of being in league with the devil and of practicing the black art of necromancy (conjuring up the spirits of the dead for nefarious purposes). The principles upon which his ghostlike projected images were called forth were not well understood, or were deliberately misunderstood by his enemies, even among the most highly educated people of the time.

Kircher went on to refine his apparatus. He, too, had a flair for the dramatic, and he arranged ways in which stories could be told, illustrated with projected slide images. A number of later inventors added refinements to the "magic lantern" and still others exploited its use as a means for entertainment. The solution to the first basic technical problem of the motion picture was thus complete by about 1645.

The Illusion of Continuous Motion

The second of the major problems requiring solution was to discover the way in which the human being perceived the *illusion of continuous motion*. Unlike the problem of the projector, this involved a relatively large number of elements. Complex discoveries in the theory of human vision and human perception had to be worked out. Essentially, the problem was to discover how a rapid series of drawings, or other figures, could be presented to the human eye in such a way that the afterimages and the visual lag occurring within the neural-perceptual processes would cause the figures to be consciously experienced as a single figure in smooth motion.

In the early 1800s children in London and Paris were playing with a device called the Thaumatrope. It was a small disk about the diameter of a teacup mounted on a shaft. It had a figure on the front and another on the reverse side. By twirling the device with the aid of short strings or threads, various illusions could be created. Several forms of the toy were prepared

49

with amusing figures of one kind or another. There has been some controversy about the origin of this device, but it is generally attributed to a London physician, John Paris (born 1785). It was described and discussed by David Brewster, the student of the polarization of light and the inventor of the kaleidoscope, in one of his scientific works. The toy is not of particular significance in itself except insofar as it depended upon the phenomenon of visual lag and suggested that an illusion of motion might be produced by rapid presentation of slightly changed figures in sequence.

One of the great students of the so-called persistence of vision or visual lag was the Belgian scientist Joseph Plateau (born 1801).[7] Early in his career, he became interested in various aspects of vision and particularly the way in which the human being perceives motion and color.

Plateau's doctoral thesis from the University of Liege outlined the problems of vision that had to be considered in producing the illusion of motion in the human perceiver. First, each individual figure, drawing, or picture in a rapidly presented series had to remain stationary for a brief but sufficient amount of time for the neural-perceptual process to apprehend it clearly. The eye does not operate absolutely instantaneously. It takes a certain amount of exposure time for a given scene to register an impression. The rapidly whirling blade of a fan seems to "disappear" because of this feature of the human eye. The second point is also a time factor. An impression once registered within the neural-perceptive mechanisms of vision does not stop registering at the instantaneous moment the stimulus itself is withdrawn. There is a substantial lag as the impression lingers briefly. The simplest demonstration of this principle can be made with a common "sparkler" such as children use on the Fourth of July. If this bright light is moved quickly in a figure-eight pattern in the dark, the individual "sees" a complete figure eight, and not simply a rapidly moving dot of light. This is what is meant by visual lag.

With these principles in mind, Plateau worked out a rather cumbersome apparatus of belts, cranks, pulleys, disks, and shutters that enabled him to create a simple illusion of movement, based upon the rapid successive presentation of a drawing. He refined this to a large disk, around whose circumference was arranged a series of drawings, each of which was slightly varied so that the same basic figure advanced to a slightly different position from one drawing to the next. When suitably shown to a subject, a moving figure was perceived. This machine was called the Phenakistiscope or Fantascope. It was the first true motion picture device. A system had thus been invented, based upon known principles of vision, that permitted a human observer to perceive an illusion of smooth and continuous motion from serially presented still figures. Professor Plateau pursued his quest for the principles of vision to the point where he experimented on himself by testing the effect of prolonged staring at the most powerful light he could think of—the sun. As a result of such experimentation, he became permanently and tragically blind, and much of his important work had to be done after his sight had gone completely. The irony of a blind scientist establishing the visual principles of the motion picture is paralleled only by the tragedy of the deaf Beethoven, who wrote some of the world's great symphonic music after his hearing totally failed, and Edison's invention of the phonograph when he himself was deaf. Joseph Plateau moved the accumulation of technology a great step closer to the day when the motion picture would be used as a form of mass entertainment.

Capturing the Image of the Camera Obscura

Only the last of the three important technical problems needed to be solved before the culture complex of the motion picture as a form of mass communication could be synthesized out of these elements. The technology of *photography* in general, and of taking rapid sequence photographs of objects in motion in particular, remained as prerequisites to the motion picture.

The scientific struggle to achieve a workable photographic process is in itself a story of tremendous difficulties, great complexity, and deep fascination. It depended upon developments within the growing science of chemistry and in particular upon that part of the science concerned with chemical changes in substances produced by the action of light. The development of photography also involves the already familiar camera obscura. When sufficiently reduced in size, provided with a lens and a removable reflecting surface coated with a light-sensitive chemical, it became the camera with which we today capture the inverted images of scenes reflected within. In so doing we are still utilizing principles known in the time of da Vinci. The problem, then, was not the camera itself, but the film. What chemical processes and techniques could be used in order to fix the image of the camera obscura? Even here knowledge was well advanced by the beginning of the nineteenth century. In the early 1700s it had been shown experimentally that there were particular chemical compounds, such as various salts of silver, that were rapidly altered by exposure to light. This realization permitted speculation about the possibility of capturing the image of the camera obscura. It was not until the third decade of the nineteenth century, however, that the mechanical and chemical techniques for preparing, exposing, developing, and fixing an actual picture from the camera obscura were worked out.

The Daguerrotype   Solutions to this problem were in fact reached by at least three separate individuals. Each worked without knowledge of the other; each employed a somewhat different approach; and each announced his discoveries at almost the same time (between January and March of 1839), Louis Daguerre in France, William Talbot in England, and John Herschel, also of England, all succeeded in producing photographs based upon the same general chemical principles but upon rather different specific mechanical techniques.[8] The Daguerre process produced a sharp image of exquisite detail on a polished plate of copper that had been coated with silver metal and exposed to iodine fumes (to form silver iodide). Light striking this plate, when correctly exposed in the camera, caused the silver iodide to be drastically altered where bright light struck but to remain relatively unaffected where light of less intensity fell on the plate. The resulting *daguerreotype* produced an excellent picture with sharpness and clarity. There were no negatives; only one picture could be obtained at a time. The processes of Talbot and Herschel employed paper treated with similar light-sensitive chemicals and produced negatives, from which it was necessary to make a second (positive) print. Although the latter procedure proved in time to be by far the most useful, it was in its early form very crude, cumbersome, and unreliable. Furthermore, the pictures produced on the paper of the time lacked the precision of the daguerreotype. For this reason, the daguerreotype was an instant success, and the name of Louis Daguerre became very well known. In a world that had never seen a photograph, the daguerreotype seemed an almost incredible accomplishment. Such pictures were, in fact, when carefully produced, the equal of the finest and most carefully made photographs of today. The use of a polished metal plate of silver gave them a great brilliance and sharpness. They were less "grainy" and showed more detail than even a very good modern paper print. Some indication of the world's astonishment and delight with this new product of science can be gained from the following account, written in 1839 by the editor of a popular American magazine, who had just seen a display of the new daguerreotypes:

> We have seen the views taken in Paris by the "Daguerreotype" and have no hesitation in avowing that they are the most remarkable objects of curiosity and admiration, in the arts, that we ever beheld. Their exquisite perfection almost transcends the bounds of sober belief. Let us endeavor to convey to the reader an impression of their character. Let him suppose himself standing in the middle of Broadway, with a looking glass held perpendicularly in his hand, in which is reflected the street, with all that therein is, for two or three miles, taking in the haziest distance. Then let him take the glass into the house, and find the impression of the entire view, in the softest light and shade, vividly retained upon its surface. This is the "Daguerreotype!"[9]

The acceptance of the Daguerre photographic process was immediate and enthusiastic. Improvements in technique were quickly made so that portraits were possible in indoor "salons." Rigid iron head clamps were used, and light was reflected from overhead skylights. The first daguerreotypes were made in the United States in 1839, the same year that the process was announced in Paris by various scientists and enthusiasts, among whom was Samuel F. B. Morse. While Morse is best remembered for his work with the telegraph, he was actually a portrait painter of some distinction. He was also a professor in the arts of design at the University of the City of New York. The daguerreotype was closely related to both these interests. He was immediately enthusiastic about the new art, and he actually visited Daguerre in France in 1839. Morse became an active daguerreotypist in New York and is said to have supported himself financially by making portraits, and by training students in the process, while awaiting recognition and financial support from the U.S. government for his telegraph.

The Demand for Portraits   The production of portraits provided an immediate link between the art of daguerreotype and the art of making money. Here was a new kind of profession, requiring a relatively brief period of technical training and a small outlay for equipment, that had the potential of financial success. The 1840s in the United States were a period of economic depression. A number of enterprising young people were looking about for an opportunity to enter into some venture whereby they could make a living without investing large capital and without having to undergo extensive university professional training. The occupational role of daguerreotypist was almost made to order. There were villages, towns, and cities all over the settled part of the United States that had not yet seen the new process. The cost of having one's portrait made, especially in the smaller sizes, was not prohibitively expensive. A family of average means could easily afford it. Daguerreotype equipment was loaded on wagons, flatboats, oxcarts, and mules. The photographer's art spread out over the country. In all the major cities, daguerreotype salons were established, and business was exceedingly brisk. Quality of work varied greatly. The roving daguerreotypist with poor training and little skill turned out a dreadful product, paying attention neither to graceful poses nor to technical precision in the production of the plates. Some combined the photographic art with other occupational pursuits. A given individual might be a combination blacksmith, cobbler, watch repairer, dentist, and daguerreotypist. It was possible to have one's boots resoled, watch oiled, teeth pulled, horse shod, and portrait made all at one stop—all in a "package deal" so to speak.[10]

At the other extreme were the beautiful and luxurious salons that developed in the principal population centers. Mathew Brady gained an international reputation as a fine portrait artist in Washington, D.C., long before the beginning of the Civil War.[11] Stretched between these two extremes were establishments large and small that were producing over *three million portraits a year* in the 1850s![12]

The insatiable demand for portraits was undoubtedly related to a number of characteristics of the times. The United States was a society on the move. People were no sooner settled on one frontier than another opened up farther on. The males often left their families in more settled areas until they could be brought out to reasonably favorable accommodations. The movements of population associated with the various gold rushes, land rushes, oil booms, and other events separated men from their wives and children from their parents. Along the Atlantic seaboard, the Yankees were a maritime people, with menfolk often "gone awhaling" or engaged in world commerce and shipping. The vast upheaval and movement of persons during the Civil War gave portrait photographers a decisive boost. Portraits were a way of reducing the pain of the separations in some small measure. In some degree, they even breached the great gulf between the living and the dead. They were prized reminders of significant primary-group ties.

The product of the portrait artist also had a deep tradition as a status symbol. To be able to display portrait paintings of assorted ancestors testified to a family's place in time. It was a society where aristocratic birth or family background was decreasingly related to power and wealth. Still, there was a pronounced cultural lag that permitted such symbols to suggest high social position. Achieved criteria were becoming objectively more and more important, but ascribed criteria had not lost their significance. In the early period of the industrial revolution, some members of the newly rich are even said to have hired portrait painters to manufacture for them a set of distinguished ancestors. For the less wealthy, and for the growing middle and working classes, the silver iodide plate of the daguerreotypist provided a mass-consumption substitute for the more distinguished canvas of the portrait artist.

Some indication of the rapid adoption of this innovation can be gained by a study of the growth of the occupational classification of "photographer." Table 2 indicates the number of photographers in the United States per 100,000 population for the years 1840 to 1930. These data show the rapid diffusion of photography as a cultural innovation. This occurred in the four decades 1850–1890. By the last decade of the nineteenth century, there is little doubt that the average American was widely familiar with photographs. The transition between a still photograph and one that gave

THEORIES OF MASS COMMUNICATION

Table 2   The Growth of the Occupation of Photographer in the United States
(1840–1930)

Year	Size of Population (in thousands)	Number of Photographers	Photographers per 100,000
1840	17,000	0	0
1850	23,000	938	4
1860	31,000	3,154	10
1870	39,000	7,558	19
1880	50,000	9,990	20
1890	63,000	20,040	32
1900	76,000	27,029	36
1910	92,000	31,775	35
1920	106,000	34,259	32
1930	123,000	39,529	32

SOURCE: U.S. Bureau of Census, *Population Census of the United States* (for the decennial years 1840, 50, . . . 1930, Washington, D.C.).

the illusion of motion was not an impossible step for the imagination of the ordinary citizen.

Improvements in Photography   The technology of photography be-came increasingly sophisticated; it also became more and more important as part of the growing industrial complexes of society. Factories for the manufacture of photographic chemicals, photographic equipment, and photographic plates were developed. Among these, the name of George Eastman is perhaps the most widely known. The first daguerreotype pho-tography had given way to other techniques. The ambrotype grew in popularity and then quickly declined. The tintype was widely used during the Civil War, but was discontinued with the perfection of newer technol-ogy. Wet-plate processes, with light-sensitive chemicals suspended in a thin collodion film on glass, were widely used for many years. It was the dry plate, however, that permitted preparation in advance of glass photo-graphic plates. This led to their commercial manufacture, distribution, and sale. The miniature camera and the amateur camera were popularized when this technology became available. George Eastman went into the business of manufacturing such photographic plates in the year 1880. From a modest enterprise started on a capital of three thousand dollars, he built a business that thirty-four years later could pay five million dollars for exclusive rights to the patented process of making flexible photographic plates on nitrocellulose film.

The development of flexible film actually occurred in several places at the same time.[13] One type of film was developed in France in the early 1880s. One of Eastman's chemists applied for a patent in the United States at about the same time. Still another patent was applied for in 1889, by the Reverend Hannibal Goodwin, an obscure clergyman. These films were all based upon more or less the same process, with minor variations from one to the other. However, several years of extremely complex litigation ensued, during which the patent office reviewed and re-reviewed the various claims. The patent was finally awarded to Goodwin, but in the meantime. Eastman had been manufacturing flexible film for almost a decade. This roll film was designed for his "foolproof" camera that could be used by the novice (the famous Kodak). With the availability of this flexible film, the development of the motion picture was a step nearer. Edison had produced the light bulb, and the technology of electricity was widely understood. The study of objects in motion had progressed with the use of instantaneous still photography. As we have seen, the principle of projection had long been common knowledge. The neurophysiology of visual lag had been worked out to an adequate extent. It remained only for these various elements to be combined into a workable projected motion picture. The camera obscura and the magic lantern were about to be combined in ways that would have astonished Kircher, della Porta, and da Vinci.

Motion Pictures Become a Reality

It was Thomas Alva Edison who achieved the basic technological combination, but hundreds of others in various parts of the world also contributed.[14] From Edison's laboratory came the motion picture camera and a motion picture projector. It was early in the last decade of the nineteenth century.

Edison lacked confidence in the financial feasibility of the commercial projection of motion pictures on the ground that they would be a novelty and the public would soon lose interest. His conception of the way to exploit his device commercially was to develop a machine that could be used by only one person at a time, paying a fee to view a few moments of photographed motion. His peep show Kinetoscope was scheduled for premiere at the Chicago World's Fair of 1893, but it was not ready in time. It was in fact the following year, 1894, when the Kinetoscope was placed on public exhibition for the first time. An enterprising exhibitor opened up a "Kinetoscope Parlor" with ten of the machines right on Broadway in

New York. But the limitations of the Kinetoscope were severe, and the possibilities for a more complete exploitation of the magic lantern of movement were seen by a number of people both in the United States and in Europe. While Edison made the most significant contribution to the actual emergence of the motion picture by achieving the basic technological combination, it remained for more adventurous souls to try to perfect the technique and to turn it into a process for the mass entertainment of the multitude.

In the final years of the century, literally dozens of people were clamoring for patents in as many countries. They were looking for financial backing and for recognition of a variety of motion picture cameras or motion picture projectors. From England, France, Germany, and the United States came conflicting claims and reports that these devices had been invented, improved, modified, or perfected. It was in fact a period of high excitement, intense activity, and inventive ferment. Showmen such as Emile Reynaud in Paris were exhibiting projected motion picture stories, based upon the principle of animated drawings, with great success. It took no vast stretch of imagination to see that the commercial exhibiting of projected motion pictures could be a considerable financial success.

THE MOVIES AS A MASS MEDIUM

In 1895 an establishment called the Cinematographe was opened in Paris. For a single franc, patrons were admitted to a "salon" where they could view a few very brief films. The exhibition became so popular within a few days that it attracted thousands of viewers, and was operated on a standing-room-only basis.

The Cinematographe was soon exhibited in New York, and the system was widely imitated. In the meantime, in England, the motion picture camera was focused on such events as the Derby of 1896, and the exhibition of these projected films caused a sensation. These and other attempts at public showings stimulated further interest in the idea of projected motion pictures for entertainment of the public. It was clear that there were fortunes to be made in the motion picture business.

By this time, Edison had become convinced. He combined efforts with a young American inventor named Thomas Armat, who had obtained certain patents involved in the improvement of the projector. Together they manufactured the Vitascope, or Armat-Edison projector, which was used in the most successful of the early efforts to exhibit motion pictures to the public.

With the dawn of the twentieth century, then, all the technological problems had been solved. The motion picture theater had been more than two thousand years in the making, but it was now ready to take its place as the second of the major mass media of communication and to play its role in a growing communication revolution.

The Content and Audiences of Early Films

From the outset, motion pictures were concerned with content of low cultural taste and intellectual level. Even the very first moving pictures in the Edison Kinetoscope parlors exhibited such inspiring works as *Fatima and Her Danse du Ventre*. She was the sensation of the Chicago World's Fair in 1893. Naive and slapstick comics were popular. A view of a mischievous boy squirting a hose on a dignified dowager or even pornography (within the limits of the era), such as the brief *How Bridget Served the Salad Undressed*, were received with enthusiasm by the patrons of the penny arcades in which the Kinetoscopes were installed.[15] These first films, with their boxing matches, low comedy, and shimmy dancers, can be contrasted with the efforts of the first printers. Gutenberg's first product represented the most significant and important ideas of his time. Books in the early period were works of philosophy, science, art, or politics. The motion picture concerned itself in its early period with the trivial and inconsequential. The content mattered little to anyone; it was the novelty of movement that was the important factor. The film's first audiences stared with open mouths at any picture that moved. But even among the habitués of the penny arcades, an important principle quickly began to manifest itself. Such films as *Beavers at Play* or *The Surf at Dover* brought in fewer pennies than the brief but exciting *Danse du Ventre* or the titillating *What the Bootblack Saw*. Efforts toward the filming of more serious or artistic subjects were not received with enthusiasm. Film content aimed at more elementary gratifications brought in the money. From the first, then, systematic relationships between audience tastes and the financial structure of the infant "industry" governed the production of film content. Audiences were selective in what they would pay to see, and because of this, producers were selective in what they produced.

It would be tempting to analyze the characteristics of the clientele of the penny arcades, which were to say the least not located in the more discriminating sections of the urban centers. One might be tempted to draw the inference that it was their low level of cultural taste that left a permanent stamp of mediocrity upon the film. The problem was that the film moved out of the penny arcade very quickly, but it did not noticeably rise in the seriousness or in the artistic taste of its content. The film went from the arcade to the vaudeville house, where it was exhibited as a scientific novelty following the major acts. Again, the tastes of the burlesque theater governed the content of the films.

The Nickelodeon Era

In about the year 1900, a number of enterprising arcade owners, former circus operators, medicine showmen, ex-pitchmen, barkers, and the like, began to rent unused stores, to equip them cheaply with benches or chairs, and to project films with secondhand equipment. Their working capital was meager, their repertoire atrocious, their establishment dismal, but above all it was cheap. For only a nickel the audience member could watch an assortment of exciting short pictures, ranging from *Life of An American Fireman* to *Dream of a Rarebit Fiend*. These were either trick movies of brief length or exciting little sequences of dramatic events such as the firemen responding to a call. Various names were used but the term "nickelodeon" caught on as a popular way of referring to these enterprises. The most important things about them were that they were popular with people at the bottom of the social structure, and they made money. Then nickelodeons began to clean up their interiors and dress up outside. Many opened up in principal cities in the country. The first decade of the twentieth century, then, saw a new form of communication begin to spread. The film was about to become a true mass medium.[16]

The content of the films soon changed markedly. They became longer and more sophisticated technically. They did not rise far in taste or seriousness. Such fare as *The Great Train Robbery* was just about what the nickelodeon audience wanted to see in 1903. Films with stories became the norm in a very short time. These places of entertainment thrived in their most prosperous form in the same areas of the metropolis where the penny arcades were located. As the motion picture was establishing itself, its audience tended to be heavily weighted with poor immigrants, drifters, and the anonymous residents of the city's zones of transition. The most significant groups in numbers were by far the immigrants. The first ten years of the 1900s were a period of unprecedented immigration, unequaled in more contemporary times. People from many cultures were pouring into the United States from eastern and southern Europe. By the millions they established ethnic neighborhoods within the ecological and social structure of the city. Immigration laws were not strict by today's standards, and many of these new citizens were illiterate even in their own language. A large proportion had no knowledge of English whatsoever. Substantial numbers were agricultural peasants in their own land. For these humble people, surrounded by a bewildering and complex industrial society that they had not yet begun to understand, the primitive movie was a source of solace and entertainment. The plots were simple; the stylized acting needed no knowledge of the language in order to understand the idea. Today's viewer is amused at the stereotyped facial expressions and the gross body movements of the actors in early films. Such techniques become more understandable when it is realized that the audience had only occasional subtitles with which to follow the plot in a verbal sense. Even many of the English-speaking members of the audience could read only with difficulty, if at all, and a great many of the foreign-born knew not a word.

The immigrants, then, along with rustic Americans newly arrived in the big city were the most important audience types toward whom the early nickelodeon movies were aimed. With slapstick and burlesque they even poked fun at such people themselves and made them laugh at their own plight. The country bumpkin and the immigrant were often seen in films. The cop, the crook, the pretty girl, the jealous husband, the boss—this was about the total range of personalities that appeared in the movies. It was enough. Their antics were easily understood. In intensified form, this stereotyping and slapstick led to such content as the Keystone Cops and the pie-throwing scenes.

The Movies Mature

Within a short time the nickelodeon had spread far beyond urban centers. The movies began to be a form of family entertainment. People wanted longer films with more interesting content. The novelty of merely seeing motion had worn off. Movie producing companies sprang up to fill the demand for films, and operators worried about how they could shake the sordid image of the medium. A number of changes were made, and this booming entertainment medium was well on its way. The "star" system came; movies discovered the classics; more flexible techniques of photography were developed. The films grew longer to the feature length we are now accustomed to. This increase in technical competence was due in part to the growing enthusiasm of motion picture audiences. The dreary nickelodeons had given way by the beginning of the 1920s to much larger and more elaborate picture palaces. Some were so luxuriously decorated they almost appeared to be temples of worship for the new gods and goddesses of the screen. Such stars were receiving the adoration of millions of shop girls and factory hands. They were also receiving astronomical salaries, which made Hollywood synonymous with ostentatious consumption of wealth.

The Influence of World War I The Great War had given the American film industry an unprecedented boost. The production of motion pictures in the studios of Europe had ceased after 1914, but the demand for films had become tremendous and worldwide. This placed U.S. films in the export market with an advantage, which was retained for years. The silent film, with written subtitles easily changed to any language, was made by directors and producers who were themselves immigrants from other countries. It was a particularly flexible product for export to foreign countries. Almost inexhaustible markets were opened up when the more remote regions of the world began showing films with subtitles in Urdu, Hindi, Chinese, Arabic, or whatever local language was required. If the local audience was not literate in its own language, a "storyteller" was employed to explain to the native audience what was transpiring in the film as it progressed. Any relationship between these versions and the original intent of the film's designers was purely coincidental. The political position of the United States in World War I, then, had the most significant impact upon the American motion picture as a mass medium. It made the medium one of world significance.

The events of the Great War also point up other ways in which a society can have an impact upon its media. When the war broke out in Europe, the American public increasingly began to focus its public opinions in two opposite directions. The pacifists wanted to stay out of the European war and avoid engaging in any military expansion that might eventually lead the country into participation in the war. Those in favor of preparedness felt that the United States would more than likely have to enter the war at some point, and it might as well make military preparations to make the task easier if the need arose. These were issues of great importance during the years just before the United States declared war on Germany. When war came, a large bloc of the American public still retained attitudes, opinions, and sentiments unsuitable for total commitment and participation in the war effort. To reduce these "unhealthy" pacifist feelings, George Creel, chief of the Committee on Public Information (the official U.S. agency for domestic propaganda), mobilized motion pictures as part of an all-out effort to "sell the war to the American public." This thrust upon motion pictures a propaganda role they had not played before, at least in the United States.[17] Motion pictures had been simply a form of entertainment. They had not seriously engaged in persuasion for political partisanship, moral uplift, social responsibility, or cultural betterment. In general, they had *followed* public tastes and attitudes rather than *led* them. In the minds of some, experiences of the war opened up new possibilities and objectives for the film as a medium of persuasion. Actually, the motion picture in its form as a medium of entertainment has never become a consistent vehicle for effective political or social comment. While Hollywood has cooperated during wartime and has occasionally produced a film with a social "message," these are considered departures from the norm. The position of the film in this respect is distinct from that of the newspaper, which has consistently assumed that it has the responsibility to play a part in the political process.

Talking Pictures During the last part of the 1920s the sound track came to the film. By this time the motion picture theater was a permanently established and respectable place of entertainment for American families. As a business the production, distribution, and exhibition of motion pictures was firmly entrenched in the American economy, and as a cultural innovation it had become deeply institutionalized into our weekly routines. Accurate records of motion picture attendance are available on a national basis beginning with 1922. By that time, the film was so popular that the number of paid admissions in an average week in the United States already exceeded 40 million!

QUANTITATIVE PATTERNS

The adoption of the motion picture as a cultural innovation for mass use was both swift and extensive. The United States was literally transformed into a nation of moviegoers between 1900 and 1930. Table 3 shows both average weekly attendance from 1922 to 1973 and the number of households during the same period. Although attendance data are not available from 1900 to 1921, it appears most likely that this early period of movies followed the estimated trend as shown in Figure 2.

Perhaps the most significant aspect of the adoption pattern for the film is its *variability*. This is particularly apparent in the middle section of the curve, when attendance figures fluctuated wildly. These were the Great Depression years; hard times in the early 1930s had a sharp impact on moviegoing. Admissions dropped by more than 30 percent between 1930 and 1932. However, the late 1930s and the decade of the 1940s were Golden Years for the film. Even so, functional alternatives were becoming increasingly available. As these grew in number and popularity, their impact on motion picture attendance was to be little short of disastrous. Clearly, the rapid rise of television, beginning at the end of the 1940s and continuing through the next decade, had the deepest possible impact on the mass use of the motion picture. Even though the society as a whole was moving toward unprecedented economic affluence, average weekly attendance per household dropped from 2.37 in 1946 to only .53 in 1960. This

Table 3 Motion Picture Attendance in the United States (1922–1977)

Year	Average Weekly Movie Attendance (in thousands)	Total Number of Households (in thousands)	Weekly Attendance per Household
1922	40,000	25,687	1.56
1924	46,000	26,941	1.71
1926	50,000	28,101	1.78
1928	65,000	29,124	2.23
1930	90,000	30,000	3.00
1932	60,000	30,439	1.97
1934	70,000	31,306	2.24
1936	88,000	32,454	2.71
1938	85,000	33,683	2.52
1940	80,000	35,000	2.29
1942	85,000	36,445	2.33
1944	85,000	37,115	2.29
1946	90,000	37,900	2.37
1948	90,000	40,523	2.22
1950	60,000	43,468	1.38
1954	49,000	46,893	1.04
1958	40,000	50,402	.79
1960	28,000	52,610	.53
1965	21,000	57,251	.37
1970	15,000	62,875	.24
1971	14,000	64,374	.22
1972	15,000	66,676	.22
1973	16,000	68,251	.23
1974	18,000	69,859	.26
1975	20,000	71,120	.28
1976	20,000	72,867	.27
1977	20,000	74,142	.27

SOURCES: U.S. Bureau of Census, *Historical Statistics of the United States, Colonial Times to 1957* (Washington, D.C., 1960), Series H 522, p. 225; Series A 242–44, p. 15.

U.S. Bureau of Census, *Historical Statistics of the United States, Continuation to 1962 and Revisions* (Washington, D.C., 1965), Series H 522, p. 35.

U.S. Bureau of Census, *Statistical Abstract of the United States* (Washington, D.C., 1968), tables 11 and 302, pp. 12, 208 (1973); tables 53, 347, 349, pp. 41, 211, 212.

U.S. Bureau of Census, *Current Population Reports: Population Characteristics*, Series P-20, No. 166 (24 August 1967), pp. 1, 4.

U.S. Bureau of Economic Analysis; U.S. Bureau of Labor Statistics, Industry and Trade Administration, *U.S. Industrial Outlook*, 1979, p. 503

NOTE: Figures do not include Alaska and Hawaii. Some figures have been revised from previous editions because of revisions in source materials.

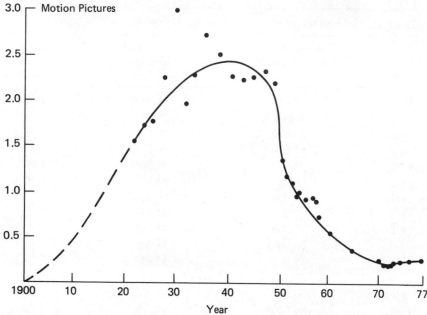

Figure 2. The cumulative diffusion curve for motion pictures; average weekly attendance per household in the United States (1900–1977).

drop continued to the remarkably low rate of .23 in 1973. It was still only .27 by 1979.

The movie industry struggled mightily to slow the rate of decline. As competition with television increased, numerous experiments were tried. At one point, moviegoers were issued special glasses so that they could see the picture in three dimensions. Screens widened—to almost unbelievable proportions in some cases. Special sound effects, with speakers in various parts of the theater, were tried. These gimmicks did not help much; the decline continued. Perhaps more significantly, the older moral standards governing film content collapsed. At an earlier time, motion pictures shown to American audiences were about as racy as the proverbial Sunday school picnic. Solid, middle-class America didn't need to be titillated with taboo themes to get them to pay at the box office. Today, unless a movie promises a blood-bath shock, or frank sex it may not be a big money-maker. Much legal maneuvering and litigation has accompanied this change, and the issues of "freedom of speech" versus "obscenity" have been widely discussed in connection with motion picture portrayals. Currently, public officials and others are sharply criticizing film violence as well as explicit sex.

Whatever the eventual significance of these issues within the context of the motion picture, it seems reasonably clear that the real pressure for change has been an economic one. The most logical projection for the future would be that the decline will continue, and that the movie theater as we now know it will eventually disappear. This does not mean that films will no longer be made. Television provides an insatiable demand for even the dullest films—as any viewer of the Late Late Show will testify. Thus, while the industry may survive, or even prosper, the behavioral forms of its consumers appear likely to continue their present trend. The strong shift of interest of the American public from the movie screen downtown to the television screen at home is likely to continue as color television achieves saturation, and as TV moves toward codes concerning content which will probably eventually resemble those of contemporary movies.

The conditions and factors related to the abandonment of a given behavioral form within a social system have largely been neglected in the recent surge of interest in the innovation process. Obsolescence is a natural counterpart of innovation, and a necessary feature of an adequate theory of social change. There are undoubtedly systematic principles that govern the way in which a given item, trait, or culture complex is abandoned by a population. We no longer make much use of quill pens, detachable collars, automobile cranks, the Townsend Plan, and the chaperoned party for young adults. These forms undoubtedly followed some reverse pattern of declining usage, symmetrical in form to the usual S-curve of adoption. In spite of the obvious significance of such obsolescence patterns for under-standing social and cultural change, no systematic theory is available concerning the conditions under which they are generated.

In the case of the motion picture, the causes of obsolescence are not particularly obscure. The depression, the population shift to the suburbs, and, of course, the continued growth of the electronic media have cut deeply into paid attendance. To these fairly obvious factors could be added the increasing congestion of central business districts where most theaters were located and the burden of mounting labor costs, which has resulted in continuous box-office increases and a correspondingly smaller number of consumers.

Overall, our analysis has shown the long and complex evolution of the motion picture. That evolution has been characterized by an accumulation of culture traits and technological innovations that were necessary for the emergence of the film as a medium of mass communication. It has indicated the many social and cultural conditions, such as wars, population shifts, and conflicts in the economic institution, that were significantly related to the eventual widespread adoption and possible impending obsolescence of motion pictures as a behavioral innovation on the part of the American population.

The impact of a society on a communication medium could not be more clear than in the case of the motion picture. As a technology, and as an industry, it will undoubtedly continue to occupy a place in our social system. However, there are considerable doubts concerning its survival in the form in which it was originally adopted by our population.

NOTES

1. Martin Quigley, Jr., *Magic Shadows: The Story of the Origin of Motion Pictures* (Washington, D.C.: Georgetown University Press, 1948), pp. 18–20.
2. Helmut Gernsheim and Alison Gernsheim, *The History of Photography From the Earliest Use of the Camera Obscura in the Eleventh Century Up to 1914* (London: Oxford University Press, 1955). See esp. Chap. 1, "The History of the Camera Obscura," pp. 1–19.
3. Quigley, *Magic Shadows*, pp. 29–35.
4. A reproduction of this famous work has recently been made available. See John Baptista Porta, *Natural Magick*, ed. Derek J. Price (New York: Smithsonian Institute for Basic Books, 1957).
5. Ibid., pp. 364–65.
6. Quigley, *Magic Shadows*, pp. 48–61.
7. Ibid., pp. 85–97.
8. Josef M. Eder, *History of Photography* (New York: Columbia University Press, 1945), pp. 209–45, 263–64, 316–21.
9. Robert Taft, *Photography and the American Scene* (New York: Macmillan, 1938), p. 3.
10. Ibid., p. 48.
11. Ibid., pp. 55–62.
12. Ibid., p. 76.
13. Ibid., pp. 384–404.
14. Quigley, *Magic Shadows*, see esp. Chaps. 15 and 16.
15. Richard Griffith and Arthur Mayor, *The Movies* (New York: Simon and Schuster, 1957), pp. 1–8.
16. Ibid., p. 19.
17. Ibid., pp. 113–19.

Broadcasting today represents the contemporary outcome of a long and continuing evolutionary process that includes an almost staggering number of technological innovations, scientific advances, and new economic and social forms.

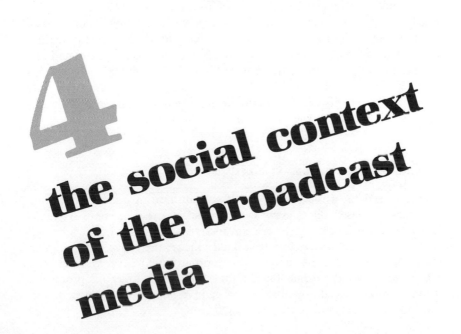

4
the social context of the broadcast media

Like the evolution of the other media, the development of broadcasting as a mass medium has been influenced by numerous conflicts, and its characteristics today have been shaped by the resolution of those conflicts. Huge corporations fought over patent rights; rival transmitters competed on the same frequencies to a point where the federal government finally had to intervene with emerging forms of control unique to this medium; radio fought newspapers for the right to broadcast the news; advertisers have fought regulatory agencies over false claims and puffery; and in recent times, battles have been waged over the portrayal of violence on television. Both the evolutionary and the conflict paradigms, therefore, provide essential frameworks for interpreting the way in which broadcasting has been shaped into the media we know today.

THE EVOLUTION OF TELECOMMUNICATION

In tracing the principal ways in which society has influenced the broadcast media, three somewhat distinct issues require clarification. First, there are the numerous and complex social factors that established the need and consequent search for an instantaneous medium of communication that could leap across oceans and span continents. Second, there is the chain of scientific and technical achievements that accumulated as one invention led to another when various means of fulfilling the need were sought. Finally, there are the events that resulted in the translation of commercial wireless-telegraphy and radio telephone technology into a mass medium with which to broadcast programs to the home receivers of entire nations. We might add, of course, the growth of television out of radio as still another issue; but as will be made clear, the newer medium not only shared a common history with radio but inherited its financial basis, traditions, structure of control, and even much of its talent.

Expanding Communication Needs

People's need for a reliable means of communicating rapidly over long distances increased relentlessly as their society grew in complexity. As long as their social activities were confined to a small band, which moved about together or stayed close to a fixed village, the range of the human voice, or at most the distance a strong runner could cover without rest, proved sufficient as a means for handling their communication problems. But as complex social organizations were invented for military, commercial, and governmental purposes, such groups were continuously faced with the problem of coordinating their activities without a really reliable method of transmitting information quickly over long distances.

Human ingenuity is vast, and people of every age have shown a remarkable ability to take the technology of their time and apply it in some fresh way to the solution of practical problems. So it was with long-distance communication. Our earliest records tell of military commanders who signaled information at night from the tops of hills with the use of torches arranged in previously agreed upon patterns or crude codes.

The word *telegraph* itself comes from the Greeks, fully three hundred years before Christ. Its two component words imply "at a distance" and "to write." In the Greek, Persian, and Roman civilizations social organization in military affairs, government, and commerce had far outstripped communication technology, and the inability to coordinate complex activities was a frequent source of great difficulty. Armies were defeated, navies were sunk, governments collapsed, and fortunes were lost, all for the want of a word.

The Search for Solutions   An impressive array of technical gadgets was invented and pressed into service over the intervening centuries to find a solution to this cultural lag. Even primitive people, needing to communicate but sorely handicapped by their crude technology, were able to burn out the inside of a log and stretch the skin of an animal over one end to form a drum. With this they could conquer surprising distances using coded sounds. Smoke signals are another familiar example; carrier pigeons are still another (used right up into the twentieth century). Flashing mirrors, lantern signals, cannon shots, and fire beacons were all used in the struggle to surmount distance and time. But these early communication techniques were severely limited. Most were terribly cumbersome and distressingly unreliable. Many depended upon good weather, and the others could handle only very simple messages.

In more recent times, many interesting communication systems were invented. All were in some way dependent upon line-of-sight vision between communicator and receiver. By relaying a message along a series of stations, however, complex messages could be sent over surprisingly long distances. During the height of Napoleon's power in France, that country actually had a total of 224 semaphore stations that spanned over a thousand miles in all.[1] This type of system was the most elaborate and widely used of all the line-of-sight communication devices. An outgrowth of a simple idea developed by three French schoolchildren for sending messages to each other, it depended upon positioning a pair of large wooden arms on top of a tower in such a way that given configurations represented the letters of the alphabet in agreed-upon patterns. The signals could be read and interpreted by a receiving operator in another tower several miles away. This operator in turn sent the message along to the next station, and so on. It was expensive and cumbersome, but the system was in use in a number of European countries right up to the time that the electrical telegraph replaced it. The semaphore still has some limited applications, especially aboard naval vessels maintaining radio silence.

As Western society came into the nineteenth century, the need for a means of communication that would quickly transverse even the oceans themselves began to become critical. The tempo of commercial intercourse between nations had increased greatly with the advent of the industrial revolution. Great Britain was developing a colonial empire so vast and far-flung that it would be able to boast with impunity that it was one upon which the sun never set. Britannia ruled not only the waves but also a substantial portion of the world's land surface and a sizable segment of the world's population. Other nations, too, were building mighty navies and great merchant fleets. They were consolidating new political systems, developing colonial markets, and exploiting new sources of raw materials. Along with all of this came fundamental changes in the organizational nature of Western society. These changes have been discussed by social scientists in various terms such as complex organic evolution analogies, the movement from Gemeinschaft to Gesellschaft, the change from mechanical to organic solidarity, and the trend from a sacred to a secular society, to mention only a few. There can be little doubt that a communication medium such as the electrical telegraph was sorely needed in the face of growing societal complexity and could have been put to immediate, practical, and important use long before it was finally available.

The Dream of Instantaneous Communication The idea of an instantaneous telegraph based upon magnetic principles had been around in one form or another for a long time. Giovanni della Porta, the author of *Natural Magick,* had discussed a very special kind of lodestone (a type of iron ore with magnetic properties).[2] If two similar compasses were to be fashioned by using this mineral to magnetize their needles, it was said they would be locked together by some mysterious force so that if the needle of one were forced to point in a given direction, the other would then instantly and automatically move to the same orientation, regardless of intervening space. With the alphabet fixed around the circumference of the compass, the telegraphic possibilities which such a system might provide were obvious. But sadly, search as they might, scientists, philosophers, and learned people were never able to find quite the right variety of lodestone needed to construct such a marvelous *sympathetic telegraph.* Like

THEORIES OF MASS COMMUNICATION

the philosopher's stone, the Golden Fleece, and the fountain of youth, it remained forever beyond their grasp.

Scientific Progress in Understanding Electricity

Although the legendary lodestone failed to provide the means for a telegraph, the scientific laboratory eventually would yield devices that would transcend the hopes and dreams of all the ancient wise ones. The development of an adequate understanding of electricity came during the nineteenth century as part of the great surge of accomplishment in the physical sciences. Radio itself was a by-product of a long, continuous, and basic inquiry into the nature of electrical energy.

The theorizing and research that led to this communication medium occupied the lifetimes of large numbers of scientific workers, only a few of whom ever achieved popular recognition, financial success, or even lasting scientific honors. The list of problems these people solved is simply staggering. Today's teenagers who tune in to their favorite program of popular music while lying on the beach and the factory workers who prop up their feet at night and view their favorite ball team in action are acting in ways dependent upon the end products of centuries of brilliant scientific advances, the solution of which absorbed some of the most creative imaginations and most tireless workers of the last two centuries. These pioneers grappled with an endless list of conceptual, theoretical, and mechanical-technical problems whose solutions permitted today's systems of broadcasting.

The problems needing solution before radio could become a reality included the basic theory of electricity and elementary circuitry, including generating, conducting, and measuring electric currents. Also included were the theories of electromagnetic fields, coils, and the electromagnetic radiation and detection of high frequency oscillations. Another series of problems centered around the alteration of currents, such as rectification and amplification. The diode and triode electron tubes were required to couple voice transmission to the dot-and-dash wireless telegraph. Finally, for television, an offspring of radio, the problems associated with broadcasting patterns of light and shadow and receiving these on a viewing screen had to be solved. The light-sensitive photoelectron tube in the heart of the television camera was a substantial advance, as was the kinescope-receiving picture tube. The latter two opened the way for commercial television.

The Elements of Electrical Theory   The principles by which sound or light are converted to electromagnetic waves that can be broadcast through space, to be received and converted back into sound or light, involve the most basic of the physical sciences. Some of these principles govern the nature of matter itself.

The key to radio transmission and reception and to television is the *electron*. In oversimplified terms, the electron is conceptualized by physicists as an infinitesimally small *particle* that has the electrical characteristic of being negatively charged. Electrons, of course, are one major type of particle that make up *atoms*, but there are other kinds such as protons and related types that constitute the *nucleus* of a given atom. These tiny nuclear particles have positive electric charges that exactly match the negative electrical charges of the atom's electrons. It is this balance of electrical forces that holds the particles together in a given atom.

Each atom of the elements has a different number of electrons and other particles, making up its overall structure. The heavier a given element is, the more electrons it has in its atoms, and vice versa. An atom of a given element is a tightly organized structure of particles that are electrically balanced against each other in a tiny system. Some elements, however, have atoms whose outer electrons for various reasons are less solidly attached to their structures.

For some elements (like copper and many other metals), electrons can be temporarily picked off or added to the outer parts of these systems by chemical or electromagnetic processes, thus throwing the atom into a temporary electrical imbalance. When this happens, the atom attracts an electron from its neighbor to replace the one lost. Or if it has too many it passes one on to its neighbor. Then the neighbor reacts similarly with *its* neighbor, and so on. If the element is a good "conductor" of electricity, and is arranged in a long thin wire, the result will be a "flow of electrical current" along that wire. Nothing really "flows," of course, but the successive electrical imbalances in the atoms of the wires making up an electrical circuit can be thought of in this way. Storage batteries, generators, fuel cells, and many other devices are capable of producing these electrical imbalances at the end of a wire. This disequilibrium creates an energy source in the form of an electrical charge at the other end. From this comes our familiar host of applications of the resulting energy. It is used to create magnetic fields, heat, light, and other effects such as radio and television. If the foregoing seems complex, it is an indication to the reader of the difficulties that were overcome as part of the accumulation of ideas and technology prior to the invention of radio.

Electrical Technology: Applications of Theory All during the period from the Greeks up to the latter part of the eighteenth century, experimenters had marveled at the phenomenon of electricity. Static electricity was easily produced by friction, and with that principle in mind, experimenters built larger and larger devices for generating charges. The Greeks rubbed an amber rod on a piece of cloth and generated weak electrostatic induction currents capable of attracting a light pith ball suspended on the end of a thread. Centuries later, European scientists of the 1700s had elaborated the mechanics of this process to a point where they could generate awesome charges of static electricity with ponderous friction machines. Huge rotating disks with cloth pads to pick up the electrical charges were constructed. They astounded their friends by letting those charges smash between two metal points in lightninglike fashion up to a distance of several feet. Such machines were capable of attracting bits of thread or other objects from as much as thirty feet away. But actually, they were still using the same principle that had fascinated the Greeks, and they really did not understand why it all worked! While they must have been having a great deal of fun with their dramatic devices, they had not been able to solve the critical problem of *storing* electricity so that it could be used when and where it was needed.

Several people seem to have found a crude solution to this problem at about the same time. A jar half filled with water and corked with a wire down through the middle of the cork can "store" a charge of electricity. One end of the wire must dip into the water and the other end must be temporarily attached to the business end of a friction machine that is generating static electricity. An unsuspecting soul who later grasps the wire coming out of the jar will receive a bone-jarring shock if a large enough static charge has been fed into the storage jar. Called a Leyden jar (after the place where it seems most likely to have been invented), this device was used by Benjamin Franklin in his well-known experiment with the kite. He succeeded in charging up a Leyden jar with a kite flown into an electrical storm. One end of the (wire) kite string is said to have been attached to a key dipped into the water. The experiment demonstrated that the electricity of lightning and the electricity of the laboratory are the same. Why Mr. Franklin was not instantly electrocuted remains a mystery. It definitely is not advisable to attempt to repeat this interesting experiment. The storage battery of Alessandro Volta eventually replaced the Leyden jar, and more adequate devices for generating electrical currents were under development by Faraday and others.

A key element in the inexorable movement of technology toward the electrical telegraph was the development of the electromagnet. By the 1830s the various technical traits prerequisite to an electrical telegraph were available within the scientific culture. It remained only to put them together in the required pattern. The idea of the sympathetic telegraph had tantalized people for centuries. The need for such a communication device was critical, and the technological base had accumulated to a point where no fundamental problem remained to be solved.

Several people at about the same time seem to have hit upon one scheme or another that would constitute a workable telegraph. But it was the American Samuel F. B. Morse whose patents and system prevailed. Morse, the portrait painter, was not a scientist, and in his naiveté he seems to have blundered onto solutions for making a workable telegraph that scientists had overlooked as unlikely possibilities. He had set up a workshop in one of the buildings of the University of the City of New York, where he served as professor of literature and the arts of design. He tinkered with numerous gadgets and frequently sought the advice of several of his somewhat skeptical scientific friends. He eventually worked out a telegraph system that permitted him to transmit messages through ten miles of wire strung around and around in his workshop.

Morse immediately applied for a government grant to enable him to perfect the device (which he had promptly patented). After a great deal of fumbling, hesitation, and delay, the federal government eventually financed a telegraph line between Washington, D.C., and Baltimore, Maryland. The historical message "What hath God wrought?" flashed between the two cities on May 24, 1844, and the world entered into the era of instantaneous electric communication.

After an initial period of hardship, hesitation, and financial loss, the electric telegraph was gradually accepted by business, the military, and other groups; and the thin wires soon led to most major centers of population. The federal government, which had financed the original long-distance line, threw away its opportunity to control the patents and relinquished all its rights. They became the property of private corporations, with Morse as a major stockholder, and the development of this medium was left to private enterprise. It is clear now that the failure of the government to maintain itself in the telegraph business *set a precedent* that would be followed in the United States, where private ownership of the media of public communication constitutes a central condition in determining the type of content the audiences of the broadcast media now enjoy. It was this seemingly unimportant turn of events that forged an important link in the chain of development of the mass media in this country. As the telephone came, then the wireless telegraph, the wireless telephone, and eventually home broadcasting, the federal government was never again a serious contender for controlling rights to these media (although on one occasion it obtained and relinquished control of radio). This was certainly not the case in other countries.

After conquering tremendous financial and technical problems, cables were laid across the Atlantic Ocean by Cyrus W. Field, and on July 27,

1866, a message crossed the great sea with incredible speed. Within a very short time, networks of cables were laid under the oceans to the principal population areas of the world. By 1876 Alexander Bell and his brilliant assistant had succeeded in transmitting the human voice over electrical wires, and the pace of cultural accumulation in the area of communication technology was increasing swiftly. Soon the huge cultural lag between communication technology and complexity of social organization would begin to close. From the telegraph and the telephone it was only a short and very natural step to elimination of the wires to achieve a wireless telegraph and eventually a wireless telephone.

The Wireless Telegraph

While the development of the telegraph had been occurring, scientists like Volta, Ampère, Henry, Faraday, Maxwell, and Hertz were continuously working to understand the basic nature of electricity. The growth of increasingly sophisticated theory permitted an ever more elaborate technology for generating, storing, measuring, transmitting, modifying, and variously harnessing electrical power. Along about the time of the American Civil War, James Maxwell in Scotland had worked out a mathematical theory of mysterious electromagnetic waves which were supposed to travel at the speed of light. By 1888 a young German, Heinrich Hertz, had demonstrated the actual existence of these waves and built a laboratory apparatus for generating them and detecting them. The scientific world became intensely interested in this phenomenon, and experiments with the Hertzian waves were being carried on in laboratories in many countries.

Marconi's Gadget   In the early 1890s Guglielmo Marconi, who was then only twenty years old, became acquainted with these experimental studies of Hertzian waves and the apparatus used to generate and detect them. He reasoned logically that if their distance could be extended beyond the few hundred feet of the laboratory devices, signals in code might be transmitted with them in a kind of telegraph without wires. He promptly purchased an apparatus and began experimenting with it, sending its signals across the garden on his parents' estate. Although not a scientist, he was an imaginative tinkerer, and he succeeded in modifying the laboratory device and strengthening it to a point where he could send dot-and-dash messages up to about a mile. His apparatus had become the first wireless telegraph.

Marconi's work was never intended to advance basic science. His experiments had immediate practical and commercial goals rather than theoretical or scientific ones. He hurried to England in 1897 to patent his wireless telegraph. It was essentially a system of fairly common laboratory devices built on a very large scale for sending and receiving the Hertzian waves in the dots and dashes of Morse's telegraph code.

> There was a well-defined raising of eyebrows among the scientists when they learned that their laboratory gear had found its way into the patent office. Only a few, notably Crookes, Sir Oliver Lodge, and Ernest Rutherford, had given any thought at all to its practical use.[3]

Achievement of the Ancient Dream   Marconi soon built larger and larger devices that reached out over longer distances. Eventually even the Atlantic was spanned. Although Marconi's work may not have advanced basic science noticeably, it did represent a most significant step in the development of radio as an instantaneous medium of long-range communication. It brought the end product of more than a century of scientific research out of the laboratory and into the hands of groups who desperately needed a device with which to communicate rapidly over long distances.

"Marconi had come to England from Italy because he believed that England with her large mercantile marine, would prove the more profitable market for the discoveries he had made."[4] The wireless was by no means a mass medium at this time. By the end of the first decade of the new century it was in the hands of commercial, military, and governmental groups for the transmission of confidential information. It was especially suitable for use on ships, which could carry its heavy and bulky apparatus. The general public knew of the wireless telegraph only through what they occasionally read in the newspaper. The thought that they would ever have one in their homes or that it would begin to alter their family's daily routines surely never entered their heads.

FROM WIRELESS TELEGRAPH TO RADIOTELEPHONE

When radio had proved itself capable of performing the task Marconi and others had envisioned, powerful economic resources were brought to bear upon its development. The British and American Marconi companies soon had strong rivals. The naval establishments of powerful countries lost little time in adopting the wireless. Shipping firms found at last a practical means of keeping in contact with vessels at sea. Inevitably, ships with wireless apparatus found themselves colliding with icebergs or otherwise in difficulties. Dramatic messages of distress brought other ships similarly equipped to the rescue. These events attracted great popular attention. Meanwhile, radio technology continued to develop. Involved legal battles were fought over invention after invention during the time that radio's pioneers were improving the reliability, power, distance, and clarity of wireless messages. International conferences attempted to work out rules governing the transmission and receiving of messages. Hundreds of shore stations were built along coastlines by commercial, marine, and official naval interests. In the years just before World War I, wireless telegraphy was a widely used, commercially sound technique that had substantially begun to close the great cultural lag between communication technology and the development of complex and far-flung social organization. But no one had yet thought of the device as a medium of communication for the ordinary member of society.

Transmitting the Human Voice

The transmission of the human voice by wireless was the next step, and a number of inventors and scientists were working on the idea. It was not really such a tremendously difficult problem. The existing dot-and-dash wireless system had been developed in such a way that it was technically capable of receiving such broadcasts if they could be properly incorporated into the radiated signal. It was on Christmas Eve 1906 that wireless operators on ships up and down the Atlantic sea lanes off the coast of the United States first heard a human being speak to them through their earphones. They could scarcely believe their ears!

Reginald A. Fessenden had prepared an apparatus that permitted the broadcasting of infinitely more complex signals than those of the simple tone of the dot and dash. He had also constructed a very powerful transmitter to use in his experiments. Several persons spoke over the wireless on that eventful evening; one made a speech, one read a poem, and one even played the violin. The radiotelephone had become a reality.

In spite of Fessenden's early success with radiotelephony, it was to be many years before Americans had regularly scheduled radio programs to listen to in their own homes. Yet there was a growing popular interest in radio. In that same year, 1906, it was discovered that several mineral substances were capable of detecting radio transmissions when used in an extremely simple circuit. A very inexpensive "crystal set" radio receiver could be built by almost anyone with elementary mechanical skills. The cost of the parts was insignificant. This meant that people all over the country, even youngsters, could listen in on the code signals in the air. Once the code was learned, the sport had great appeal, and they never knew when they might eavesdrop upon an agonized signal of distress from some vessel sinking in mid-ocean.

> Thus at the very period when it was important that the general public be educated to the possibilities of radio the efficient crystal detector came along to boost the industry. The Morse code had great appeal to boys and young men, but when music and spoken words might occasionally be picked up out of the ether there arose a veritable army of enthusiasts for the new science. Boys love to tinker, to experiment with chemistry or mechanics, and here was the opportunity of the ages.[5]

The first decade of the new century brought many refinements, improvements, and significant new ideas. One of these was to revolutionize radio broadcasting and was even to provide the basis of an entire electronics industry that would follow. Its inventor, Lee De Forest, called it an *audion:* in the technical jargon of early radio it was called a *valve:* today we would call it a *vacuum tube.* Only recently has it been displaced by the transistor, a device which performs approximately the same task. De Forest's audion was the key element in electronic amplifiers that could enlarge both broadcast and received radio signals. After refinement, it permitted the human voice to be transmitted to all parts of the globe. Radio receivers became far more reliable and the clarity of reception improved. Refinement followed refinement. The heterodyne circuit and superheterodyne circuit significantly improved reception. Radio equipment, which was once so huge and heavy that only ships could easily transport it, now became increasingly light and portable. In fact, during World War I, radiotelephones were successfully mounted in airplanes for the purpose of informing gun batteries on the ground of the accuracy of their fire.

Private Ownership and the Profit Motive: Sources of Social Conflict

In some ways, one of the most crippling of the social conditions surrounding the early development of radio was the concept of private ownership and the profit motive. Every minor and major invention was immediately patented in the United States, in Britain, and in other countries as well. It became nearly impossible to make needed improvements in radio components or to market equipment thus improved without falling into bitter court entanglements over patent claims. In fact, all the major pioneers in radio, from Marconi on, frequently found themselves battling each other in court. Lee De Forest, one of the principal inventors of major radio components, was actually arrested and charged with fraud. The problem was, of course, that there were fortunes to be made in wireless, and the competition to tie up important inventions for exploitation was intense.

At the same time, it is also true that millions of dollars were expended by private individuals and syndicates to aid inventors in improving their ideas to the point where they could be turned into marketable devices. In the final analysis, this financial support for research may have compensated for the many problems that the concepts of private ownership, corporate profit, and commercial exploitation brought to radio.

World War I brought urgent military needs for the improvement of radio systems. It brought not only new organization, manpower, and funds to bear upon unsolved technical problems but it had another important effect. All patent litigation and restrictions were temporarily suspended for the duration of the war. The federal government was in complete control of the infant industry, and this brought new cooperative efforts to the task of technical advancement which would have taken much longer in peacetime.

THE RADIO MUSIC BOX

A young radio engineer by the name of David Sarnoff had advanced rapidly in the ranks of the American Marconi Company. He had achieved considerable public attention during the sinking of the ill-famed *Titanic* when it was ripped by an iceberg in mid-Atlantic. David Sarnoff remained at his telegraph key in a radio station in New York City decoding messages from the disaster scene. For three days and three nights he kept a horrified public apace of developments concerning the tragic incident. He later moved up from his post to more important positions in the company. In 1916 Sarnoff sent a memorandum to his superiors. This now-famous memorandum in a sense did for radio what Benjamin Day did for the press almost a century earlier. It showed an economically profitable way by which radio could be used as a medium of mass communication for ordinary families. While the company did not immediately follow Sarnoff's advice, he successfully predicted the major outlines of radio as a mass medium. He wrote:

I have in mind a plan of development which would make radio a "household utility" in the same sense as the piano or phonograph. The idea is to bring music into the house by wireless.

While this has been tried in the past by wires, it has been a failure because wires do not lend themselves to this scheme. With radio, however, it would be entirely feasible. For example—a radio telephone transmitter having a range of say 25 to 50 miles can be installed at a fixed point where instrumental or vocal music or both are produced. . . . The receiver can be designed in the form of a simple "Radio Music Box" and arranged for several different wave lengths, which should be changeable with the throwing of a single switch or pressing of a single button.

The "Radio Music Box" can be supplied with amplifying tubes and a loudspeaking telephone, all of which can be neatly mounted in one box. The box can be placed on a table in the parlor or living room, the switch set accordingly and the transmitted music received. . . .

The same principle can be extended to numerous other fields as, for example, receiving lectures at home which can be made perfectly audible; also events of national importance can be simultaneously announced and received. Baseball scores can be transmitted in the air by the use of one set installed at the Polo Grounds. The same would be true of other cities. This proposition would be especially interesting to farmers and others living in outlying districts removed from the cities. By the purchase of a "Radio Music Box" they could enjoy concerts, lectures, music, recitals, etc. While I have indicated a few of the most probable fields of usefulness for such a device yet there are numerous other fields to which the principle can be extended.[6]

If Sarnoff had added the singing commercial and the soap opera, his description of radio as it would develop into a system of mass communication would have been almost perfect. Within ten years he was to see radio grow into a medium for household use, following almost to the letter the outline that he had dictated. David Sarnoff's suggested application of existing radio technology to this imaginative, new, and practical usage ranks as an insight with that of Marconi's idea of taking existing laboratory devices and using them as a wireless telegraph. Sarnoff himself played a major role in bringing about this transformation; he became in a short time the manager of a new corporation in the radio field and was able to help make his dream become a reality.

The Issue of Control

Feeble attempts to perpetuate governmental control over radio at the close of the Great War were crushed by outcries by private interests. Just as the federal government had allowed control of the telegraph to fall into the hands of private persons, it similarly handed over this important new medium of public communication to commercial interests. Radio was defined by this act as an *arena of business competition* as opposed to a public medium of communication to be operated by organizations of government. This decision was to have far-reaching effects and ramifications with which we live today. Other societies formulated different definitions concerning the control of broadcasting, and the systems of broadcasting that have developed in such countries as Great Britain, the Soviet Union, and others offer interesting contrasts with our own. That is not to say that they are better, only that they are very different due largely to historical decisions and events.

Once direct governmental control was eliminated, British and American commercial interests, which had prospered during the war, fought each other to gain control. The General Electric Company finally bought up the British shares of American Marconi and formed a new corporation with a patriotic name (apparently designed to dispel fears of foreign control). The new Radio Corporation of America (RCA) was able to consolidate a number of conflicting patent interests, and it gave control over wireless telegraphy and radio broadcasting in the United States to American stockholders. In 1919 David Sarnoff, who had forecast the "Radio Music Box," was appointed its first commercial manager.

Scheduled Broadcasting Begins

Shortly after World War I, the Westinghouse Company, a major American manufacturer of electrical equipment, attempted to move into the international wireless telegraph field. It was not particularly successful. This was due largely to the fact that its rival RCA owned most of the important patents. However, some of its directors were interested in the newer field of wireless telephony, and the company had done considerable research in this area. Dr. Frank Conrad was in charge of experiments with new and powerful transmitters of this type. In connection with this work, he not only built such a transmitter for experiments at the Westinghouse laboratory, but he constructed one at home over his garage so that he could continue his work in the evening. He licensed his home transmitter nearly a year later as station 8XK in April 1920. He started to broadcast signals during the evening hours as he worked with his apparatus in attempts to improve its design. He soon found that people in the area were listening in on their amateur receiving sets. This proved to be a boon at first because their letters, cards, and phone calls gave him some indication of the range and clarity of his transmitter. Before long, however, his circle of amateur radio listeners began to become a problem. To create a continuous sound, he had started to play the victrola over the air. His listeners began to demand particular songs and would even call him at odd hours to ask him to play a favorite record. Dr. Conrad solved the problem by regularizing his broadcasts, and with the cooperation of a local phonograph dealer, he was able to present continuous music for a two-hour period two evenings a week. The number of listeners grew rapidly, and his family enthusiastically joined in the fun to become the first "disc jockeys."

Stimulating the Sale of Sets   All this activity increased the demand for receiving sets in the area, and it became increasingly clear that there might be money to be made in the manufacture of such sets for home use. The commercial possibilities of this did not escape the attention of officials of the Westinghouse Company. They decided to build a larger transmitter in East Pittsburgh for the purpose of stimulating the sale of home receivers of their own make and the sale of the components from which amateurs built such sets. It was in this way that Station KDKA, Pittsburgh, came into existence in the year 1920.

Although David Sarnoff had forecast the radio music box several years earlier, it was the decision of Harry P. Davis, vice-president of the Westinghouse Electric and Manufacturing Company, that concretely gave birth to commercial household radio. He decided that a regular transmitting station, operated by the manufacturer of receivers, would create enough interest in the sale of sets to justify the expense of operating the station. Although this financial basis for broadcasting has long been replaced by the sale of air time for advertising, it was sufficiently practical at the time to get radio started as a medium for home use.

To stimulate interest in the new station and, of course, to promote the sale of receiving sets, it was announced that the transmitter would broadcast the results of the 1920 presidential election over the air. Bulletins were phoned to the station from a nearby newspaper, and the returns were broadcast during the evening of November 11 as they came in. An audience of between five hundred and a thousand people heard the word through the air that Warren G. Harding had been elected President of the United States. The event was a sensation; the dream of David Sarnoff had become a reality.

Growing Public Interest   The Pittsburgh experiment was so successful that other stations were quickly launched. Transmitters began regular broadcasts in New York in 1921, followed by stations in Newark and other cities. Westinghouse soon had several competitors. The public's interest in radio had been growing. Its appetites for the new signals in the air had been whetted by the glamor and excitement of radio's brief history. The dramatic stories of rescues at sea, of daring flights over wild terrain with radiotelephones, and the struggles of giant corporations to gain control over wireless telegraphy had all contributed to this surging interest.

82   THEORIES OF MASS COMMUNICATION

When radio stations actually began to broadcast during regular periods with music and voices people could receive at home in their own cities, this latent interest suddenly burst into a fullblown craze. The public began to clamor for radio. By 1922 the manufacture of home receivers was lagging hopelessly behind the receipt of orders. New stations were being built at a staggering pace. In the last half of 1921 licenses were issued for 32 new stations, but in the first half of 1922 this number had risen to 254! Although there were still many problems to work out concerning its financial base, its content, and its technical functioning, radio as a mass medium was off to a flying start.

The Problems of Interference and Finance

One of the earliest problems that household radio encountered was brought on because of its own popularity. There is a limited spectrum of frequencies available that are suitable for broadcasting. In the beginning, no attempts were made by either government or private groups to regulate the frequencies that transmitters in a given area would use. The Radio Act of 1912 did not specify frequencies for privately operated broadcast stations. The Secretary of Commerce, who licensed all new transmitters, had selected two frequencies, 750 kilocycles and 833 kilocycles. All stations were assigned one or the other.

Conflict on the Airways: Competing Transmissions   As the number of transmitters operating grew quickly, there developed an annoying number of instances where two stations were operating near enough to each other so that the program of one would be imposed upon the sound of the other. This type of interference could not easily be controlled. Many stations worked out informal agreements to divide up available time. There was no legal authority that could assign different positions on the radio band for every station to use and could rigorously enforce such regulations. Obviously, such a problem could be handled only by some form of governmental agency, but there was no adequate provision by Congress or by the states for such a controlling body. The Department of Commerce issued licenses to operate transmitters, but did little else. Because of the lack of control over this technical problem, confusion began to mount.

In the meantime, radio was advancing at a tremendous pace. In 1922 station WJZ in Newark successfully broadcast the World Series. Stations began to broadcast opera, concerts, news, dance music, lectures, church services, and a great variety of events. Voluntary experiments were tried by having nearby stations broadcast on wavelengths at least twenty meters different from each other as a means of avoiding overlap. In spite of efforts to combat interference, the problem continued to grow.

Successful experimentation with networks was tried, and it was found that several stations linked by wires could simultaneously broadcast the same program. The rush to build new transmitters continued, and by 1923 stations were to be found in most major cities across the nation.

Paying for the Broadcasts But two major problems continued to plague the medium. The technical problem of interference was already badly out of hand, but there was also the problem of paying for the broadcasts. While the larger electrical manufacturers could afford to finance their stations out of their profits on the sale of sets, this was a limited expedient at best, and it was no help at all to the owners of stations who were not electrical manufacturers.

By the end of 1923, some of the initial enthusiasm for constructing radio transmitters began to sag as the hard financial facts had to be faced. There was simply no profit as such, and only those with other financial resources were in positions to continue in operation.

> Now that a full year of nation-wide radio broadcasting had been completed the summer of 1923 afforded an opportunity to cast up the accounts, so to speak. This was indeed a disturbing experience, since the studio ledgers of every station disclosed entries almost entirely in the red ink. Fortunes had been squandered in the mad rush. . . . As early as December, 1922, the Department of Commerce reported the suspension of twenty stations for that month alone. With every succeeding month the casualty list had grown more appalling. Between March 19 and April 30, 1923, forty-two stations gave up their franchises. In the month of May there were 26 failures. June, 1923, saw fifty radio stations become silent. In July twenty-five franchises were surrendered. Thus in the period from March 19th to July 31st of this fateful year 143 radio stations went out of business.[7]

Unless some viable financial basis could be found, radio as a medium of communication to the American home was doomed.

Attempted Solutions But the public was not to be denied radio. The mid-1920s were years of prosperity for most Americans. The grim remembrances of the Great War were fading, and the nation was entering a period of industrial and financial growth. The new practice of installment buying was part of a great expansion of credit that was taking place in the entire economic structure. No one had any inkling of the eventual collapse that would begin in October of 1929. Installment buying made it easier for families of modest means to purchase consumer goods such as radio receivers. Radio listening was becoming increasingly popular, and pressure was being exerted on Secretary of Commerce Herbert Hoover to do something about the interference problem. He did work out a system for assigning different wavelengths to various broadcasting stations, but the attempt to implement it was not completely successful. People who owned sets capable of picking up only one major frequency did not like the idea. Also, there was no actual way of enforcing the assignments, and some transmitters simply ignored the plan. On the other hand, many of the major stations, which were engaged in regular broadcasting, tried to follow the secretary's assignments and did so with success.

The industry itself was exerting great pressure upon the Department of Commerce not only to regulate frequencies but to limit the number of stations that could be licensed in a given area. The public, too, was becoming disenchanted with the cacophony that came out of their sets night after night. The problem of interference was getting unbearable. Ancient spark transmitters used for marine broadcasts, Morse code amateurs, powerful stations that broadcast regularly, and local fly-by-night operators were all blasting each other over the airwaves.

Four major conferences were held during the years 1922–1925 in Washington, D.C., to discuss the problems of broadcasting. The position of government was that it was up to the industry itself to clean up its own house. The newspapers had gotten along without government control. In fact they had fought it bitterly. The film industry was cleaning up its products. In a political system that stressed private initiative, it was felt by many government officials that federal control over broadcasting would be a dangerous precedent. In fact, Congress had repeatedly refused to consider bills on the subject. The only legislation in existence on radio was the old Radio Act of 1912, which was hopelessly out of date.

The problem was not an easy one to solve, even by government control. Since wireless telegraphy would also need regulation, the matter had international complications. In addition, there were the thousands of amateurs whose rights had to be protected. Not only were there more than 500 major stations operating on a regular basis, but there were approximately 1400 small stations of very low wattage that operated when their owners had the urge. Yet, to pick up this jumble of signals, Americans spent $136 million for receiving sets in 1923 alone.[8]

Secretary of Commerce Hoover struggled valiantly to find a solution. He tried limiting the power and hours of operation of some stations so that they could share a given frequency. By 1925 every spot on the frequency band was occupied, some by several stations. The broadcast band could not conveniently be extended without severely infringing upon other important kinds of radio and wireless operations. There were 175 additional stations clamoring for licenses that could not be accommodated.

Chaos Revisited   In 1926 this arbitrary system collapsed. A federal court decided that the Secretary of Commerce had no legal basis to impose any restrictions on a station's power, hours of operation, or transmitting frequency. In that same year also, the Attorney General issued the opinion that the only existing legislation, the Radio Act of 1912, really did not provide a legal basis for any of the regulations he had been using. Hoover simply had to abandon the entire attempt in disgust, and he issued a public statement that urged radio stations to regulate themselves. They were unable to do so.

In the face of the utter chaos that followed, President Coolidge asked Congress to enact appropriate legislation to regulate broadcasting, including provisions for adequate enforcement. They did so in 1927. They first enunciated the important principle that *the airwaves belong to the people* and that they can be used by private individuals only with the formal permission of government on a short-term license basis. Licenses were to be granted or revoked when it was in the public interest, convenience, or necessity to do so. All licenses of existing stations were automatically revoked; and the industry had to start all over by applying formally for a franchise to operate and by providing adequate statements and explanations as to why it would be in the public interest for them to do so.

Government Regulation of the Medium   The Radio Act of 1927 was to be a temporary solution. After a seven-year period of observation, trial, and some readjustments, a new and more permanent set of statutes was written and a Federal Communications Commission (FCC) was established to enforce the provisions. The Federal Communications Act of 1934 has since become, with appropriate amendment from time to time, the principal regulating instrument for the broadcast industry in the United States.

Meanwhile, the boisterous new industry continued to seek an adequate means of financial support. By the mid-1920s, broadcasters were still grappling with this problem. A committee of New York business people tried the experiment of soliciting funds directly from the listening audience for the purpose of hiring high-quality talent to perform over one of the larger stations in the area. While a trickle of funds came in, most listeners decided they would rather listen free to whatever happened to come their way than pay directly out of pocket to be assured of higher-quality programs. This response typifies the feelings of the majority even today. It also explains in part why the public eventually accepted advertising messages as a means of financing broadcasting. They would rather put up with somewhat objectionable commercials than pay directly for their entertainment.

Other schemes were proposed. David Sarnoff felt that wealthy philanthropists should endow radio stations just as they did universities, hospitals, or libraries. Others suggested charging a license fee for operating a home receiver, the proceeds of which were to be divided among broadcasters. Many felt that the industry itself would solve the problem. The larger manufacturers of receiving sets were said to have an obligation to provide something to hear on their products. It was thought that this would eventually result in a small number of networks, each operated by a different manufacturer or group of manufacturers, and that there would be few if any independent stations.

Radio Goes Commercial

But while these debates were being carried on, advertising was quietly creeping in as a dependable source of revenue for radio broadcasts. In fact, as early as 1922, station WEAF had sold radio time for ten-minute talks on behalf of a Long Island real estate company that was selling lots. Then major companies began to sponsor programs. A department store paid for an hour-long musical program. A tobacco company sponsored a radio variety show. A candy company presented two comedians. The public was much drawn to these, and audiences wanted more. At first, these sponsors made no direct advertising appeal for their products. They simply mentioned their name as sponsor or titled the program after the name of their product. This form of subtle advertising found little criticism. The general goal of sponsoring such a program was to create goodwill among the audience.

The Secretary of Commerce was dead set against open huckstering on radio. He said, "It is inconceivable that we should allow so great a possibility for service, for news, for entertainment, and for vital commercial purposes to be drowned in advertising chatter."[9] Many other voices were added to this view. Responsible officials in government, leaders of the industry, and many groups of listeners concurred.

But in our society, such an idealistic position was doomed from the outset. With listeners more interested in "free" entertainment than quality programming; with government playing only a technical role, primarily to keep frequencies unscrambled; with ownership of the media in the hands of profit-seeking companies and corporations, the noble views of the Secretary of Commerce and his supporters were not consistent with the value system, the political structure, and the economic institution of the society within which the new medium was developing. The same socioeconomic forces that led newspapers to turn to selling space to advertisers so they could sell their products to a mass audience were to result in a parallel pattern for radio. The surrender to advertising was strongly resisted for some time, but inevitably it came. It was somewhat artificially held back briefly by the policies of the American Telephone and Telegraph Company, which controlled many patents, transmission lines, and radio equipment used by broadcasters. But even this opposition was relaxed, and the way was opened for the flood of commercial messages that are now so much a part of broadcasting in the United States.

At first, advertising was restrained and dignified. But soon it became increasingly direct and to the point. It would be incorrect to say the public welcomed advertising, but it is certainly true it welcomed what advertising revenue made possible. People were willing to hear the sponsor's pitch in order to be able to listen to their programs. One reason for this was that programs were quickly designed to have great popular appeal. Money from advertising made it possible to hire effective talent. Individual comedians, singers, and bands soon developed large and enthusiastic followings. Weekly drama programs became popular. Programs for children were developed; sports broadcasts drew large audiences. A great variety of content was designed to capture the interest of different large components of the population.

By the end of the decade, the major problems of radio as a mass medium of communication were solved. Almost everyone could buy a reasonably priced and reliable receiving set on time payments. The broadcasters received generous profits from selling their time to advertisers; sponsors sold products effectively over the air to a mass market; and talent with great popular appeal captured the nightly attention of the public. In the background, the new federal legislation had brought order out of chaos with respect to the interference problem. Only the ominous event of the crash of 1929 threatened to muddy the picture. But as it turned out, this was to have little negative impact on the growth of radio.

The Golden Age of Radio

Radio flowered during the 1930s and 1940s. These were very trying decades for the American society. The Great Depression and World War II were events that affected the destinies of every citizen, but they had little inhibiting effect on radio.

An overview of radio's growth in the American society can be obtained from table 4, which shows the number of receiving sets in operation for selected years. By the end of the 1930s there was slightly more than one set per household in the United States. This remarkable growth in the use of radio receivers had occurred in spite of ten years of economic depression following the stock market collapse of 1929. It should be emphasized for those who did not experience those tragic days that this was a period of

Table 4 The Growth of Radio Set Ownership in the United States (1922–1977)

Year	Total Number of Sets Home and Auto (in thousands)	Total Number of Households (in thousands)	Sets per Household
1922	400	25,687	.015
1925	4,000	27,540	.145
1930	13,000	29,905	.434
1935	30,500	31,892	.956
1940	51,000	34,855	1.463
1945	56,000	37,503	1.493
1950	99,000	43,468	2.277
1955	120,000	47,788	2.511
1960	156,000	52,610	2.965
1965	227,000	57,251	3.964
1970*	320,700	62,875	5.100
1971	336,000	64,374	5.219
1972	353,500	66,676	5.301
1973	408,500	68,251	5.985
1974	458,000	69,859	6.556
1975	501,000	71,120	7.044
1976	536,000	72,867	7.356
1977	580,000	74,142	7.823

*The development of transistors increased the numbers of radios in use sharply.

SOURCES: New York World Telegram Corporation, *The World Almanac, 1970* (New York, 1970).

U.S. Bureau of Census, *Historical Statistics of the United States, Colonial Times to 1957* (Washington, D.C., 1960), Series A 242–44, p. 15.

U.S. Bureau of Census, *Current Population Reports: Population Characteristics*, Series P 20, no. 106 (9 January 1961), p. 11; no. 119 (19 September 1962), p. 4; no. 166 (4 August 1967), p. 4

National Association of Broadcasters, *Dimensions of Radio* (Washington, D.C., 1974).

Electronic Market Data Book (Washington, D.C.: Electronic Industries Association, 1979).

NOTE: Figures after 1960 include Alaska and Hawaii. Some figures have been revised from previous editions because of revisions in source materials.

great distress for American families. Millions of workers were unable to find employment, and there were few public agencies to turn to for relief. The trauma of such conditions cannot be adequately appreciated without having been personally involved. It was a time when the people of the United States were gravely depressed in spirit as well as in an economic sense.

Quantitative Patterns   In spite of the hardships of the times, radio seemed to thrive on the depression! Advertising revenue, instead of drying up, grew at an ever increasing pace. The number of radio sets owned by Americans about doubled every five years. Families who had reached the limit of their financial resources would scrape together enough money to have their radio receiver repaired if it broke down. They might have to let the furniture go back to the finance company or stall the landlord for the rent, but they hung grimly on to their radio sets.

Radio fit the needs of millions of hard-pressed people during that trying time. It had music to restore their sagging spirits, funny people to cheer them up, and dramatic news to divert their attention from their personal problems. Amateur nights, evening dramas, soap operas, Western adventures, and variety shows were all followed avidly by loyal listeners night after night. On a summer night people could walk down a street on the evening that a particularly popular comedian was on the air and hear the program uninterrupted through the open windows of every house they passed.

By the time the depression eased and the war was about to begin, radio was reaching every ear. In mid-1940 there were nearly one and a half sets per household in the United States. Radio had also become increasingly sophisticated in every sense. It was technically excellent. It was possible for direct broadcasts to be picked up and relayed to listeners in their homes from almost any point on the globe. News broadcasting had become a sophisticated art, and outstanding journalists had established themselves within this new medium. The press and radio had learned to live with one another after prolonged feuding, and radio had full access to the world's wire services.

During World War II, the radio industry made all its resources available to the federal government. War information messages, domestic propaganda, the selling of war bonds, campaigns to reduce the civilian usage of important materials, and many other vital services were performed. It should be noted that the manufacture of home receiving sets was completely curtailed during the war years. Figure 3, the cumulative diffusion curve for radio sets, shows that from 1940 to 1945 few new sets were acquired by American households. Special attention should be

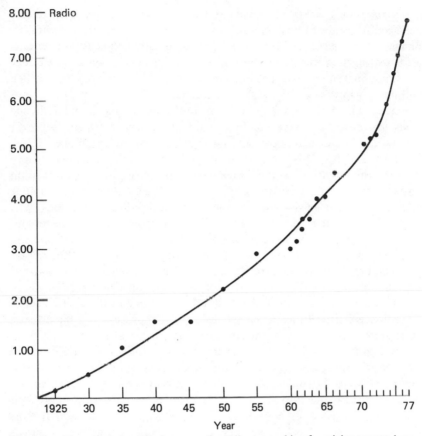

Figure 3. The cumulative diffusion curve for radio; ownership of receiving sets per household in the United States (1922–1977).

called, however, to the sharp rise in sales during the following five-year period, when the cumulative diffusion curve recovered from the retardation of the war years and resumed its regular pattern of growth.

Competition from Television   Of greater sociological significance are the postwar years when radio was faced with vigorous competition from television. If radio had retained its original format and content, it would have remained a direct competitor of the newer medium, which was apparently capable of gratifying the relevant needs of the mass audience in a more effective manner. At first, radio attempted to do this with the somewhat optimistic argument that over the years people had built up a deep loyalty to radio, which had served them so well, and they could not easily be lured away to a flashy new thing like television. The public turned out to be completely fickle, however, and as soon as families could afford television, they gleefully abandoned radio in favor of the tube. To put it in the language of structural functionalism, radio had been satisfying certain needs within the American society as a social system. When a more effective functional alternative became widely available, however, the earlier medium began to show signs of obsolescence.

Faced with the prospect of oblivion, radio was forced to find audience needs to satisfy that were not being effectively served by television. It successfully found such needs, and radio remodeled itself along new lines. During the 1930s, '40s, and even the early '50s, radio had successfully captured the attentions of the American family during the major evening hours. People turned to their radio to listen to the country's most popular entertainers. As television grew, it took over these entertainers along with the family's evening time. Radio was displaced from the living room and had to be content with the bedroom, the kitchen, the automobile, and the beach. Transistor technology, which opened up a huge market for miniature sets, helped keep radio from the type of postwar decline that occurred with motion picture theaters as a result of television (Figure 2).

At present, radio seems to have found a workable formula. It caters to its audience during times when television is inappropriate. People listen when they wake up in the morning, while they are working, driving, playing, and the like. But when evening comes and they settle down in their living rooms, the radio dial is turned off in favor of the television set. Nevertheless, radio remains as one of the most massive of our mass media in terms of the ownership of sets. Table 4 shows that Americans now own more than five sets per household. Figure 3 suggests that the curve of diffusion for radio has not yet begun to level off; it has by no means reached its peak. The trend toward miniaturization will probably continue, and set ownership will soar even higher. Needless to say, the impressive number of sets owned by American families does not imply that they spend a corresponding amount of time in radio listening.

DEVELOPMENT OF THE TELEVISION INDUSTRY

The newest of the broadcast media inherited many of the traditions of radio. Several factors worked together to make its technological development and its diffusion through the American society a much more rapid and less chaotic process than was the case with its parent medium. The technology of television was really quite sophisticated before mass-manufactured sets were placed on the market for the public. There was no period comparable to the "crystal set" era in any widespread sense. The new medium did not have to work out a structure of control with the government. The FCC and its supporting legislation were simply taken over from radio. The financial basis of television was clear from the start. The public was completely accustomed to "commercials," and television promised to be even more effective as a vehicle for the sales pitch. No great problem was foreseen in attracting advertising money. There was no period of feuding with newspaper and wire-service interests. These arrangements were simply extended from established radio interests. The network idea was already popular from the older medium. An adequate coaxial-cable technology was available, and only the physical facilities needed to be constructed. The public was already completely familiar with the moving picture, and its transmission through broadcasting was not difficult for them to accept. For this reason, little public resistance to adoption of the new device was anticipated.

The TV Set as Status Symbol

Actually, the television set quickly became a status symbol. In its early period of diffusion, families who could ill afford a set would sometimes scrimp on necessities to be able to buy one. The "easy payment plan," by now a deeply established American folkway, was widely used by families of modest means to acquire their sets. The urge to be identified as a set owner in the initial period of diffusion was so strong that in some cases families are said to have purchased and installed television antennas conspicuously on top of their dwellings long before they actually had sets to hook on. Stories of this type were widely circulated during the late 1940s. The definition of the television set as a luxury and as a status symbol led to occasional public outrage when it was discovered that people on public welfare or other forms of relief owned sets. Apparently the experiences of the depression years when radio sets were regarded as extremely comforting to people in trying economic circumstances had been forgotten.

Impediments to Growth

Actually, television might have been a household medium even earlier had it not been for two factors that held back its growth—World War II and a government imposed freeze. The electronic technology of television was worked out during the 1920s and '30s. By 1939 television broadcasts were being made in the United States. The World's Fair of that year featured demonstrations of this latest marvel of science, and President Roosevelt gave an address over the new communication medium. This particular broadcast was viewed by only a handful because commercial manufacturers had not yet begun to mass-produce sets. In 1941, on the eve of World

War II, the FCC approved home television, and the communication industry began to work out elaborate plans for its development. By this time there were nearly 5000 television sets (mostly in the New York area) in private hands, and several small stations were broadcasting regularly for two or three hours a day.

World War II The war interrupted any further development for the duration. In some ways this block to development may have accounted for the very rapid growth of television when the country returned to a peacetime economy. Electronics manufacturing techniques that aided in overcoming problems of television receiver production were developed during the war. Furthermore, the war completely ended the depression of the prewar period. In fact, with minor fluctuations the country entered a period of continuous economic growth, that was uninterrupted for more than two decades. The purchasing power of the average family rose to a point where television ownership was within the means of almost everyone.

The Freeze With the bitter lessons of the interference chaos in the early days of radio before them, the government took a much more active role in controlling the broadcasting frequencies of television. By 1948 there were about seventy stations in operation and several million sets in use. Applications for new permits began to come in rapidly. Since television has only thirteen VHF channels for the whole nation, a rigorous means of control was needed to avoid interference. Fortunately, the television signal does not follow the curvature of the earth as does a radio signal. This means that two stations broadcasting on the same channel would not interfere with each other if there were sufficient distance between them. A master plan for the whole United States had to be worked out so television channels could be fairly allocated. There was also the need to study competing color systems to see what problems lay there. In addition, there were a substantial number of UHF channels on the spectrum, and these had to be allocated among competing interests. With these and other technical problems in mind, the FCC stopped granting new permits for television stations in 1948. Those stations in operation were permitted to continue, but time was needed to work out a master plan in detail so that as many problems as possible would be avoided when television reached its maturity. Actually, the stations already in operation (about seventy) were located in urban centers and were concentrated in the more eastern, and therefore more populated, sections of the country. Thus, the sale of sets could continue, even though no new stations were being built.

The Rapid Adoption of Television

Table 5 shows that in spite of the "freeze," which continued until 1952, the sale of sets rose steadily through the early 1950s. When the freeze was discontinued, a large number of applications for stations was received, and areas of the United States that had been without a television signal began to find television stations in their midst. These factors stimulated the sales of sets, and Figure 4 shows that the period 1950 to 1955 was one of very rapid diffusion. By 1960 the statistical average shows approximately one television set per household. As shown in Table 5, a slower but steady rate of increase continued, so that by 1971 there were more than 1.5 sets per household. Figure 4 shows that the purchase rate for monochrome sets started to decline around 1965, brought about largely by reductions in the cost of a color television set. The diffusion rate of television will probably continue upward into the near future, but an increasing proportion of the television sets purchased will be color sets.

It is difficult to predict when the saturation point of television will be reached or when a functional alternative to conventional television will emerge. It is conceivable that ongoing technological developments might allow television to become truly portable so that it, like transistorized radio, could be used in a car, on the beach, or in numerous other environs outside the home. Or technological innovations, such as cable TV and the video cassette, might emerge to compete effectively with conventional television. Or, even more probable, the conventional television set might take on new functions, such as serving as a receiver and transmitter for two-way cablevision or in a computer-based data processing system.

Another difficulty in forecasting the final outlines of television in the United States is the future role of subscription television. There is clearly a portion of the population that is dissatisfied with current popular fare on television and that is also sufficiently affluent to pay for better programs. "Pay" television has not been a popular idea with the general public. Many seem to see it as some kind of threat to the "free" television they now enjoy. Similarly, educational television is a confusing issue. Many residents of a community without an educational television channel bitterly complain about it. When such a channel begins to operate in their city, however, many of those who formerly complained do not view it.

One of the most constant factors about our electronic mass media is their continuous change. The television set of today is a vastly different object from what people were viewing in the late 1940s. The sets that will be used in the decades to come will make present equipment appear quaint and amusing. As electronic technology continues to advance, media that

Table 5 The Growth of Television Set Ownership in the United States (1946–1977)

Year	Monochrome Sets in Use (in thousands)	Color Sets in Use (in thousands)	Total Number of Households (in thousands)
1946	8		37,900
1947	250		39,138
1948	1,000		40,523
1949	4,000		42,107
1950	10,600		43,468
1955	37,400		47,788
1960	56,900	200	52,610
1961	59,500	400	53,291
1962	61,900	800	54,652
1963	64,000	1,600	55,189
1964	65,800	3,000	55,996
1965	66,400	5,000	57,251
1966	66,100	9,700	58,092
1967	64,370	14,630	58,845
1968	62,900	20,100	60,444
1969	61,900	26,400	61,805
1970	61,400	31,300	62,875
1971	61,100	37,500	64,374
1972	60,600	45,400	66,676
1975	58,640	48,850	71,120
1976	57,346	51,230	72,876
1977	58,338	54,870	74,142

SOURCES: U.S. Bureau of Census, *Historical Statistics of the United States, Colonial Times to 1957* (Washington, D.C., 1960), Series A 242–44, p. 15.

U.S. Bureau of Census, *Current Population Reports, Population Characteristics*, Series P 20, no. 106 (9 January 1961), p. 11; no. 119 (19 September 1962), p. 4; no. 166 (4 August 1967), p. 4.

New York World-Telegram Corporation. *The World Almanac, 1970* (New York, 1970).

are beyond our imagination may become as commonplace in the future as a radio receiver or a television set is today.

AN OVERVIEW

As each of our mass media was invented and converted to a form suitable for use by American families, it was diffused more or less rapidly throughout the population. The longer adoption period of the newspaper stands in

Monochrome Sets per Household	Color Sets per Household	All Sets per Household
.0002		
.0063		
.0246		
.0949		
.2438		
.7826		
1.0549	.0038	1.06
1.0801	.0075	1.09
1.1326	.0146	1.15
1.1596	.0289	1.19
1.1750	.0535	1.23
1.1598	.0873	1.25
1.1378	.1669	1.30
1.0938	.2486	1.34
1.0406	.3325	1.37
1.0015	.4271	1.43
.9765	.4978	1.47
.9491	.5825	1.53
.9088	.6809	1.59
.8245	.8330	1.51
.7870	.8933	1.49
.7868	.9440	1.53

National Association of Broadcasters, *Dimensions of Television* (Washington, D.C., 1974).

Trends in Television, 1950 to Date (New York: Television Bureau of Advertising, 1 April 1978).

NOTE: All figures after 1960 include Alaska and Hawaii. Some figures have been revised from previous editions because of revisions in source materials.

contrast to the swift diffusion of television. The decline of the newspaper reveals the impact of functional alternatives. The drastic reduction in motion picture attendance indicates what happens when a new medium becomes capable of gratifying the entertainment needs of a society in a more effective way. Clearly, the older media are showing signs of obsolescence, while the newer electronic media have not yet reached their maximum points of diffusion. As even newer media are invented, different patterns of usage can be expected to emerge.

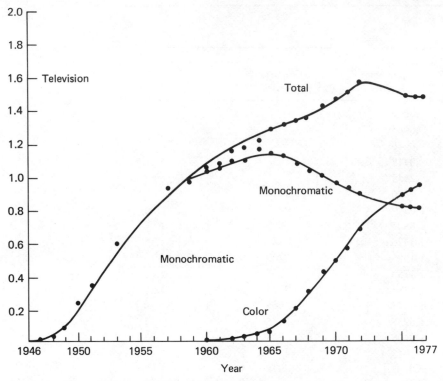

Figure 4. The cumulative diffusion curve for television; ownership of receiving sets per household in the United States (1946–1977).

The foregoing chapters on the newspaper, the film, radio, and television have attempted to show some of the details concerning the impact of a society on its mass media. The study of the media within this perspective emphasizes the evolutionary process of social change. That is, it focuses on the accumulation of technological culture traits. It notes their invention as new configurations of such traits. It follows their transformation from technical devices known only to a few to forms that can be used by the multitude. It traces their diffusion patterns as they spread through the society and studies their curves of obsolescence as they are replaced by functional alternatives. This type of analysis says little about the psychological processes of individuals as they decided to adopt the various media or as they were influenced by the absorption of media content. Such an analysis also stresses the broad social, economic, and political conflicts that characterize the society during the development of each medium. Such factors as war, depression, affluence, immigration, urbanization, the spread of education, and the presence of given technological elements in

THEORIES OF MASS COMMUNICATION

the culture of a society produce strains that facilitate, inhibit, or otherwise affect the development and adoption of a given mass medium. Thus, the many events that make up the history of our mass media cannot be interpreted in a theoretical vacuum. Viewing them as part of the complex evolutionary processes that occur when a society becomes more differentiated and achieves greater specialization of functions places them in a context of social change. Showing the media to be a part of the broad evolutionary process of industrialization and urbanization relates them to the two master trends in modern society. The older idea that the media are independent forces shaping and molding the society as they wish is simplistic and outmoded. The media are shaped by events in the society as a whole, and they are deeply influenced by the dialectic process of conflict among opposing forces, ideas, and developments within the media system and between the media and other institutions of society. In other words, there are numerous and pervasive ways in which a society has profound influences upon its media.

NOTES

1. Gleason L. Archer, *History of Radio to 1926* (New York: American Historical Society, 1938).
2. John Baptista Porta, *Natural Magick,* ed. Derek J. Price (New York: Smithsonian Institute for Basic Books, 1957).
3. Monroe Upton, *Electronics for Everyo* (2nd rev. ed.; New York: American Library Association, 1962), p. 137.
4. S. G. Sturmey, *The Economic Development of Radio* (London: Gerald Duckworth, 1958), p. 17.
5. Archer, *History of Radio,* p. 91.
6. Ibid., pp. 112–13.
7. Ibid., p. 312.
8. Girard Chester, Garnet R. Garrison, and Edgar Willis, *Television and Radio* (3rd ed.; New York: Appleton-Century-Crofts, 1963), p. 24.
9. Alfred N. Goldsmith and Austin C. Lescarboura, *This Thing Called Broadcasting* (New York: Henry Holt, 1930), p. 279.

In previous chapters we saw
how the emergence of new
forms of mass communication
have both reflected and afffected
the societies in which they developed.
The present chapter explores
some major innovations

5
emerging media
systems

that, if not themselves candidates for mass media of the near future, most probably lay the technological foundation for the emergence of new media systems. Our discussion of another emerging communication revolution begins with a brief description of its key technological components—computers, cable television, and communication satellites. We then move to consider several sketches of communication systems that may become mass media in the near future. We conclude with an examination of some potential effects of those technological developments on individuals and their societies.

COMPUTERS

The computer opened the door to the mass media of the future. Parker states: "It is already evident that the primary social significance of the computer is not as a calculator, or even as a basis for factory automation, but as a versatile device for storing, manipulating, and transmitting information, in other words, as a medium of communication." [1] Until recently, only corporations or agencies with a lot of space and money could use computers. As developments in electronics reduced the computer's size, improved its efficiency, and increased its storage capacity, a time-shared computer system emerged. Time-shared customers do not have to install a computer; rather, they install transmission and reception devices that link them to a computer. Such transmission and reception devices include touch-tone phones, teletypes, and visual display panels. Because customers share both time and cost, computers are economically available to many business, educational, governmental, and other organizations.

Travelers have frequent opportunities to witness such time-shared computer operations at work. When airline passengers make reservations, the ticket agent punches certain keys on a typewriterlike panel and sends a request to a central computer to sort through all the schedule information it has stored to see if there is space remaining on the desired flight. If the agent has transmitted the request properly, an immediate reply is sent from the computer, which may be received on a visual display or teletype panel. Similar procedures are employed by many hotels to identify stolen credit cards, check a customer's credit, or make room reservations.

The time-shared computer system, while available to increasing numbers of organizations, is not yet a mass medium. Most people have neither the resources nor the skills necessary to have access to these systems. A mass communication system centered on the time-shared computer, however, may emerge as a result of the development of cable television.

Another factor to ponder today is the future linkages between minicomputers and mass communication. The cost and size of computers has decreased greatly in recent years to a point where the home computer is fast becoming a reality.

CABLE TELEVISION

Community antenna television (CATV) was originally developed to serve geographically remote or small rural communities with limited over-the-air television reception capabilities. But CATV soon appealed to urban residents because it increased both picture fidelity and the number of channels they could receive. Channel capacity and picture fidelity are increased because cable transmissions are relatively unaffected by the air-space limitations and interference problems of conventional over-the-air television. Approximately 20 percent of American households now subscribe to CATV, a figure that is expected to increase rapidly in the next decade.[2]

Development of cable television is a relatively inexpensive and simple technological matter in countries equipped with an over-the-air television system. Very tall antennas with considerably greater reception range than conventional TV are installed on hills in relatively unpopulated areas. Large dish antennas receive satellite transmissions in other areas. Transmissions are sent via coaxial cable to the subscriber. The initial cost of connecting households with the CATV antenna is made relatively modest by piggybacking coaxial-cable lines on existing telephone-pole routes, and by using the conventional TV set as the receiver. The subscription fees paid by cable TV customers substantially reduce cable companies' reliance on advertising revenue.

In addition to picking up over-the-air and satellite transmissions, cable companies can also transmit their own local programs. Such programming was initially limited to a time, weather, and community-announcement station. Some cable companies have since expanded their production capacities to include local and national news, sports, theater, and other kinds of programs.

While the technological requirements of a mass cable television system have been resolved, legal, political, and economic problems continue to slow its growth. Independent cable television has not been allowed unchecked growth largely because of its economic threat to the broadcast television industry. Recently, however, broadcast corporation strategy seems to have changed from attempts to block CATV to one of incorporating CATV companies.[3] Such action raises antitrust and First Amendment issues.[4] Political issues raised by the prospect of centralized ownership of CATV in a few national corporations include the loss of a community-based and, thus, to some extent, community-controlled television system. To date, the Federal Communications Commission, which is supposed to regulate the electronic media ensuring that its development serves the public interest and protects a free marketplace of ideas, has not indicated the capacity to solve such basic issues.[5]

COMMUNICATION SATELLITES AND OTHER COMMUNICATION INNOVATIONS

Technological advances in rocketry and electronics that propelled human beings into space also broke barriers to worldwide mass communication. A communication satellite system has recently been completed that allows television audiences to receive international transmissions with a speed and fidelity equal to, or better than, present national transmissions. Airspace limitations that have kept the number of over-the-air channels small will be substantially reduced. Present limitations on transmission-reception range that prevent groups living in remote areas from having access to television will be virtually removed. The Canadian government, for example, is using its communication satellite system to bring television to its Northwest Territories.

The initial expense and resources required to install a communication satellite system are enormous relative to the costs of a cable television system. This fact has meant that only governments or large corporations can develop and own satellite communication systems. Moreover, control over the content of TV transmissions will most probably reside with a few wealthy industrialized nations that have the resources to build a communication satellite system. Such a system could have serious implications for processes of cultural invasion and diffusion. On the other hand, it could also provide an efficient vehicle for technical assistance to any community or nation equipped with a television receiver. The opportunities and dangers of a world television system will create the need for international agreements on communication policy.[6]

Other by-products of advances in communication technology, such as the videophone, the video cassette,[7] and the videodisc, may become products for mass consumption in the near future. Such developments may enrich communications by combining visual and audio dimensions. They may also affect the fortunes of some communication industries. The traditional movie industry, for example, already faced with severe competition from television, would be seriously undermined by the advent of inexpensive video cassettes. Nevertheless, the addition of these communication gadgets would probably not produce basic changes in the process of mass communication or in the nature of mass media systems.

POTENTIAL MASS MEDIA FOR THE NEAR FUTURE

The emergence of time-shared computers, mini-computer networks, cable television, and communication satellites has led analysts such as Parker, Goldmark, Drucker, Schwartz, and Henderson to forecast the development of fundamentally new *modes* of mass communication.[8] They see the potential for basic alterations in the process of mass communicating and in the goals and functions of mass media systems. Such alterations could have far-reaching consequences on our political, economic, and social life. We will limit our discussion to descriptions of two media systems that knowledgeable observers think could and should emerge—an "information utility" and two-way cablevision.

Information Utilities

Parker describes an information utility in the following manner:

> This new communication medium, which is coming to be called an information utility, will have one radical new property that previous mass media lack: what is transmitted over the communication channel can be controlled more directly by the receiver than by the sender of the message. It may look like a combination of a television set and a typewriter, function like a combination of a newspaper and a library, and permit a communication network that is something like a combination of a telephone and telegraph system.[9]

The telephone is the only mass medium in use today that permits customers to control the content of what is sent over the channel. All other mass media are essentially monological in form. The roles of communicator (source) and audience (destination) are fixed. Communicators control what messages are and are not sent over the channel. Thus, the prospect of equalizing or even transferring control over message to receivers portends a major change in the process of mass communicating.

Parker identifies five component parts of an information utility: (1) a time-shared computer system, (2) a storage medium, (3) a console or terminal device, (4) a communication link connecting the terminal with the system, and (5) a set of computer programs.[10] The time-shared computer system is the heart of an information utility. It is linked to the storage

THEORIES OF MASS COMMUNICATION

medium, which contains vast amounts of information either in digital form, such as magnetic tape, or analogue form, such as microfilm. Persons wishing to retrieve or process a portion of the sorted information use terminal or console devices such as a teletype or touch-tone phone. Coaxial-cable and telephone lines are the most common communication links between the terminal and the system. The only remaining component required to set the information utility into motion is the set of computer programs that speak the computer's language. A request for information is translated into computer language, sent from the terminal over phone or cable lines to the computer, which retrieves and processes information from the storage medium and then transmits that information back for reception by the terminal device.

Like most innovations, information utilities became available first to those economic and political organizations that could afford to underwrite their development. The primary impetus for bearing the costs of developing information utilities is the increased speed and efficiency they provide in performance of information functions vital to the health of all complex organizations. An information utility, for example, increases the efficiency of information gathering, producing, processing, and communicating powers vital to production, evaluation, marketing, and development dimensions of economic activity. An information utility likewise increases the efficiency of social control, intelligence gathering, or forecasting and policy formation dimensions of political activity.

Various partial or full information utilities are already in operation or in the process of development.[11] Medical facilities and universities and the Library of Congress have installed computerized libraries. Law enforcement agencies have developed regional and national information utilities which greatly expand their recordkeeping and retrieval capabilities. In addition to the airlines and credit agencies mentioned earlier, banks, oil companies, and virtually every other large corporation make use of some kind of information utility. Probably the most rapid adoption arena today is mini-computers in small business. But even more important is the growth of such computers purchased by private citizens. Present estimates are that more than half a million American households have their own home information utility in the form of minicomputers hooked up to telephone lines and to their television receiver.[12]

Telephone companies are also increasingly dependent on information utilities for their functioning, as in the direct-dial system. But most information utilities are also dependent on telephone companies for their functioning, which is why an increasing portion of the telephone companies' revenue comes from their information as opposed to traditional communication services.

Access to efficient information systems is not only essential to the survival of powerful economic and political agencies but is also necessary for effective public action. To date, most of the public have had sparse access to information utilities. A few groups, like the People's Computer Corporation, have tried to provide public access, but most citizens lack the resources and skills necessary to take full advantage of information utilities and the public services they could provide.[13] A few public information service organizations, such as Ralph Nader's or Common Cause, are gathering, processing, and disseminating information that may assist ordinary citizens to protect their health, or their political or economic interests. But there is really no adequate substitute for a mass information utility accessible to all persons regardless of their socioeconomic status, residential locale, or level of training in information technology.

It seems most economical to use the ordinary television set modified by coaxial-cable receiving and transmitting hookups between customers and time-shared computers as the basis for such a mass information utility. Let's say, for example, that information about available community, state, regional, and national services (e.g., legal, medical) was contained in retrievable form in a central storage medium, which in turn was connected to a time-shared computer. Cable television sets outfitted with transmission and reception devices would be linked to the time-shared computer. Through community educational programs or instructional manuals included as part of the CATV company service, people would learn how to talk to the time-shared computer. Whenever subscribers wanted assistance or how to go about coping with problems for which there were community, state, or other service programs, they could request and receive the desired information through the two-way cable time-shared computer information utility system without having to leave their homes.

Mass information utilities, if developed, would probably replace some traditional media and force changes in others. For example, if most persons had a terminal hookup to a news information utility in their homes, newspapers and news magazines could become obsolete. People might be able to formulate their own newspapers by requesting the information content they desired and receiving it in their homes over a telephone, teletype, or cable television receiver. Rather than have wire services like the AP or UPI, news gatherers or reporters might send their stories directly to a central storage medium. Information utility customers could be their own editors. While information gathering and processing activities would still be necessary, decisions about what subjects were most important and how much of the available information deserved dissemination could be made by news consumers. This is one illustration of why Parker sees the shift in control over content away from transmitters to receivers as the most potentially revolutionary aspect of mass information utilities.

Two-Way Cablevision

While two-way cablevision may serve as the receiving-transmitting arms of some future mass information-utility, a two-way cable system could also become a mass medium in its own right. The present one-way cable system could be modified by adding a parallel cable so that subscribers could transmit as well as receive messages. The key revolutionizing component of two-way cablevision is its capacity for mediated dialogue. The monological form of conventional television is broken. Participants in dialogue mediated by cablevision communication systems could break out of passive audience-receiver roles to become both communicator and communicatee, transmitters and receivers.

The numerous practical and legal problems that would have to be resolved make it difficult to determine how a two-way cablevision capacity would be transformed into a concrete media system. Nevertheless, one model for such a system is the two-way conversations between news commentators located at TV stations in different parts of the world that are broadcast periodically in news programs. The TV audience watches the conversation, but the news commentators are engaging in mediated dialogue in which they not only see and hear one another, but are also able to respond to or even interrupt each other. In this case, dialogue is mediated by an over-the-air and satellite media system.

Dialogue between everyday citizens could theoretically be carried out in much the same manner with the mediation of two-way cablevision. It might be possible, for example, to create an "electronic townhall." Citizens could through some agreed upon procedure receive time to debate a specific issue announced well enough in advance so that all interested parties would have an opportunity to participate in the debate. The nature of such mediated interchange could include some important aspects of face-to-face communication which heretofore have been absent from mass communication, such as immediate verbal and nonverbal feedback.

A few two-way cablevision systems are already in operation that could be utilized to establish "electronic townhalls." For example, in Tulsa, Oklahoma, twenty-six cable stations are linked together so that persons in each station can engage in dialogue with persons in the other stations.[14] Two-way cablevision could, of course, be adapted to serve almost infinite numbers of other political, educational, business, or even recreational functions. World chess or bridge tournaments, for example, could be held without the players or observers leaving their living rooms.

POTENTIAL SOCIAL IMPACT OF NEW MEDIA SYSTEMS

The information utility based on a time-shared computer and the two-way cablevision system, separately or together, open doors to new ways of living which have both optimistic and pessimistic implications.[15] Much of the public discussion has focused on the dehumanizing or otherwise pessimistic implications, such as invasion of privacy, "big brother" systems of surveillance, and centralization of power brought about by centralization and mechanizations of information systems. Our discussion focuses on a few optimistic implications, but does so in the context of identifying the forces that will ultimately determine whether future mass media undermine or improve democratic processes and the quality of life.

Distribution of Power

Innis's elementary premise—the nature of a society's communication systems has a limiting effect upon the nature of its social structure—is as applicable to these new communication-information systems as it was to analyses of the impact of former communication revolutions discussed in Chapter 1.[16] The potency of these communication technologies derives primarily from the dynamic reciprocal relationship between information and power—economic power, political power, social power.

Information as a power resource and product is necessarily rooted in communication systems. Access and control are the key factors that will determine the consequences of new information-communication systems upon the distribution of freedom and equality in our society. Perhaps this can best be illustrated by referring to contemporary predicaments encountered by everyday citizens, members of Congress, minority groups, and credit applicants. The struggle of ordinary citizens to "fight city hall" usually means trying to get some person (rather than a computer) not only to talk to them but also to give them the specific information they need to get a license, challenge a utility bill, or a thousand other things. Members of Congress have come to recognize that their outdated information systems have resulted in considerable loss of power to the Executive, in large part because Congress no longer has sufficient control or access to the information required to construct and oversee the national budget. Minority groups encounter frustration when excluded from informal communication networks because such exclusion means lack of access to and control over information that may need to gain real, as opposed to token, equality. People who have been denied credit by a company or a bank can run around in circles trying to find out the reason for the denial. In one way or another, all these groups face problems of insufficient access to and control over information processes. Such inadequate access and control limits their power, thwarts their chances for equality, or restricts their freedom.

Some of the many factors that mitigate against increased public access to and control of present and future information-communication systems are lack of computer, videotaping, and other technical skills necessary to operate such systems: legal barriers, such as natural security classifications and FCC regulations; economic barriers, such as increasing corporate control over computer and cable systems as well as the sheer cost of the necessary hardware.

History may buttress pessimistic predictions that such information-communication systems as information utilities and two-way cablevision will be used primarily to increase the power of already powerful groups. Nevertheless, as Parker suggests, there may be some lead time that could be used to promote citizen participation in shaping the next communication revolution. Some specific efforts being made to enhance public access and control over media systems are: a proposed reinterpretation of First Amendment rights of free speech to include the right to be heard via rights of public access to the media;[17] legislative proposals to guarantee privacy and freedom of information; citizen action programs that teach the public how to use the new communication technology and that increase public understanding of how information can be used as a political tool; and taking advantage of the FCC regulation that all towns of ten thousand persons or more with cable television must make at least one channel available for strictly public use.

It is tempting to ignore the fact that social, political, and economic forces largely determine how technological innovations are used. Like the powerful networks were able to slow the growth of cable television, other powerful groups, fearing a decline in their political power as a direct consequence of a new mass medium, probably have the resources to prevent its development. Thus, the information-communication systems that are most likely to emerge from technological advances are those that alter economic, political, or social structure in ways that serve the interests of powerful groups.

Work Style

New information-communication systems could also dramatically alter how we work. Some forecasters expect the homes of the near future to resemble a communication center. If homes are increasingly equipped with a variety of information-communication devices including information utilities, videophones and cassettes, and two-way cablevision, then all the hardware necessary for the performance of many work activities would be available in the home. Hundreds of jobs are based heavily upon information or communication activities that could be accomplished at appropriately outfitted residential communication centers. A few of these activities are research, diagnosis, advertising, marketing, policy formation, diplomacy, engineering, evaluation of programs or products, education, investment and trade, sales, recordkeeping and retrieval, testing, and conferring. Some jobs would, of course, still require at least part-time on-the-spot presence of a worker. Surgeons, for example, could diagnose, test surgical procedures, and arrange for operations at home communications centers; but they would still have to travel to a "hospital" to conduct surgery.

Being able to perform some or all of one's work at home would have substantial consequences for the organization of economic activity, workers' life styles, family life, ecology, and the nature of urban and rural communities. A few of the advantages for employer and worker would be reduced costs of transportation and work facilities, savings in time required to commute from home to work, reduced need for day-care centers, more humanistic work atmosphere, and increased choice of place of residence.

Goldmark foresees the potential for development of new rural communities as a consequence of the reduced need for centralized urban work centers.[18] Many workers could choose to live in relatively unpopulated areas because they no longer needed to live close to their place of work. Such redistribution of the population may not only be advantageous to workers but may also revitalize small towns or rural communities which have been deteriorating in recent years. Goldmark suggests that video cassettes and narrow-band cable TV channels exclusively designed to carry cultural activities from anywhere in the world could provide rural residents with access to culture and arts now available only in large population centers.

It would take considerable energy to run such home-work communication centers. These energy costs could be at least partially offset by reduction in energy requirements for travel to and from work, conferences, sales trips, speaking engagements, and the like. Moreover, decreased work-related travel would lessen traffic pressures and reduce air pollution. Highway construction funds might be freed for the development of efficient mass transit systems, which, by the way, could also be run by computers and monitoring devices from residential communication centers.

Mass-Mediated Dialogue

The conventional electronic media have, for the most part, failed to provide communities not only with positive feedback but also with any feedback of relevant information. Schwartz has said that "when a community or group gets feedback on itself, it changes."[19] Klapp notes that a communications system which allows groups to receive positive feedback about themselves is essential for development and maintenance of a strong collective identity.[20] Two-way cablevision has the potential for "socio-cybernetic" feedback, which Weiner and Klapp might regard as necessary for community growth and strong community identity. In contrast with biofeedback or psycho cybernetics where individuals get feedback about their biological or psychological selves, socio-cybernetics refers to *groups* (e.g., families, communities, or even nations) getting feedback on themselves. Mediated dialogue provided via two-way cablevision could revitalize socio-cybernetic feedback processes vital to group identity, growth, and social cohesion.

Two-way cablevision could also enhance democratic processes of decision making. While the mediated dialogue of the "electronic townhall" might not completely recapture the rich interaction and debate of the New England townhall, it would provide more equal opportunity and freedom to participate in political processes. The quality and quantity of such public discourse would probably surpass that presently fostered by one-way information-communication systems. More direct public opinion polling might also be feasible whereby viewers vote via the cable system. Many problems, such as establishing that a person is a bona fide voter, would have to be solved before the "electronic townhall" system could be used to conduct elections. But the obvious advantages of decreased election costs and ease of voting might encourage the development of cable voting devices.

With satellite communication, these processes of feedback and debate could extend beyond national borders to a townhall of the world. As the "hot line" telephone between Moscow and Washington, D.C., was hailed because it provided improved communication opportunities, worldwide cablevision could enhance the fidelity and scope of communication between nations. The effectiveness of the United Nations, for example, may be furthered by the opportunity for nations to engage in regular mediated dialogue.

If mass information-communication media of the future permit *mediated dialogue* and receiver *control over content*, then not only will the nature of mass communication have been radically changed but so will the social functions of the media. The mass media of the future could serve such new or expanded functions as aiding individuals in their attempts to cope with social agencies and city hall; work-related functions; political functions, particularly in the area of public debate; conflict resolution functions; and community-integration functions.

It may seem necessary to conclude that if some version of the communication revolution forecast here is actualized, present mass media will become obsolete. We cannot now know what information-communication systems will, in fact, emerge. Therefore, attempts to predict exactly which media will survive, and what alterations in media systems will occur, are necessarily speculative. Economic and technical limits on the amount of information that can be stored, processed, or transmitted at any one time make it unlikely that new information-communication systems would entirely replace present mass media. But one thing seems clear: Media capable of transformation into *mass information systems* have the best survival chances.

NOTES

1. Edwin Parker, "Technological Change and the Mass Media," in *Handbook of Communication*, ed. Ithiel de Sola Pool et al. (Chicago: Rand McNally, 1973), pp. 619–45.
2. Barry Schwartz, "The Anatomy of Cable Television," in *Human Connection and the New Media*, ed. Barry Schwartz (Englewood Cliffs, N.J.: Prentice-Hall, 1973), p. 84.
3. Nicholas Johnson, *How to Talk Back to Your Television Set* (New York: Little, Brown, 1970).
4. D. Gillmor and J. Barron, *Mass Communication Law: Cases and Comment* (St. Paul: West Publishing, 1969).
5. Johnson, *How to Talk Back to Your Television Set.*
6. See: Rita Cruise O'Brien, "Technological Factors in International Communication," *Communication* 5, no. 1 (1980): 89–106.
7. Barry Schwartz, "Video Tape and the Communication Revolution," in Schwartz, *Human Connection*, pp. 66–79.
8. Parker, "Technological Change"; Peter Goldmark, "Tomorrow We Will Communicate to Our Jobs," in Schwartz, *Human Connection*, pp. 172–79; Peter

Drucker, *Landmarks of Tomorrow* (New York: Harper & Row, 1957); Schwartz, "The Anatomy of Cable Television"; Hazel Henderson, "Information and the New Movements for Citizen Participation," *Annals of the American Academy of Political and Social Science* 412 (March 1974): 34–43.

9. Parker, "Technological Change," p. 621. Our discussion of information utilities is based on Parker's discussion.
10. Ibid., p. 623.
11. Ibid.
12. Bart Preecs, "Get Personal with a Home Computer," *Spokesman Review*, 21 December 1980, p. E1.
13. Henderson, "Citizen Participation."
14. "Symposiums Examine Values," *Tulsa Daily World*, 12 May 1974.
15. See Parker, "Technological Change," pp. 627–39, for a discussion of both the "optimistic" and "pessimistic" implications of two-way cable and information utilities.
16. Harold Innis, *Empire and Communication* (London: Clarendon Press, 1950).
17. Jerome Barron, "An Emerging First Amendment Right of Access to the Media," in Gillmor and Barron, *Mass Communication Law*, pp. 178–86.
18. Goldmark, "Tomorrow We Will Communicate."
19. Schwartz, "The Anatomy of Cable Television," p. 84.
20. Orrin Klapp, *Currents of Unrest* (New York: Holt, Rinehart and Winston, 1972).

Having seen in some detail a number of ways in which evolutionary processes and social conflict have had an impact on the development of the mass media in American society, we now turn our attention to how human

6

the nature and consequences of human communication

communication takes place, with or without media. There are two critical reasons why it is necessary to understand this process fully. First, mass communication depends upon the basic principles of interpersonal communication. Clearly, the use of media such as print, film, and broadcasting introduces special conditions and consequences into the process, but these cannot be assessed and understood in the absence of an adequate basic theory of the elementary characteristics of the communicative act. Second, the communication process is fundamental to all our psychological and social processes. Without repetitively engaging in acts of communication with other people, none of us could possibly develop the human mental processes and human social nature that distinguish us from other forms of life. Without language systems and other important tools of communication, we could not carry on the thousands of organized group processes we use to coordinate our societal activities and lead our intensely interdependent lives. Yet, in spite of the awesome importance of the communication process to every human being, every group, and every society, we know less about it than we do about the life cycle of the bat or the chemical composition of the soil on Mars!

In the present century only two major theoretical paradigms have been formulated that attempt to explain comprehensively both the nature and consequences of human communication. These are the core concepts and conclusions of *semantics* and the insights and generalizations of *symbolic interactionism* (which we discussed very briefly in Chapter 1 in terms of its assumptions about the nature of society). Given the critical role that communication plays in human affairs, it is difficult to understand why so little attention has been devoted to the development of *basic* theories about its nature and consequences. Perhaps one reason for this is that human communication is such a formidably complex process that the task of formulating a theory explaining its nature seems to be one of unmanageable proportions. Another reason may be that we are now in an era of communication science in which it is seen as more important to accumulate findings around narrowly focused issues than to attempt to sketch ideas in broad strokes. Still a third reason may be that there are now so many separate scientific disciplines contributing to our understanding about various aspects of communication that bringing them together would be difficult indeed. In spite of these problems, the present chapter attempts to describe and explain communication in basic terms and to spell out some of its major personal and social consequences. This formulation draws on many perspectives of the past and brings together a number of ideas, insights, and findings from contemporary fields of science.

EXISTING PERSPECTIVES

Human communication has been a concern of scholars since the beginning of intellectual inquiry. One of the original analyses of the nature and importance of communication in human life was published by John Locke in 1690. According to Locke, mind was directly linked to the language process:

> God having designed Man for a sociable Creature made him not only with an inclination, and under a necessity to have fellowship with those of his own kind; but furnished him also with language, which was to be the great Instrument, and common Tye of Society. *Man* therefore had by Nature his Organs so fashioned, as to be *fit to frame articulate Sounds*, which we shall call Words. But this was not enough to produce language; for Parrots, and several other Birds, will be taught to make articulate Sounds distinct enough, which yet, by no means, are capable of Language.
>
> Besides articulate Sounds therefore, it was further necessary that he should be able to *use these sounds*, as Signs of Internal Conceptions; and to make them stand as marks for the Ideas within his own Mind, whereby they might be made known to others, and the thoughts of Men's Minds be conveyed from one to another."[1]

In his theory, then, Locke described a relationship among *words, internal meanings, and the role of language as the basis of both mind and society.*

More recently, human communication and the consequences of such behavior have been studied in many fields. The findings of these disciplines have led us to conclude that human communication must be viewed within at least five major perspectives:

1. Communication is a *semantic* process; it is dependent upon symbols and rules for their use that have been selected by a given language community.
2. It is a *neurobiological* process in which meanings for particular symbols are recorded in the memory functions of individuals. Thus, the central nervous system plays a key role in the storage and recovery of internal meaning experiences.
3. It is a *psychological* process; the meanings of words or other symbols to a given individual are acquired through *learning*. Such meanings play a central part in perceiving the world and responding to it.
4. Human communication is a *cultural* process; language is a set of cultural conventions. That is, the language of any society is a set of postures, gestures, symbols, and their arrangements that have shared or agreed-upon interpretations.

116

5. Communication is a *social* process; it is the principal means by which human beings are able to *interact* in meaningful ways. Thus, through symbolic interchange, human beings can play roles, understand the norms of a group, apply social sanctions, and appraise each other's actions within a system of shared values. This integration of perspectives shows once again how indispensable communication is to human beings.

The Semantic Perspective

How can we more completely understand the nature and consequences of this significant human activity? It is toward this problem that the present discussion is addressed. We begin by reviewing briefly the semantic perspective. This review has two purposes. First, human communication is differentiated from other forms, such as exist in the animal world. Second, the review defines a number of *terms* that will become important later in our analysis. In the next section, communication is discussed as the *basis of society*. The chapter continues by setting forth a *comprehensive theory of human communication* as an interpersonal process. Finally, the significance of this theory is discussed in terms of the sociocultural construction of reality.

A basic review of the concerns of semantics would emphasize the following points: The field of semantics originally emerged as part of linguistics.[2] It is a science that attempts to understand the principles of meaning. Most centrally, it is concerned with the relationship between words and that to which they refer.[3] In addition, semantics attempts to categorize types of meaning and the principles that govern language usages. Semanticists point out, first, that we use words that have *standardized* (denotative) meanings if we want to communicate with others in our language community. It is such standardization, semanticists point out, that makes communication possible.

Denotative and Connotative Meanings This focus on semantic study is not as simple as it may sound. It is also important to note that each of us has private connotative meanings for a given word in addition to those that are supposedly standardized in our language community. The semanticist would also note that standardization is always less than perfect. Many words can mean much the same thing (e.g., *flower, blossom, bloom*). Furthermore, many words have multiple meanings: The word *head* denotes a part of a body, a person in charge, or toilet facilities on a ship, depending on the context within which it is used. It is also easy to understand that to a specific person every one of these usages can have connotative meanings somewhat unique to that individual. For example, to a given worker, the department *head* may mean not only the person in charge of the unit but also (privately) "nice fatherly man," "a clever woman who is very fair," or "a conniving sneak." All these aspects of meaning need to be understood before an accurate theory of human communication can be formulated.

Human versus Animal Communication   One way of providing a perspective on the semantic principles of meaning in human communication is to contrast it with animal communication. John Locke pointed out long ago that communication of a particular kind exists in the animal world, and much research continues on the issue today. One kind of animal communication is based on signs. One important category of signs is both *natural* and *unlearned*. Such signs include odors, sounds, postures, or activities that are genetically built into the behavioral repertoire of a given species. (An example would be the "honey dance" of certain bees that communicate the direction and distance of food sources.) Other signs used in the animal world are products of *learning*. Some of these occur in nature, as when the young are taught to respond to parental sign behavior. Other learned signs are easily observed among animals that interact with human beings. In some cases the link between sign and meaning may be a product of unplanned pairings of events that come to "stand for" some experience to follow. In other cases they may be products of deliberate human contrivance. For example, through a series of unplanned situations, the dog learns that the jingling of keys (a sign) "means" that the reward of a ride in the car will follow. Pet owners often observe anticipatory behavior in their animals that indicate the presence of such "meanings."

Although such animal sign behavior reveals little of the nature of human communication, it does provide a baseline against which human communication can be compared. Stated very simply, signs in the animal world are events initiated by one organism to which another responds in some patterned way. In this manner, the animals follow genetic mechanisms or patterns of learning that have established the link between the sign and the response it calls out. In either case important limitations exist in this process that set it apart from human communication. These limitations include the way in which the particular sign is selected and the degree to which animals *lack shared understanding* as to what responses are linked to which signs. Natural signs in the animal world are not really "selected." Generally, they are part of the genetically endowed response capabilities of the creatures involved. Even when the signs are learned, animals can exercise very little choice over what acts, noises, and the like they will use or how they will respond to such events. In other words, semanticists insist, signs among animals are not *arbitrarily* selected. Arbitrary selection means that *any* particular sign can be chosen to stand for a particular meaning. Once selected, however, the sign always stands for the same meaning. Shakespeare illustrated the point long ago when he pointed out that human beings can arbitrarily select signs and then agree upon their meaning: "a rose by any other name would smell as sweet." Moreover, we do not postulate that animals have inner understandings, definitions, and mutual expectations of behavior for a given sign that is shared. But, as a matter of fact, semanticists conclude that *it is precisely these factors of arbitrariness and sharing that characterize human communication.*

Symbols and Referents To discuss human communication, semanticists use the term *symbol* rather than sign. For example, because of its arbitrary and conventional features, the (gunshot) sign used to start the race can be classified as a symbol. It is, to be certain, an elementary nonverbal symbol and its agreed-upon meaning lacks complex intellectual content. But it is a symbol nevertheless. More common, of course, are the symbols of language that we all use extensively in everyday life. In this sense a symbol is commonly defined as an arbitrarily selected object or event (e.g., a noise) that has a culturally "agreed-upon" referent. Referents are not the same as *meanings*. (The nature of "meaning" will be addressed in a later section.) A referent indicates those situations, objects, or events in the world for which a given symbol is a sign or label. In summary, then, the relationship between symbol and referent is established by a cultural convention. New members into the group sharing the convention must *learn* the connection between the symbol and the referent.

Semanticists also explain that whereas most of our symbols are words, nonverbal symbols are very common in human communication, and throughout history they have played an important part in guiding behavior. This was especially true before literacy was widespread. For example, in Roman times, each legion had its own distinguishing *signa*. Such nonverbal symbols for each unit were clearly displayed on standards and banners carried into battle. This permitted soldiers to regroup around their unit if they became separated. Communication scientists recognize that nonverbal symbols play a significant part in our communication processes even today. They include such phenomena as common road signs, cattle brands, company logos used in advertising, and military insignia, to mention only a few. However, while nonverbal symbols are important, their significance should not be overestimated. Most of our communication is accomplished with words.

Generally, then, an elementary examination of the semantic aspects of language reveals that the arbitrary and conventional symbols used by human beings are vastly more intricate than the signs used by other animals. The use of symbols depends upon training individuals in symbol/referent conventions. Conventionalized symbols permit the paralleling of inner experiences, which is the heart of the human communication process. Nevertheless, although the semantic perspective effectively clarifies many of the foregoing issues, it offers few details as to how such paralleling of experience takes place or of the nature of social and personal consequences of communication. A formulation that focuses more clearly on these problems has been advanced by sociologists.

Mead's Symbolic Interactionism Paradigm

In the 1930s George Herbert Mead elaborated many ideas set forth by John Locke centuries earlier and added some ideas of earlier sociologists such as Charles H. Cooley. Mead synthesized a new theoretical paradigm called "symbolic interactionism."[4] We noted earlier (Chapter 1) that its emphasis was on the personal and social consequences of participating in a language community. As did Locke, Mead maintained that language is the basis of human *thinking*—including thinking about one's *self*. And, following Locke, he maintained that symbolic interaction made *society* possible.

Meaning as Responses to Gestures Mead began his analysis of human communication with the concept of *gesture*. For Mead, "gesture" referred to an action. His analysis can be summarized in the following terms: When a responding organism (e.g., human being) has learned that the beginning phases of another's action are a "sign" for the full action to follow, then a response to the sign can be initiated (as though it were the entire action of the other). The "gesture," then, is the beginning phase of the action—in other words, a kind of sign. When two organisms can respond to the same gesture (sign) in a parallel way, communication becomes possible. They can both have the same response pattern, either implicitly or explicitly, to the gesture or sign (as the beginning part of the act).

While the above formulation can apply to animals, Mead illustrated this process with the example of boxers. When two boxers begin a match, each is anticipating the actions of the other. The beginning phases of one boxer's blow becomes a sign (gesture) for the other, who responds by ducking even before the blow arrives. The other boxer does the same. Each, in other words, understands that the beginning phases of such an action *stand for* the whole. Thus, a kind of ongoing "conversation of gestures" takes place as the boxers jab and feint, weave and stab. Each is responding to the beginning phases of the actions of the other. Such gestures have "meaning" insofar as the boxers adjust their behavior according to the actions of the other. Or, as Mead put it: "The meaning of the gesture on the part of one organism is the adjustive response of another organism to it."[5]

Vocal Gestures as Significant Symbols Mead went on in his analysis to maintain that in human communication words are "vocal gestures" that also call out adjustive responses (of an inner subjective nature) among both the parties that use them. Here, however, meaning is a more complicated idea than simply an adjustive response. He termed vocal gestures that call out parallel forms of inner adjustive response in *both* parties "significant symbols."[6] Thus, to define it formally, a significant symbol, in Mead's formulation, is any gesture that calls out in the person initiating it the same (or very similar) inner adjustive responses (of a subjective nature) as it calls out in the person apprehending it. According to Mead, communication is possible because of the similarity of such responses among those who use a given significant symbol.

Taking the Role of the Other Two additional extensions of Locke are important for present purposes. First, Mead used the phrase "taking the role of the other." This meant that the user of a significant symbol must make certain assumptions about those toward whom the symbol is directed. Mead discussed this idea as role taking. He pointed out that those who wish to influence the behavior of others through the use of significant symbols must *anticipate* and *forecast* what adjustive responses will be called out when that other person apprehends the symbols. Taking the role of the other, then, implies mentally predicting the understanding of the other person toward whom communication is directed. *Accurate role taking* permits the communicator to select symbols that will trigger the desired adjustive responses in that receiving person. Following this perspective, skilled communicators must anticipate accurately the kinds of responses that their selection of words will *arouse* in members of their audience.

Mind, Self, and Society as Symbolic Behaviors A second important feature of Mead's theory is that it advances an explanation of *thinking*.

Thinking takes place when a communicator initiates a symbol and responds to it in a way that is parallel to the adjustive response anticipated from others. The insight that people can express their own thoughts to themselves is an old one. Locke pointed out that we use words "for *recording* our own selves."[7] Such self-responses to significant symbols are what are commonly called *thoughts*. Viewing "thinking" as a self-arousal of internal meanings takes much of the mystery out of the process. Thus, "mind" is the *facility* or capacity to behave in such ways. Symbolic interactionism maintains that mind, thought and thinking, as human beings engage in such behavior, would not be possible without significant symbols.

Because individuals can initiate and respond to their own symbols, and because they can take the roles of others in communication processes, they are able to *assess their own qualities* as human beings. Once community standards for judging human qualities have been acquired through symbolic interaction, individuals can develop a conception of *self*. Finally, the development and maintenance of any human group is possible only because goal-oriented activities can be coordinated through symbolic interaction. Thus, the same communication processes—the same symbol-meaning relationships that permit thinking and self-conception—are said to be the basis of all social behavior. The definition of society, or of any other human group large or small, is that it is a system of mutual influence between interacting parties (such interaction is patterned into norms, roles, social controls, and hierarchies or ranking).[8] In other words, social behavior is possible because people can exchange significant symbols and do so in patterned ways. Mead's perspective, therefore, maintains that the process of exchanging significant symbols is fundamental to the development of *mind, self,* and *society.* Each of these is a consequence of the same underlying communication process.

Clearly, George Herbert Mead greatly extended the ideas of Locke. Mead's formulation provides valuable insights into the consequences of communication in human affairs. Nevertheless, it should also be noted that symbolic interactionism is somewhat limited. It seems to "make sense" out of important aspects of our behavior, but it does not provide detailed information that explains the basic processes of human communication. For these reasons, additional perspectives are needed that not only build upon the ideas of semantics, and extend the ideas of Mead, but that also bring together a number of other important conclusions about communication from contemporary fields of science. In the section that follows, therefore, such additional perspectives are set forth. They explain human communication as a biosocial process and summarize some of its consequences for individuals and society.

HUMAN COMMUNICATION AS A BIOSOCIAL PROCESS

Human communication begins when one person decides that he or she wants to arouse a specific set of internal meaning experiences in another individual by initiating a significant symbol. The process of communication has been completed when the internal experiences of the receiving person are more or less parallel to those intended by the communicator. At first glance, such a one-symbol case seems to be too simple as a means of explaining the complex process of human communication. As will be shown, however, even such a basic act of human communication involves a number of stages. A complete understanding of the process requires making use of many ideas from several different sciences. Also, viewing human communication as a biosocial process, as presented below, can explain not only the single-symbol or one-word case but more elaborate forms of communication that make use of sentences and other more complex message structures.

Stages in the Process

In overview, what stages are involved in the basic act of communication? Reviewing these briefly in the case of communication with a single symbol will enable us to understand the concepts and principles that govern all forms of human communication, despite their complexity and regardless of the various media that may be a part of the process. To gain such understanding we first present a brief summary of the stages involved in the face-to-face situation where the message consists of a single word. These stages are then discussed in considerably greater detail. Finally, more elaborate forms of communication are taken into consideration.

Briefly stated then, human communication depends, first on specific neurological and psychological memory functions occurring in the central nervous system of the participants. Because of the existence of these memory functions, the communicator is able to have a rich variety of cognitive and/or affective experiences from which given messages can be formulated. As the communicator begins to create a message, these internal experiences are not yet at the verbal level. As the process continues, the preverbal experiences are brought together and implicitly labeled using a learned symbol that is culturally standardized in the relevant language community. The implicit symbol is then made explicit. That is, it is transformed into sounds and/or visual events that the receiver can apprehend. The message can then be moved across space or through time. At the receiving end the person perceives these physical events. He or she recognizes them as a culturally defined symbol and interprets the message. Interpretation implies that the symbol arouses in the receiver a set of subjective experiences that are similar to those aroused earlier in the communicator. A necessary condition, of course, is that both parties have learned the same cultural conventions for interpreting the symbol. Ultimately, however, the parallel internal experiences of the receiver are possible because of the neuropsychological processes of memory occurring in his or her central nervous system. Thus, human communication is a series of processes in both communicator and receiver that begin and end in the biochemistry of their respective central nervous systems. Included in this basic act of communication are precognitive and cognitive mental and/or emotional activities, habits of perception, cultural conventions, overt behaviors with the mouth or other parts of the body, and events in the physical world that overcome time and space. Because of the complexity of these processes, even in the one-word case, the possibility of communication failure is ever present. To understand the complexity of the above stages and processes, each must be discussed in detail.

The Role of Memory

It is assumed that a person would not be able to initiate a communication process making use of conventional symbols unless he or she had an adequately functioning *memory*. The same assumption is made about the receiving individual; unless parallel internal experiences can be aroused in the memory functions, as he or she responds to the symbol, no communication can take place. Paralleling of experience requires that both parties have been exposed to the cultural conventions concerning the link between the symbol and its referent. Thus, both adequately functioning memories and a similarity of prior experience with the symbol being used are necessary (but not sufficient) conditions for both communicator and receiver.

The Trace   Remembering is dependent upon events that occur in the central nervous system of the human being. Understanding human memory requires a grasp of specific biochemical and electrical processes that take place within the molecular structure of nerve tissue. Such concerns seem to be far removed from the interests of communication researchers. Therefore they have seldom been included in basic theories of the nature of the human communication process. Because of their centrality, however, human memory functions can neither be ignored nor glossed over.

How does the human memory work, and what are the implications of the memory functions for the basic act of communication? The most important single concept that aids in understanding the workings of human memory is the *trace*.[9] Scientists who have studied the neurodynamics of memory functioning have concluded that every experience of which the individual is aware is *indelibly imprinted* within the nerve cells of the brain. This imprinting seems to involve some of the most basic biochemical processes of living organisms. However, the actual details of how traces of experience are imprinted into neural tissue is still a subject of much debate:

> One theory is that memory stems from RNA (ribonucleic acid) changes in neurons, brought about by experience; it has also been suggested that memory involves the formation of new neural circuits developed in the learning situation. Moreover, there is some evidence that there is more than one kind of memory, and that each may involve different processes.[10]

Even though the precise mechanics of the biochemistry of memory are not clearly understood, it does seem reasonably clear that every experience of which we are aware imprints a trace—a permanent record of that experience. Each of the billions of cells in the brain seems to have a capacity for storing many "bits" of recallable experience. The total capacity of human memory is simply enormous! On the other hand, everyday experience tells us that not every biochemical record is immediately available for conscious recall. Furthermore, it seems well established that some memories are painful or disturbing, and they may be difficult for a person to recover into consciousness.

Even though we all forget things, impressive research seems to support the idea that our psychoneural traces provide for the storage of *all* our prior experiences, whether we can readily bring them to consciousness or not. In fact, medical research has shown that an incredible amount of detail is available in the trace "data banks" for potential recovery and recall. For example, one neuroscientist has been able to show that delicate electrical stimulation of various areas of the brain with minute currents can trigger elaborate recoveries of experience. Such electrode stimulation can result in a "replay" in rather vivid detail of earlier personal experiences that had long been forgotten. The process is not unlike a videotape that can be replayed to view a scene again. Patients undergoing such stimulation were able to reexperience activities they had undergone years before. This "reliving" occurred at the same speed as the original experience and was complete in every detail. One patient experienced a play that she had seen in childhood. Another experienced a visit with friends and relatives in a gathering that had taken place long ago. One of the most dramatic accounts shows the degree to which our imprinted traces of earlier experience can retain even the most insignificant details:

It was fascinating to learn that it is not only the important events that can be summoned from the past (by electrode stimulation), but even everyday, humdrum occurrences that had been long forgotten. It seems that even extremely minute details of our lives are stored in the brain, literally millions of bits of information, which we may not be able to summon through normal attempts at remembering. The amount of information that we store away unaware has also been demonstrated by hypnosis. For example, an elderly bricklayer under hypnosis described in detail the bumps on the bricks in a wall he had built when he was in his twenties. When the wall was checked, it was found that the bumps were there, just as he had said.[11]

At present no one knows why some individuals can voluntarily recall experiences more readily from their psychoneural traces than others. People with "photographic memories" can recall experiences quickly and in detail even without electrode stimulation or hypnosis. The majority of people, of course, have only partial conscious access to their stored experiences.

From all these considerations, we may assume two things about a trace: It is a permanent biochemical change in nerve cell structure, and it provides a psychological record of subjective experience. While the exact nature of the biochemistry is not yet understood, it seems clear that the imprinted trace is the basis of human memory. Again, the trace has two distinct aspects: On the one hand, it is a neural modification; on the other hand, it has an associated capacity to store details of prior experience for potential recall. It is not at all clear what the conditions are that limit or facilitate retrieval or recall of the experiences stored in a given set of psychoneural traces. It is likely that repeated experiences may have a higher probability of recall than those of casual or one-time occurrences.

The Basis of Selective Recall   We have already noted that recall is highly selective. Often recall can occur only under hypnosis, electrical stimulation, or applications of specialized drugs. We need, therefore, to explain the *basis* of the selective nature of recall of imprinted traces. Frankly, no one really understands the process. Recent work by neuroscientists suggests some possibilities. For example, special substances are manufactured by the brain. These seem to play a critical role not only in selective recall but also in controlling our moods, our experiences of pain, and (potentially) even in emotional disorders:

What makes the brain different from the heart or big toe is that it processes information. Nerve cells, or neurons, communicate with each other by releasing a variety of chemical messengers called neuro-transmitters. The emergence of a new class of such transmitters—called peptides—has recently proved very exciting to scientists. So much so, indeed, that some speak optimistically of a "peptide revolution."[12]

Thus, it may be that traces are activated biochemically on a *selective* basis by these peptides. We assume, therefore, that the biochemistry of the central nervous system acts in such a way as to inhibit some traces and bring others into awareness at any given time. Our content of awareness, from moment to moment, therefore, may be a product of the psychotropic influences of brain chemistry interacting with the protein structures of traces.

Such an interpretation is consistent with observations of human behavior that would otherwise be difficult to explain. For example, in the absence of sensory input (in bed at night in a dark room with eyes closed and no noise) a person can have rich imagery and a flow of internal experience. And, when brain biochemistry is altered with drugs, fatigue, alcohol, and so forth, stored traces can trigger involuntary hallucinations, compulsive imagery, and the like. Even during so-called normal states, stored traces can thrust into awareness troubling ideas, tunes that keep "running through our head," and unwanted imagery.

With these biological concepts in the background, it is possible to account for the beginning point of the act of human communication. Specifically, dynamic traces operating under selective psychotropic influences of brain biochemistry generate a pattern of recorded experience into the awareness of the communicator. He or she then begins the process of selecting a suitable symbol (or symbols) for potential expression of that experience to a receiver. Clearly, then, only a portion of our stored traces are made active at any given moment. Although temporarily passive, the many remaining traces are available for recall, depending upon biochemical conditions at the moment.

Meaning as Configurations of Traces   The importance of the trace explanation of human memory is that it enables us to understand the beginning phase of the basic act of communication. That is, it enables us to understand how a communicator can formulate meaning experiences and associate them with a given symbol. As a result of socialization in our culture, and other imprinting of experience, each of us has billions of such traces. Stored in our memories, these traces can be selectively recalled or retrieved in various *configurations*. The meaning for a given word, or other symbol, is a specific trace configuration that we have learned to link (because of language conventions) to that symbol.

From Trace Configuration to Significant Symbol

In initiating an act of communication a person must first decide upon the intended meaning by identifying an appropriate configuration of traces and then determine if a given symbol likely to be known to others is a suitable means of potential expression of the desired meaning. To accomplish this, the individual must first *search* his or her array of psychoneural traces for appropriate recorded subjective experiences. This searching is a kind of a *comparison* process, analogous to a computer searching through a vast data bank. When the intended configuration of subjective experiences has been *identified*, it can be *labeled* by assigning to it a language symbol likely to be understood by the receiver.

Labeling Meaning In labeling, a person's private meaning (trace configuration of imprinted experiences) is assigned a significant symbol (that is likely to be understood by others). This is the end stage of the process described above in terms of searching, comparing, identifying, and (finally) labeling. These activities are possible because human beings have that capacity referred to by Locke and Mead as *mind* and because they have learned through socialization to participate in a language community.

The activities of searching, comparing, identifying, and labeling spell out in more detail what psychiatrist Harry Stack Sullivan has described as three "modes of experience": In Sullivan's *protataxic mode,* (subjective) experiences are not yet organized, either logically or symbolically, and cannot be communicated readily either to self or others. The *paratataxic mode* describes an intermediate stage in which experiences are partially organized in a quasi-logical manner. However, they are only partially available to conscious introspection or for communicating to others. On the other hand, in the *syntaxic mode* experiences are highly organized and logically ordered into symbolic formulations. Such experiences can readily be consciously reviewed and communicated to other persons.[13] It should also be noted that both the labeling process as described above and Sullivan's modes of organizing experiences allow a place for subverbal and precognitive behavior without the need to assume an "unconscious mind."

It is through such steps that what has been a subverbal and precognitive process now becomes an implicit verbal and cognitive activity. Recognizing subverbal and precognitive trace records as patterns of subjective experiences and linking them to implicit cultural symbols is what Locke, Mead, and others have referred to as *thinking,* a form of self-communication. When we are engaged in the act of communicating to another person, however, the implicit message is ready to be made *explicit*—that is, to be presented to the receiver in a form to which he or she is capable of responding.

It is important to stress that we are describing in great detail the stages in the complex process of communication. We are slowing the process down, like a movie shown in very slow motion. In reality, the actions of the communicator in searching and comparing traces, identifying a potential configuration, and labeling it with a suitable significant symbol are virtually *instantaneous*. They proceed at a pace that rivals or exceeds the fastest computer. The same is true of the counterpart processes that take place in the receiver. Once the symbol comes to his or her attention, the processes involved in interpretation are virtually instantaneous.

Transferring Information   How is the significant symbol converted by the communicator into a form that can be perceived by the receiver? This is a process by which a set of cognitive events becomes a set of physical events. This change of form in the message is a result of voluntary actions of the part of the communicator. He or she makes use of those parts of the anatomy involved in speaking, gesturing, writing, or typing. These overt activities are governed by the same principles of behavior as any other form of voluntary action and need not be elaborated here. For present purposes we need simply note that it is through such overt actions that the communicator transmutes what began as trace configurations of internal experience into events in the physical world that can be apprehended by the receiver.

We will use the term *information* to refer to such physical events. They include the vibrations of air molecules that make up sound waves, or patterning in light intensities that form visual stimuli. Such physical events can be perceived via the visual and auditory senses by the receiving person. In our one-word case, where we are discussing face-to-face interpersonal communication, no particular mechanical medium is required to move the information between the two parties.

From Significant Symbol to Trace Configuration

The receiver—the person toward whom a message is directed—engages in a number of activities that are in many ways the reverse of those we described in originating and presenting a message. Nonetheless, there are a number of important differences. First, it can be assumed that the receiver is *attending* to the presentation of the communicator. This implies that the receiver is in a state of readiness to *perceive* the patterns of information produced by the sender. Perception is commonly defined in general terms as that complex psychological process by which various kinds of sensory stimuli are changed into culturally defined cognitive experiences. In other words, perception is the mental activity by which sensory input is classified into recognizable categories of experiences. For example, a receiver perceives a word; he or she must first *identify* the incoming pattern of information (physical events) as a distinctive, culturally defined symbol. A necessary condition here is an understanding by the receiver that a conventionalized form of internal meaning response is expected by the communicator. Once the symbol has been perceived and *classified*, the process of assigning meanings begins.

Reverse Labeling The term "reverse labeling" refers to the assignment of meaning to a symbol by the receiver. Earlier, we discussed labeling in terms of a communicator assigning a significant symbol to a specific configuration of psychoneural traces. In reverse labeling, a receiver assigns such a configuration to a perceived significant symbol. To assign a specific configuration, the individual undertakes a search/comparison process by which candidate configurations are reviewed. Once a decision has been made as to which configuration of internal experiences corresponds best to the significant symbol, the receiver has *interpreted* the incoming message. In other words, the perceived symbol arouses a pattern of subjective experiences that have been stored in the memory functions of the receiver via psychoneural traces imprinted as a result of earlier learning. Communication has taken place if both parties have followed the cultural conventions of the language being used and if the internal experiences of the receiving person are more or less parallel to those intended and built into the message by the communicator.[14]

Nonverbal Dimensions of Meaning It should be noted that in addition to standardizing the linking of referents and symbols, cultural conventions also direct much of the nonverbal activity that accompanies language behavior. In addition, although the nonverbal aspects of human communication do not possess as well-defined denotative meanings as do language symbols, they can be an integral part of a given configuration of psychoneural traces. Thus, nonverbal meanings can play a role in labeling, perception, and interpretation. In fact, it is precisely through the *configuring* of traces that nonverbal activities acquire specific referents. That is, such referents are acquired when experiences that are nonverbal in origin are associated with those that are verbal. It is assumed that all traces are imprinted on the central nervous system in the same manner whether they are the consequence of a verbal or a nonverbal experience.

Complexity and Accuracy in Communication

Thus far, our analysis of the act of human communication has been limited to the one-word case. This was done so that the principles and stages could be set forth clearly. We need, at this point, to consider more complex messages in which communicators make use of combinations of words that follow specific rules of grammar and syntax. We need also to review briefly those processes by which human communicators strive to increase accuracy—to ensure a close paralleling between the meanings of source and receiver.

Metasymbols Common observation tells us that when words are put together in various patterns according to culturally defined rules, meanings are introduced into the resulting messages that *go beyond* those associated with each of the individual symbols that make up the pattern. Communicators formulating complex messages, and receivers responding to them, take these patterns or *metasymbols* into account in both assigning and interpreting meanings to the message as a whole. Thus, metasymbols are culturally defined patterns and structures of configurations (configurations of configurations) that introduce meanings beyond those related to each specific symbol in a given message.

The metasymbol concept can be illustrated by considering three common words, each of which has an agreed-upon cultural convention in the English language. The word *bear* arouses in us the experience of a large mammal. The symbol *ate* stimulates in us commonly recognized meanings of food intake. Finally, the term *man* implies still another meaning, a member of the genus and species *homo sapiens*. Placing these words in the pattern "the bear ate the man" adds meanings not contained in the individual words. Thus, the pattern is a distinctive *metasymbol*. Using the same words in the pattern "the man ate the bear" arouses a very different interpretation. Thus, patterns arouse meanings just as individual symbols do.

The use of metasymbols by communicators and receivers follows the same general principles and stages described in the one-word case. Such metasymbols correspond to configurations of learned psychoneural traces aroused in both communicator and receiver. Thus, the biosocial view of communication is by no means limited to one-word messages. Its concepts and principles govern more complex human communication as well.

The Problem of Incongruence If the meaning experiences of the communicator were exactly similar to the meaning experiences of the receiver, communication would be *perfectly congruent*. Complete congruence is another way of saying "perfect accuracy." We know, however, that absolutely parallel meanings between the two parties is unlikely, except in the case of very trivial messages. Thus, perfectly accurate communication will seldom or never exist. There will always be disrupting factors that reduce the similarity of meanings between communicator and receiver.[15] Many factors lead to such disruption and cause incongruence.

Incongruence can be defined as any reduction in the correspondence between the trace configurations of the communicator and those used in interpreting the message on the part of the receiver. The causes of incongruence take two general forms: Physical factors such as dim light, disruptive sounds, electrical static, malfunctioning circuitry, or any similar condition that interferes with the transferring of information can produce incongruence. However, any biological, psychological, social, or cultural conditions that bring about differences between the meanings of source and receiver can also produce incongruence. These could include memory failure, faulty perception, unfamiliarity with symbol-referent conventions, or even brain damage. Obviously, the greater the amount of incongruence, however caused, the less accurate the communication will be.

With meaning and accuracy of communication defined in terms of congruence of trace configurations of sender and receiver, the way is opened for developing more rigorous statements concerning the relationships between these concepts. For example, the meaning (configuration of psychoneural traces) of the sender can be conceptualized as a matrix (M_s) of rows and columns, in which the entries consist of 1's and 0's, to signify the presence or absence of specific imprinted traces that together make up the pattern of internal responses of the sender to a given significant symbol. The meaning of the receiving person can similarly be conceptualized as another matrix (M_r). The rows and columns of such matrices obviously need definition in any specific case. However, they can identify *dimensions* of meaning such as denotation versus connotation, verbal versus nonverbal elements, factual versus evaluative modes of response, and so on. Many other possibilities for defining the significance of rows and columns exist. The measurement of such phenomena has been pursued with instruments such as semantic differential scales and similar devices for many years.

Whether or not empirical content can be obtained for such matrices at this point is not our main issue. What is important is that, at least in principle, meaning can be conceptualized in such a manner. The problem of specifying rigorously the meaning of accurate communication then becomes one of assessing quantitatively the degree to which M_s and M_r are parallel in their structures of elements. That is, the degree to which they are congruent. In principle, this is an elementary problem in matrix algebra. The development of the necessary equations goes beyond the scope of the present book, but the end result would be an index ranging from zero (for complete incongruence) to one (for complete congruence). Thus, the biosocial theory of communication lays the foundation for further work ahead in the mathematical specification of both the content of communication and its level of accuracy.

Reducing Incongruence   The discussion above has described human communication as essentially a *linear* process in which a message is originated by one person, goes through the various stages described, and is completed by the receiving individual. In reality, human communication is far more complex and dynamic than this. For one thing, the communicator in the face-to-face situation is ever alert to various verbal or nonverbal cues on the part of the receiver that provide *feedback*. These are taken into account to reduce incongruence as the message is formulated, transmuted, and transmitted.

Feedback is essentially a reverse communication process initiated by the receiver and directed back toward the communicator. It may be largely nonverbal, largely verbal, or both. Feedback is usually provided on an ongoing basis—as is suggested above—in such a way that it can have a substantial influence on message formulation by the communicator. Thus, when two people are in the act of face-to-face communication, meanings are transferred back and forth as the messages of the one stimulate feedback from the other.

When the communicator reduces incongruence by interpreting feedback cues correctly and adjusting message content to achieve greater accuracy, he or she is engaging in what Mead referred to as *role taking*. In the present analysis, role taking is a process by which the communicator assesses which configurations of meaning for given symbols will arouse parallel configurations in the experience of the receiver. An important corollary follows from these propositions: The greater the amount of feedback provided, the more adequate the communicator's role taking. This in turn implies that less incongruence will result in the communication. Thus, the process of communication is a reciprocal one, at least partially under the control of both parties.

Interpersonal versus Mediated Communication

In our analysis thus far, communication has been described in terms of face-to-face or interpersonal situation. An important question is whether or not the introduction of a medium into the process alters its principles in some fundamental way. Does talking on the telephone, for example, depend upon a set of biosocial principles that are different from those used to describe and explain unmediated communication? It would seem that the answer is no. Even if the communicator is using a television transmitter and the receiving person is viewing many miles away, the same underlying biological, psychological, social, and cultural processes discussed in earlier sections of this chapter are necessary conditions for a paralleling of meanings between the two parties. Human communication is still a process that begins in the memory functions of the communicator and is completed when experiences of a more or less parallel nature are aroused in the memory functions of the receiver. The fact that there may be many receivers in the case of mass communication makes it somewhat unique, but the underlying principles remain the same.

At the same time, introducing a medium into the human communication process does have consequences. The nature of these consequences depends very directly on the nature of the particular medium. As we noted in earlier chapters, human beings have been using various media to overcome distance and time for as long as they have used language. Media can range from such simple devices as stone slabs on which carvings have been made, or hollowed logs that can be beaten in rhythmic patterns, to the intricacies of modulated radio waves and the transmission/reception technologies upon which modern intercontinental television depends. Whatever their form, the most significant factors in the use of media that make mediated communication different from unmediated communication are feedback and role taking. There is also, of course, the ever present possibility of physical causes of incongruence. Obviously, such factors as dim light, competing noises, and electrical static can introduce inaccuracies in communication.

More important, when a medium is used in the process of human communication, the related processes of feedback and role taking are less effective as means of increasing accuracy. When talking on the telephone, as we all know, one has less in the way of cues from one's receiver as to how well the message is being understood. These may be nonverbal gestures such as facial expressions, or nuances of spoken words that do not transmit readily via phone. In the case of mass communication via print, film, or broadcast signals, feedback is, of course, at a minimum or even nonexistent. One could say that it is not entirely absent because listeners or viewers can write or telephone to the media to voice their complaints or satisfactions. The rating services also provide forms of feedback. Still, it is correct to say that in an immediate sense very little feedback exists. Normally, the communicator simply has no ongoing cues from his or her receivers as the message is being delivered. In turn, audiences have little or

134

no control over the communicator or over the content, structure, or pace of media presentations. All of this leads to the conclusion that much less accuracy, as we have defined it, can be expected in mass-mediated communication. In other words, mass communication is mainly a linear and one-way process. Readers, viewers, and listeners may interpret mediated messages in distorted ways in the absence of corrective role taking and feedback processes.

THE CONSEQUENCES OF COMMUNICATION: SOCIOCULTURAL CONSTRUCTIONS OF REALITY

From the standpoint of the receiver, participation in communication processes can have a number of important consequences. These consequences can occur in both face-to-face or mediated communication. First, through such participation, meanings can be *established* for symbols and meta-symbols not previously understood. This is perhaps most easily seen in children's acquisition of language. The establishment of new trace configurations can occur in all forms of socialization, however, such as in education, propaganda, or incidental learning, where new conventionalized meanings are acquired.

Meanings can also be *extended*. New traces can be added to existing configurations of meanings for given symbols. For example, for many people the word *doctor* activates configurations pertaining to the practice of the healing arts. For more educated citizens, the term has probably been extended to include Ph.D.s and Ed.D.s or others who have undergone specialized training in one of many fields of knowledge.

Still another consequence of participation in communication may be *substitution* of new configurations of traces for previously learned meanings. Advertisers often seek to substitute new meanings for old in connection with their wares. For example, one company that advertises margarine attempts to define their spread as having the same meaning as butter. The manufacturer of one well-known brand of cigarettes has for years attempted to insert meanings of masculinity into the purchase and use of its product. In general, substitution refers to the linking of new configurations of traces to a given symbol and thus eliminating older habits of meaning.

Finally, an important consequence of human communication is the *stabilization* of meanings. The repeated use of specific words and the consequent repeated activation of their associated trace configurations can strengthen the conventionalized links between symbols and their referents. These consequences—establishing, extending, substituting, and stabilizing meanings—are most easily seen as influences on receivers, although, in reverse communication (feedback) they can also influence communicators.

The specific meanings associated with particular symbols and meta-symbols as culturally defined responses are, of course, dependent upon the particular culture within which communication participants have been socialized. The meanings that people assign to particular aspects of the physical or social world are not personally invented but are constructions of reality learned through socialization into a particular language community. We need at this point, therefore, to look at the relationship among personal meanings, social constructions of reality, and patterned behavior toward such constructions.

Perceiving the World through Language

Anthropologists have studied the languages of almost every society in the world. Consistent with our view of the consequences of human communication is their finding that the languages people use shape the way they perceive and develop beliefs about the realities around them:

> One of the most important elements of the culture we assimilated in our infancy is our mother tongue. It has become part of our second nature which is a complex assemblage of conditionings and attitudes that form our structured unconscious. We see the world through the meshes of that man-made filter; we project on the world of phenomena the relations that we have learned to observe among the parts of speech; we interpret what is happening in terms of the logic of cause and effect that is embedded in our grammar.[16]

In other words, two basic processes are vital consequences of the specific language we speak. One is *perception* and the other is *belief*. Each merits close examination. It will be recalled that perception can be viewed in our account of human communication as the process of identifying and classifying a given symbol and assigning to it a particular stored configuration of psychoneural traces. Belief, as we will show more fully, can be defined as a given pattern of symbols, each of which arouses its own configuration of psychoneural traces. In addition, the pattern itself is a metasymbol arousing additional meanings.

The idea that language shapes the way people perceive their world can be illustrated in a nontechnical way by comparing certain aspects of English verbs with verbs in the Navajo language (spoken by the Navajo Indians in the American Southwest). In English we build three major categories of *time* into the grammatical rules for the use of verbs. It seems obvious, natural, and totally logical to conjugate verbs in terms of past, present, and future actions. The division of time into these three categories is so much a part of the language and thinking patterns of English speakers that to propose that there are any alternative ways to perceive and describe action as related to time seems preposterous. Yet, the Navajo do not proceed this way at all! Navajo speakers use verbs that fall into two major categories, *neuter* and *active*.

Neuter verbs are used to report a state of being or a condition of some object or situation. They do not refer to time. For example, such verbs are used to label an absence of movement or action, such as "standing," "sitting," or "at rest." Some neuter verbs even include what English speakers would classify as adjectives, such as one Navajo verb that would be translated as meaning "a round solid object is at rest." Active Navajo verbs, on the other hand, report movements and activities in terms of no less than seven specific grammatical categories! Furthermore, each of these verb forms can take as many as five distinct stems.[17] The result is a sophisticated system for reporting events and actions in complex configurations of attributes. What this means is that the native Navajo speaker perceives the world of action in a far more complex way than the English speaker. A review of other languages reveals that people divide not only time and action into different categories but spatial directions and other aspects of the world as well. The Kwakiutl Indians of British Columbia have a unique system for indicating directions and distances.[18] The color vocabulary of the Hanunoo of the Philippines has little in common with that of the Western world.[19]

Examples of the cross-cultural differences in the naming of such matters as time, directions, and colors provide illustrations of a major principle: *The ways people assign meanings to the physical and social realities around them are very tightly linked to their language conventions.* Each language community divides up whatever aspects of reality it wants to communicate about in its own unique manner. Its participants correspondingly perceive their world in ways governed by those divisions.[19] Essentially, this is an expression of the well-known Sapir-Whorf hypothesis:

> Human beings do not live in the objective world alone, nor alone in the world of social activity as ordinarily understood, but are very much at the mercy of the particular language which has become the medium of expression for their society. It is quite an illusion to imagine that one adjusts to reality essentially without the use of language and that language is merely an incidental means of solving problems of communication or reflection. The fact of the matter is that the "real world" is to a large extent unconsciously built up on the language habits of the group. No two languages are even sufficiently similar to be

considered as representing the same social reality. The worlds in which different societies live are distinct worlds, not merely the same world with different labels attached.[21]

What are the implications of the Sapir-Whorf hypothesis for our biosocial account of human communication? Obviously, the hypothesis implies that people will have difficulty in understanding one another because of the distinctive relationships between symbols and trace configurations. Even if they can translate one another's languages, they still will report and experience their inner and outer worlds differently.[22]

Most of us have little occasion to communicate with speakers of Navajo, Kwakiutl, or Hanunoo. We may ask, therefore, are the implications of the Sapir-Whorf hypothesis really important in the communication processes in contemporary society? The answer is a decided yes! They become important when we remind ourselves that urban industrial societies, such as the United States, are divided into distinctive socioeconomic strata, ethnic and racial groups, regional subsocieties, political divisions, and other groupings that develop *specialized language usages*. In each case the groups in question are perceiving, understanding, and communicating about inner experiences that are important to them. In addition, such specialized language usages can create numerous forms of incongruence between groups. In other words, neither the biosocial view of human communication nor the Sapir-Whorf hypothesis is a set of principles that operates only among exotic peoples in faraway places. They are in full force in our daily lives.

Cultural Beliefs as Metasymbols

The manner in which a given people perceive and interpret reality involves more than developing specific symbols with agreed-upon configurations. Patterns of such symbols, in the form of cultural beliefs, are also of critical importance. Such combinations of symbols define some aspect of reality in an agreed-upon way. In this sense, *cultural beliefs are metasymbols*. In our discussion of metasymbols we pointed out that individual symbols are put together according to culturally defined rules of syntax. The resultant patterns arouse trace configurations of meanings in both communicator and receiver that include more than the meanings associated with each of the specific symbols used. It is because human beings can use such metasymbols to make *assertions about the world they perceive around them* that they can develop shared understandings about the nature of reality.

The Origins of Beliefs through Communication How do such shared beliefs become established in a culture? Over a long period of time, many individuals propose various kinds of new assertions about the nature of some aspect of reality. Most of these are ignored, but some become widely accepted and passed on as shared metasymbols. A similar process has been described by William Graham Sumner[23] to account for the origins of common folkways. In other words, as people communicate intensively over the years, selected assertions become regarded as true or correct metasymbolic representations of specific aspects of reality. Because of this process, our interpretations of reality, as well as folkways and other social norms, are *constructed* as by-products of the biosocial process of communication.

Sociocultural constructions of reality, therefore, are the means by which people collectively "interpret" the physical world that impinges upon their senses. In addition, shared beliefs about the organization of the social world permit understandings of the nature of group behavior and society. That is, people socially construct shared systems of beliefs about rules for appropriate behavior. For the individual participating in such a society, these shared beliefs make it possible to interact with others in predictable ways on a day-to-day basis.

In our stored traces we have enormous numbers of metasymbols that provide the basis of our *factual* knowledge. For example, we share factual beliefs that wood will burn, water runs downhill, the sun rises in the east, and so on. In contrast, a given culture also consists of numerous shared *evaluative* assertions. These make up an important part of our social constructions of reality. We also share thousands of metasymbols that express judgments of the nature of things, events, or situations within a framework of approval or disapproval. For example, Americans widely share the belief that "murder is bad," "hard work is virtuous," and "the United States is the best country in the world." Thus, one major category of culturally shared beliefs defines the factual nature of various aspects of the physical and social world, while another major category makes evaluative assertions about aspects of those realities.

Beliefs, Attitudes, and Behavior Beliefs are often organized into larger patterns. For example, organizations of evaluative beliefs pertaining to some object of social significance are called "attitudes." Other terms widely used in social/behavioral science can similarly be defined as kinds of belief organizations. "Values" are broad patterns of beliefs concerning what is generally desirable or undesirable in human life. Terms such as "stereotypes," "prejudice," "ethnocentrism," "opinion," and "self-concept" are combinations of factual and/or evaluative beliefs. *All such* *belief organizations are composed of metasymbols that activate meaning config-urations in the psychoneural traces of individuals.* It is such culturally shared beliefs, attitudes, values, and other cognitive and/or affective orientations that give direction to human behavior. Individual behavior, therefore, is shaped by trace configurations that are consequences of participation in symbolic interaction. In other words, human communication is absolutely basic to both personal behavior and social interaction.

What it all boils down to is that our biosocial account of communication brings together a number of diverse issues into a single perspective. John Locke provided the foundation for such a perspective in his famous essay. In more recent times, various concepts, principles, and stages involved in human communication have been studied separately within semantics, neurobiology, sociology, psychology, anthropology, journalism, speech communication, and other fields of learning. The present biosocial explanation attempts to *integrate* a broad range of ideas from these fields into a coherent account of the process and consequences of human communication. Essentially, the major points that emerge from our analysis can be summarized in the following terms:

Because of the nature of their memory functions, based on psychoneural traces, human beings can store and recover imprinted experiences (although selectively). The capacity to do this, often called *mind,* permits them to participate in language systems governed by cultural rules. However, such languages impose on their participants unique ways of perceiving and interpreting their physical and social worlds. Furthermore, the verbal and nonverbal symbols of language can be patterned into metasymbols, the meanings of which go beyond those of the individual words that compose the patterns. Because they can use metasymbols, and also engage in role taking and feedback, human beings can both think and communicate with others in sophisticated ways. They can also imprint and recall socially constructed cultural beliefs about the factual nature of reality and the evaluation of that reality. Such beliefs, derived from participation in the communication process, are a significant part of human personality and play a central role in shaping both behavioral tendencies and conceptions of self. Such beliefs also make it possible for people to form groups with complex organizational rules and ultimately to develop the social institutions of society itself.

Having seen something of the underlying principles that occur in human communication, mass and otherwise, we need next to ask, How does mass communication influence the audiences of the media? As will be seen in the next chapter, the answer to this question involves some of the most complex theories of the social and behavioral sciences.

NOTES

1. John Locke, *An Essay Concerning Human Understanding*, ed. Peter Nidditch (Oxford: Clarendon Press, 1975), p. 402. First published in 1690.
2. Charles W. Morris, "Foundations of the Theory of Signs," in Otto Neurath, Rudolf Carnap and Charles Morris, *International Encyclopedia of Unified Science*, vol. 1, nos. 1–10 (Chicago: University of Chicago Press, 1955), pp. 121–26.
3. S. I. Hayakawa, "Semantics, General Semantics, and Related Disciplines," in *Language, Meaning and Maturity*, ed. S. I. Hayakawa (New York: Harper & Brothers, 1954), p. 19.
4. George Herbert Mead, *Mind, Self and Society: From the Standpoint of a Social Behaviorist*, ed. Charles W. Morris (Chicago: University of Chicago Press, 1934).
5. Ibid., pp. 80–81.
6. Ibid., p. 54.
7. Ibid., p. 416.
8. Melvin L. De Fleur, William V. D'Antonio, and Lois B. De Fleur, *Sociology: Human Society* (2nd ed.; Glenview, Ill.: Scott Foresman, 1977), pp. 32–47.
9. Alexander R. Luria, *The Neuropsychology of Memory* (Washington, D.C.: V. H. Winston & Sons, 1976), pp. 1–16.
10. Robert A. Wallace, *Biology: The World of Life* (2nd ed.; Santa Monica, Calif.: Goodyear Publishing, 1978), p. 310.
11. Ibid., pp. 309–10.
12. David N. Leff, "Peptides, Chemicals Manufactured by Our Brains, May Affect How We Feel, Behave, React and Remember," *Smithsonian* 9, no. 3 (June 1978); 64.
13. Harry Stack Sullivan, *The Interpersonal Theory of Psychiatry* (New York: W. W. Norton, 1953).
14. Wilder Penfield, "The Uncommitted Cortex, The Child's Changing Brain," *Atlantic* 214, no. 1 (July 1964) 210.
15. Such factors have been called "noise" in one well-known analysis of the problem; see Claude E. Shannon and Warren Weaver, *The Mathematical Theory of Communication* (Urbana: University of Illinois Press, 1949).
16. J. Samuel Bois, *The Art of Awareness: A Textbook of General Semantics and Epistemics* (2nd ed.; Dubuque, Iowa: William C. Brown, 1973), p. 16.
17. Harry Hoijer, "Cultural Implications of Some Navajo Linguistic Categories," in *Language, Culture and Society*, ed. Del Hymes (New York: Harper & Row, 1964), pp. 143–44.
18. Franz, Boaz, *Geographical Names of the Kwakiutl Indians* (New York: Columbia University Press, 1934).
19. Harold C. Conklin, "Hanunoo Color Categories," *Southwestern Journal of Anthropology* 2 (1955): 339–44.
20. Harry Hoijer, "The Sapir-Whorf Hypothesis," in *Language in Culture*, ed. Harry Hoijer (Chicago: University of Chicago Press, 1954), p. 94.

21. Edward Sapir, "The Status of Linguistics as a Science," *Language* 5 (1929): 209. Reprinted in David G. Mandelbaum, ed., *Selected Writings of Edward Sapir* (Berkeley: University of California Press, 1949), p. 209.
22. Benjamin L. Whorf, *Collected Papers on Metalinguistics* (Washington, D.C.: Department of State, Foreign Service Institute, 1952), p. 5.
23. William Graham Sumner, *Folkways* (New York: New American Library, 1960). Originally published in 1906.

To try to explain the consequences of mass communications for the audiences whose attentions are turned toward them, a wide variety of ideas, assumptions, theories, and hypotheses has been advanced over a consider-

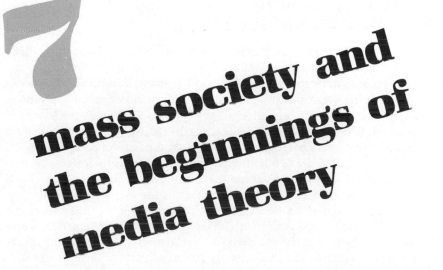

7

mass society and the beginnings of media theory

able number of years. In their theoretical thinking about the impact of the mass media, scholars, critics, and enthusiasts have all been influenced in greater or lesser degree by the conceptions of the fundamental nature of human beings and of society that have been current in their time. Such paradigms describing the social order and individual psychological organization have undergone considerable change during the century that saw the rise of the media. As the media developed, an increasingly pressing need arose to understand how they operate within that social order and the manner in which they influence individual members of society as well as the social process.

Although the lines of influence between general behavioral science theory and conceptualizations of the mass communication process have by no means been perfectly clear, it is important to show some of the ways in which students of communication have been influenced by general theorists. This can clarify in part why media scholars, or others who have commented on the nature of the mass communication process, have come up with the particular notions that they have. Effective contributions to mass communication theory have been made by the various behavioral sciences. However, the present chapter will treat in somewhat greater detail those from some of the earlier sociological theories of the general nature of society that eventually led to conceptions of *mass* society. This conception, in turn, played a key role in early thinking about the influence of *mass* communications.

GENERAL PARADIGMS VERSUS MASS COMMUNICATION THEORY

The task of showing these lines of influence involves two basic difficulties. First, theories of the nature of society have never been uniform at any given point in time. In fact, sociologists of different theoretical persuasions have seen the organization of societal processes and changing patterns in societal relations from very different perspectives all through the history of sociological thought. Theories of society in the nineteenth century were mainly evolutionary paradigms developed on the basis of complex organic models. Later, the rise of quantitative research procedures introduced new ideas that substantially influenced the analysis of the nature of society and brought additional schisms into sociological theory. More recently, the introduction of conflict models, symbolic interactionism, structural/functional paradigms, and the growth of interest in "social systems" has produced still further divisions. Second, on the other side of the coin, there have really never been any rigorously articulated sets of theories concerning mass communication. As we shall see, even at the present time there is no body of relatively consistent, agreed-upon, and formalized assertions that can truly be called "mass communication theory." To be sure, there has been a great deal of speculation about the way in which mass communication takes place; much energy has been spent on charges and countercharges concerning the manner in which the media may or may not influence individuals and groups; and from time to time various conceptual schemes or even broad hypotheses have been widely discussed with respect to some phase of mass communication or some aspect of the media. There has also been a substantial accumulation of empirical data that illuminates particular communication processes or specific effects. But, as yet, even though we use the phrase "mass communication theory," the field has not been unified by the development of a standard set of concepts, an interrelated body of hypotheses, or an overall explanatory framework. In fact, it is even fair to say that there is no final agreement in this interdisciplinary area of study as to exactly what constitutes the subject matter of the field of "mass communication." By the late 1950s one writer even proclaimed the field to be dead.[1] About the best one can do is to reconstruct in retrospect the types of theoretical assumptions that seem to underlie the analyses of problems associated with mass communication at particular times.

Given the above-mentioned lack of coordination, the task of tracing relationships between general thought concerning the nature of society and more specific interpretations of the nature and effects of mass communication may seem hopeless. Yet it is a necessary task; thinking about mass communication has changed, and this change has not been random. There has been something like a progressive development and increasing sophistication of ideas concerning the media and their impact, in spite of the fact that this development has often been, and remains, halting and disorderly. Clearly, we now know more about mass communication than we did in 1920; we also know more about it than we did in 1940 or even 1980. But we must account for the direction of this change and formulate some idea of where it has led us. Only when we understand clearly what have been the underlying postulates concerning the nature of societal processes in general can we begin to understand why hypotheses related to mass communication have been formulated in the way they have. The importance of establishing such linkages between general paradigms and mass communication theory is not so much that we may more clearly view in retrospect the factors that have influenced thinking about the media in the past but that we may formulate more adequate theories in the future and fully understand their underlying postulates. With this perspective in mind, we turn to an overview of general paradigms of societal structure and change that influenced students of the mass media during the early development of explanations of media influence.

THE EVOLUTIONARY PARADIGM AND THE CONCEPT OF MASS SOCIETY

Society is large and organized. It also seems to grow more complex. These two elementary observations were the foundations upon which the systems of thought of the founders of sociology were developed. Speculation about the nature of the social order—the manner in which it is changing or how it might be improved—had been the subject of philosophical writing since the beginning of recorded human experience. However, the founding of sociology as a systematic discipline devoted specifically to the study of societal processes did not take place until the first half of the nineteenth century, at about the same time that Benjamin Day started selling his newspaper on the streets of New York for a penny a copy.

Comte's Conception of the Collective Organism

Auguste Comte is usually credited with giving the new field its name, and he also advocated the application of the Positive (Scientific) Method to the study of society. Comte's major contributions to the task of studying social phenomena scientifically were more philosophical than substantive. Nevertheless, he did include in his voluminous writings an *organic conception of society*, that was widely used by pioneer sociologists.

The concept of society as organism was not original with Comte, but he made it a fundamental postulate. The significance of this idea is that important consequences follow from it. In simple terms, society can be thought of as a particular type of organism, namely a *collective organism*. This did not mean for Comte that there is just a rough analogy between the organization of some individual biological organism, such as a particular plant or animal, and a human society. Comte assumed that society was an organism in its own right. He saw that it had structure, that specialized parts functioned together, that the whole was something more than the sum of its parts, and that it underwent evolutionary change. These characteristics were those of organisms in general, and so society could be properly classified as such, recognizing that it clearly differed from other specific varieties of organisms.

The Role of Specialization   Comte marveled at the great diversity of tasks, goals, and functions that characterized a society and commented on

146   THEORIES OF MASS COMMUNICATION

how each individual and group can seem to be pursuing private ends and yet the overall result is that of a harmoniously functioning system. One of the basic principles of the organization of society (as organism) that accounts for this interested him greatly. That principle was *specialization*. The division of functions that people voluntarily assume, he felt, was the key not only to the continued stability of society but also to its possible disorganization.

> The main cause of the superiority of the social to the individual organism is, according to an established law, the more marked specialty of the various functions fulfilled by organs more and more distinct, but interconnected; so that the unity of aim is more and more combined with diversity of means. We cannot, of course, fully appreciate a phenomenon which is forever proceeding before our eyes, and in which we bear a part; but if we withdraw ourselves in thought from the social system, and contemplate it as from afar, can we conceive of a more marvellous spectacle, in the whole range of natural phenomena, than the regular and constant convergence of an innumerable multitude of human beings, each possessing a distinct and, in a certain degree, independent existence, and yet incessantly disposed, amidst all their discordance of talent and character, to concur in many ways in the same general development, without concert, and even consciousness on the part of most of them, who believe that they are merely following their personal impulses? . . . This reconciliation of the individuality of labour with cooperation of endeavors, which becomes more remarkable as society grows more complex and extended, constitutes the radical character of human operations [at the societal level].[2]

Comte saw great harmony and stability, then, arising from the assumption of specialized functions by individuals. He felt that inevitably these specialized activities would all contribute to the general equilibrium of society in that ". . . all individual organizations, even the most vicious and imperfect (short of monstrosity), may finally be made use of for the general good."[3]

The Consequences of Overspecialization Comte also saw danger in too much specialization. It should be added that this point is of considerable significance for the student of mass communication, because the same idea was used by later theorists to develop the concept of the *mass society*. The mass society concept was of central importance for early thinking about the media. The most important element of this idea was that ineffective social organization failed to provide adequate linkages between individuals to maintain an integrated and stable system of social control. This theme is clearly stated by Comte:

Some economists have pointed out, but in a very inadequate way, the evils of an exaggerated division of material labour, and I have indicated, in regard to the more important field of scientific labour, the mischievous intellectual consequences of the spirit of specialty which at present prevails. It is necessary to estimate directly the principle of such an influence, in order to understand the object of the spontaneous system of requisites for the continuous preservation of society. In decomposing, we always disperse; and the distribution of human labours must occasion individual divergencies, both intellectual and moral, which require a permanent discipline to keep them within bounds. If the separation of the social functions develops a useful spirit of detail, on the one hand, it tends, on the other, to extinguish or restrict what we call the aggregate or general spirit.[4]

Comte went on to discuss extensively and critically the possible consequences of an overexpansion of the division of labor. He felt that the more individuals were unlike one another in their position in the social system, the greater would be their reduction of understanding of other people. He saw that people with the same specialty would develop ties with each other, but would become alienated from other such groupings. "Thus it is that the principle by which alone general society could be developed and extended, threatens, in another view, to decompose it into a multitude of unconnected corporations, which almost seem not to belong to the same species. . . ."[5]

As the societal organism evolves (according to this paradigm), it develops harmony and stability through its division of labor. At the same time, there is the possibility that overdevelopment can lead to disorganization and decline by disrupting the basis for effective communication between individual parts of the organism. Given the postulate of the organic nature of society, the concept of specialization of function follows by definition. But an increasing degree of such specialization leads to increased social differentiation. If such differentiation reaches the point where effective linkages between parts of the system are threatened, then the equilibrium and harmony of the organism are also threatened. This theme recurs in the writings of later theorists, and is one of the *basic beginning points for discussing "mass" society.* The relationship between this idea and "mass" communication will be made clear.

It should be recalled that Comte worked out his views of the nature of society during the 1830s. This was before the industrial revolution had achieved a wide impact on Europe. Comte felt somewhat threatened by the possibility of an increasing level of specialization in the society he saw before him. But social theorists who came later were confronted with the *reality* of a great increase in the division of labor which the new industrialization was bringing. It is little wonder they were deeply impressed with its implications.

THEORIES OF MASS COMMUNICATION

Spencer's Organic Analogy

Speculation about the organic nature of society and its consequences constituted only a minor part of the work of Comte. The second founder of modern sociology, Herbert Spencer, pursued the organic concept with great vigor and in great depth. Spencer, like Comte, was primarily a philosopher and was concerned about science as a means for obtaining valid knowledge. This concern led him to formulate what he thought were the most important principles that seemed to him to pervade all the sciences. His famous *laws of evolution* (from which Darwin drew inspiration) were given complete development in his work *First Principles,* published in 1863, more than twenty years after Comte had completed his *Positive Philosophy.*

Spencer applied his evolutionary concepts to the study of society and wrote *The Principles of Sociology* in four volumes between 1876 and 1896. There are many parallels between the two writers, but Spencer claims that his own ideas were worked out independently of those of Comte. In any case, the theory of society that Spencer elaborated in great detail was a purely organic one. After defining society as a functioning system, he discussed the social order at length in terms of its growth, structures, functions, systems of organs, and so on, developing an extremely elaborate analogy between society and an individual organism.

The division of labor was a very important part of this analysis, and was regarded as the basic unifying factor which held the organism together:

> The division of labour, first dwelt upon by political economists as a social phenomenon, and thereupon recognized by biologists as a phenomenon of living bodies, which they called the "physiological division of labour," is that which in the society, as in the animal, makes it a living whole. Scarcely can I emphasize enough the truth that in respect of this fundamental trait, a social organism and an individual organism are entirely alike. . . .
>
> [Society] undergoes continuous growth. As it grows, its parts become unlike: it exhibits increase of structure. The unlike parts simultaneously assume activities of unlike kinds. These activities are not simply different, but their differences are so related as to make one another possible. The reciprocal aid thus given causes mutual dependence on the parts. And the mutually-dependent parts, living by and for one another, form an aggregate constituted on the same general principle as an individual organism. [6]

But Spencer did not go to the next step and contemplate the possible *difficulties* for society that might occur if specialization went too far. He was convinced that the most fundamental process of nature was evolution, and that evolution was natural and therefore good. The great changes he observed in English society, as the industrial order came, he regarded as an unfolding of society according to natural evolutionary laws. To suggest that social changes brought by natural evolution might be undesirable was unthinkable. So deeply did he hold these views that he became convinced that any interference in the natural development of society was completely unwarranted and was bound to have disastrous consequences. He bitterly opposed legislation aimed at any form of social improvement on the grounds that nature meant the fittest to survive, and in the long run this would benefit society. While Comte advocated planned social change, Spencer argued vigorously for a policy of almost complete *laissez-faire*.

Even so, it can be seen that the two major founders of sociology developed similar organic evolutionary models of the social order and that both postulated a process leading to increasing social differentiation. The one had grave reservations as to the possible consequences of overspecialization, and the other had grave reservations over any attempt to interfere in what he regarded as the natural evolution of the society. Neither had any full appreciation of the fundamental changes in the structure of the social order that were to come with the twentieth century. Comte, writing on the eve of the industrial revolution, and Spencer, writing during its early phases, could not foresee that the very fabric of society would be changed by the upheaval in the economic institution that the factory system and the new economic order would bring. The same acceleration in science that brought the mass media of communication, and indeed that prompted these two philosophers to found a science of society, also fashioned the forces of society's new industrial organization. The impact of this new order was to be felt in every corner of the world.

Tönnies' Theory of Social Bonds

Another important theoretical formulation came from the province of Schleswig-Holstein in Germany. In 1887 a young man of that region by the name of Ferdinand Tönnies produced a theoretical sociological analysis entitled *Gemeinschaft und Gesellschaft*. In this work he posed two contrasting types of societal organization—one preindustrial and the other largely a product of industrialization. In his analysis of the nature of society, Tönnies concentrated less on organic analogies, or the possible consequences of specialization, and focused his attention on the kinds of social bonds that exist between the members of societies and groups in two very distinct types of social organization.

Gemeinschaft versus Gesellschaft The term *Gemeinschaft* does not translate easily into English. The word "community" is often offered as its equivalent, but the complexity of Tönnies' meaning is not well captured by such a simple translation. The idea of Gemeinschaft is best illustrated by suggesting some of the kinds of interpersonal ties that are included within it. The bonds and feelings that exist between the members of a normal family offer one example. But the idea goes beyond the bounds of family. The members of a particular village or even of a given small society can be said to be characterized by Gemeinschaft. This type of relationship can develop because people are related to each other by blood and hold each other in mutual respect; it can be produced because people are tied by tradition to a particular place where they lead a deeply integrated life; there can even be a Gemeinschaft of the mind, as when members of a religious order share a deep commitment to a given set of beliefs that become a basis for a strong social organization. The Gemeinschaft organization, in short, is one in which people are strongly bound to one another through tradition, through kinship, through friendship, or because of some other socially cohesive factor. Such a social organization places the individual within the nexus of exceedingly strong systems of informal social control. In short, Gemeinschaft refers to a "reciprocal, binding sentiment . . . which keeps human beings together as members of a totality." [7] That totality may be a family, a clan, a village, a religious order, or even an entire society, but if so, it has as a basis for its common unity this particular kind of social relationship between its members.

It is clear that there probably have been few societies whose social bonds were based completely on such intense feelings of "community" in the sense of Gemeinschaft. However, even as an abstract construction, this "ideal type" can serve as a framework for discussing changes in social organization and new kinds of linkages between members that take place if the society evolves into some other form. For example, under the impact of industrialization, when the division of labor becomes vastly more complex through increasing specialization, is there a decline in Gemeinschaft? Tönnies saw his own homeland undergo a transition from a basically agrarian society to one that was increasingly urban and industrial. While he did not suggest that societal evolution was simply a movement from Gemeinschaft in social relations to some other form, it was clear to him that another constructed polar type was going to be increasingly important to describe adequately an entirely different system of social relationships between the members of the newer society. The second of his theoretical constructs was *Gesellschaft*.

The essential condition of the social relationship in the Gesellschaft is the contract. The contract in its broadest sense is a rationally agreed upon voluntary social relationship where the two parties involved promise to fulfill specific obligations to each other or to forfeit specific commodities if the contract is breached. The contract is a formal relationship (often written, and always backed by impersonal mechanisms of social control), whereas the social relationship of the Gemeinschaft is informal. In the new society of complex credit, world markets, large formal associations, and a vast division of labor, the contractual relationship is widely found between members. The buyer and seller relate themselves in this way, as do the employer and employee. In fact, throughout all the major social institutions, the economic order, the political structure, the educational system, religion, and even in some instances the family, the older Gemeinschaft bond, based upon "reciprocal, binding sentiment," is being replaced by relationships of the contractual type. In certain spheres of social exchange, it is almost the exclusive kind of relationship that can exist between two parties, for example, buying or renting a dwelling. In some spheres, it may seldom be found (e.g., within the family).

While no society has been or probably ever will be exclusively Gesellschaft, it is clear that this type of social bond has become ubiquitous and pervasive. It is also clear that Gesellschaft implies a very different outlook for individuals as they contemplate societal members than is the case in the Gemeinschaft.

In the Gesellschaft . . . everybody is by himself and isolated, and there exists a condition of tension against all others. Their spheres of activity are sharply separated, so that everybody refuses to everyone else contact with and admittance to his sphere; i.e., intrusions are regarded as hostile acts. Such a negative attitude toward one another becomes the normal and always underlying relation of those power-endowed individuals, and it characterizes the Gesellschaft in the condition of the rest; nobody wants to grant and produce anything for another individual, nor will he be inclined to give ungrudgingly to another individual, if it be not in exchange for a gift or labor equivalent that he considers at least equal to what he has given.[8]

The Impersonal and Anonymous Society The Gesellschaft, then, places the individual within a social system that is impersonal and anonymous. It is a situation where individuals are not treated or valued for their personal qualities, but where they are appreciated to the degree that they can uphold their end of contracted obligations. The Gesellschaft is a system of competitive relationships where individuals seek to maximize what they get from exchanges and minimize what they give, at the same time learning to be wary of others.

The reader will recognize that these two pictures of societal organization have been deliberately overdrawn for theoretical purposes. Nevertheless, the Gemeinshaft and Gesellschaft polarity does provide a very useful framework for interpreting the impact of changing social conditions upon the citizen of the emerging industrial order. The Gemeinschaft could easily be idealized as psychologically comforting and supporting, while the Gesellschaft could easily be condemned as psychologically distressing and tension producing. Such interpretations abound in literature, in popular thought, and even in social science, where the simpler Gemeinschaft life of an earlier or more rural society is identified as "good," while the impersonal Gesellschaft of the urban area is defined as "evil." But while many have speculated in these directions, our present task is to extract from such nineteenth-century writers as Tönnies ideas that were to influence those who turned their attentions to assessing the impact of the new media of communication on society. Just as an accumulation of theories and inventions in the natural sciences led to the physical basis upon which the media themselves were developed, the accumulation of sociological thought concerning the nature of the contemporary social order provided the basis of ideas upon which interpretations of the media were first attempted when they became realities.

Durkheim's Analysis of the Division of Labor

Before pulling together the various concepts we have examined into some kind of composite theoretical image of society as it was viewed by the end of the nineteenth century, there is one additional writer whose ideas were of particular significance. Near the end of the period (1893) Emile Durkheim published *The Division of Labor in Society*. In this important work he brought together the several related themes we have noted above from the writings of Comte, Spencer, and Tönnies.[9]

Mechanical versus Organic Solidarity The overall purpose of Durkheim's extended analysis was to show how the division of labor of a society was the principal source of *social solidarity* in that society, and that as the division of labor was altered (as for example through social evolution), the unifying forces of the society underwent corresponding change. Solidarity refers to the kinds of social psychological bonds that unite the members, and although Durkheim used a very different terminology, he was addressing himself roughly to the same general problem as Tönnies. By division of labor Durkheim meant more than simply the degree of specialization in the economic institution:

(We must ask) if the division of labor . . . in contemporary societies where it has developed as we know . . . would not have as its function the integration of the social body to assure unity. It is quite legitimate to suppose . . . that great political societies can maintain themselves in equilibrium only thanks to the specialization of tasks, that the division of labor is the source, if not unique, at least principal, of social solidarity. Comte took this point of view. Of all sociologists, to our knowledge, he is the first to have recognized in the division of labor something other than a purely economic phenomenon. He saw in it "the most essential condition of social life," provided that one conceives it "in all its rational extent; that is to say, that one applies it to the totality of all our diverse operations of whatever kind, instead of attributing it, as is ordinarily done, to simple material usages."[10]

To show the social implications of the division of labor, Durkheim contrasted *mechanical* and *organic* solidarity. Mechanical solidarity is that which unites a people who are essentially alike. Through their common life, and in the presence of only a rudimentary division of labor, the members of a given population work out a set of beliefs, values, and other orientations to which they are deeply, commonly, and uniformly committed. To the extent that these orientations are truly characteristic of every member, there is little basis for the development of extensive individuality. Where there is little or no division of labor, people not only act in like ways, Durkheim suggested, but also think and feel in like ways. In this kind of society, "solidarity can grow only in inverse ratio to personality," because personality is what distinguishes one person from another. "If we have a strong and lively desire to think and act for ourselves, we cannot be strongly inclined to think and act as others do."[11] In the extreme case, *all* individuality would be submerged, and the members of the society would be completely *homogeneous* in their personal psychic organization. In such an admittedly theoretical case, the members of the society would be completely uniform in their action.

The social molecules which can be coherent in this way can act together only in the measure that they have no actions of their own, as the molecules of inorganic bodies. That is why we propose to call this type of solidarity mechanical. The term does not signify that it is produced by mechanical and artificial means. We call it that only by analogy to the cohesion which unites the elements of an inanimate body, as opposed to that which makes a unity out of the elements of a living body.[12]

It is perfectly obvious that no society was ever characterized completely by this kind of social organization. The idea of mechanical solidarity as a basis for binding members of a collectivity to the whole is posed in

THEORIES OF MASS COMMUNICATION

this way as an abstract construct rather than a description that is supposed to portray reality with complete accuracy. The same can be said of Durkheim's second major concept, organic solidarity. The two taken together, however, offer a third useful interpretive framework in understanding the emergence of modern society.

If mechanical solidarity is based upon *homogeneity*, then organic solidarity is based on *heterogeneity*. In a society with a well-developed division of labor, all persons performing specialized tasks are dependent on others whose activities are coordinated with theirs. Spencer had elaborated in extraordinary detail the parallels between organisms and society as unified systems of reciprocally functioning parts. Durkheim saw the mutual dependency that specialization produced, and he recognized this as a kind of social force that bound the members of a society together to form a more or less harmonious functioning whole. But the important factor is that the division of labor, which produces organic solidarity, also increases greatly the degree of individuality and *social differentiation* within the society:

Whereas the previous type (of solidarity) implies that individuals resemble each other, this type presumes their difference. The first is possible only insofar as the individual personality is absorbed into the collective personality; the second is possible only if each one has a sphere of action which is peculiar to him; that is a personality. It is necessary, then, that the collective conscience leave open a part of the individual conscience in order that special functions may be established there, functions which it cannot regulate. The more this region is extended, the stronger is the cohesion which results from this solidarity. [13]

Psychological Isolation   Durkheim went on to show how the growth of the division of labor increases the dependence of each specialized person on the rest, but this does not mean that such increasing heterogeneity leads to consensus of thought. On the contrary: "Each individual is more and more acquiring his own way of thinking and acting, and submits less completely to the common corporate union." [14] Thus, while in one sense highly specialized persons are locked into a web of functional dependency upon others, they are at the same time isolated in a psychological sense as specializations lead them to develop greater and greater individuality.

Durkheim also noted that the evolution of society to a more complex form leads to an increase in social relationships of much the same type that Tönnies called Gesellschaft: "It is quite true that contractual relations, which were originally rare or completely absent, multiply as social labor becomes divided." [15] Thus, an increase in the division of labor has the result not only of increasing individual heterogeneity, but of introducing an increasing number of more formal and segmental relationships between people.

Anomie Finally, Durkheim saw that under some circumstances the division of labor could result in what he called "pathological forms." "Though normally," he said, "the division of labor produces social solidarity, it sometimes happens that it has different, and even contrary results."[16] If social functions, that is, parts of the organic structure, are not well articulated with each other, organic solidarity can break down. Commercial crises, depressions, strife between labor and management, civil upheavals, riots, demonstrations, and protests by subgroups offer various examples.

Thus, the very division of labor that produces harmony up to a point contains the seeds of social disharmony if pushed beyond a certain point. This, of course, was (as Durkheim noted) the thesis of Auguste Comte. Such a state of disharmony Durkheim called *anomie*. This is a pathology of the social organism that results when the division of labor becomes elaborated to a point where individuals are not capable of effectively relating themselves to others.

> Functional diversity induces a moral diversity that nothing can prevent, and it is inevitable that one should grow as the other does. We know, moreover, why these two phenomena develop in parallel fashion. Collective sentiments become more and more impotent in holding together the centrifugal tendencies that the division of labor is said to engender, for these tendencies increase as labor is more divided, and, at the same time, collective sentiments are weakened.[17]

In short, as society becomes more and more complex—as the members of the society become more and more preoccupied with their own individual pursuits and development—they lose ability to identify with and feel themselves in community with others. Eventually they become a collectivity of psychologically isolated individuals, interacting with one another but oriented inward, and bound together primarily through contractual ties.

THE EMERGENCE OF THE THEORY OF MASS SOCIETY

As the nineteenth century came to a close, this was in general the image of society that had emerged. The developing and accumulating body of sociological theory, uncoordinated and even conflicting though it was, seemed in one way or another to stress these themes. Society was a large and complex system. It was also growing much more complex. To some this represented Progress via natural laws of evolution to a more desirable and ultimately more harmonious system than before. To others it represented an insidious movement to a bleak and isolated existence for the individual, narrowly concerned with special pursuits, and incapable of intense identification with others. Great debates arose concerning the advisability of interfering with the evolution of society through legislation. Other arguments arose concerning the best possible strategy for proceeding with the further development of theories about these vast changes. But in spite of these divergent points of view over strategies and consequences, it seemed clear to most students of the social order that the Western world was experiencing an increase in heterogeneity and individuality, a reduction in the degree to which society could effectively control its members through informal means, an increasing alienation of the individual from strong identification with the community as a whole, a growth of segmental, contractual social relationships, and a great increase in the psychological isolation of the human being.

These general social trends were said to be leading to the *mass society*. The idea of mass society is not equivalent to *massive society*, that is, to large numbers. There are many societies in the world, for example, India, that have astronomical numbers of people but are still more or less traditional in their organization. Mass society refers to the relationship that exists between individuals and the social order around them. In mass society, as has been emphasized in the theories we have examined: (1) individuals are presumed to be in a situation of psychological isolation from others, (2) impersonality is said to prevail in their interactions with others, and (3) they are said to be relatively free from the demands of binding informal social obligations. These ideas have been carried by some sociologists well into the twentieth century, and are still important considerations, along with a number of modifications and countertrends.[18] In discussing the organization of the urban industrial social order of the contemporary Western world, Broom and Selznick have summarized the principal outlines of the idea of mass society very succinctly in the following terms:

> Modern society is made up of masses in the sense that "there has emerged a vast mass of segregated, isolated individuals, interdependent in all sorts of specialized ways yet lacking in any central unifying value or purpose." The weakening of traditional bonds, the growth of rationality, and the division of labor, have created societies made up of individuals who are only loosely bound together. In this sense the word "mass" suggests something closer to an aggregate than to a tightly knit social group.[19]

157

This view of the *social* nature of human beings was coupled with equally developed general paradigms of their *psychological* nature. Briefly, human conduct was, according to neurobiological and comparative approaches, largely a product of genetic endowment. That is, the causes of behavior were sought within biological structure. This line of thought was to have important implications for the early interpretation of the new mass media. The nature of these general psychological paradigms and their importance in interpreting the mass media will be made clear in later sections.

MASS SOCIETY THEORY AND THE MAGIC BULLET

It was against this intellectual backdrop that the mass media of communication diffused through the major Western societies during their early years. To assess the influence that such general interpretations of the "nature of human nature" had upon some of the early thinking about the media, we need to look briefly at the period when mass communication was still a relatively new social phenomenon with which the world had to contend.

Wartime Propaganda and Beliefs of Media Power

The first decade of the twentieth century had barely passed before Europe and later the United States were plunged into the Great War. The very division of labor and the resulting heterogeneity and individuality that had made the new industrial societies possible now became a problem. World War I was really the first of the global struggles in which entire populations played active and coordinated roles in the effort against their enemies. In most previous wars, the opposing military forces carried on their struggles somewhat independently of civilian populations. Unless combat happened to take place in their immediate area, the people left at home were not deeply and personally involved. This had been particularly true of England, which had not been occupied by an enemy since the Norman invasion. It was also true of the United States, which had last known foreign soldiers on its shores during Revolutionary times, although the Civil War had brought great hardships in some areas.

But the new kind of war was, in effect, a pitting of the manufacturing capacity of one nation against that of the other, and the armies in the field were backed by and totally dependent upon vast industrial complexes at home. These huge industrial efforts required the wholehearted cooperation and enthusiasm of the civilian populations who served in them. Total war required total commitment of the entire resources of the nation. Material amenities had to be sacrificed; morale had to be maintained; people had to be persuaded away from their families and into the ranks; the work in the factories had to be done with unflagging vigor; and not the least important, money had to be obtained to finance the war.

Propaganda and the Need for Gemeinschaft But the diverse, heterogeneous, and differentiated populations of the industrial societies were not bound together by that "reciprocal, binding sentiment . . . which keeps human beings together as members of a totality."[20] They were not Gemeinschaft societies but were in fact more like mass societies, which lacked such effective bonds. Yet, it was just such bonds of sentiment that were needed to unite these people into effective solidarity behind their respective war efforts. As each country became politically committed to the war, there arose a most critical and urgent need to forge stronger links between the individual and society. It became *essential* to mobilize sentiments and loyalties, to instill in citizens a hatred and fear of the enemy, to maintain their morale in the face of privation, and to capture their energies into an effective contribution to their nation.

The means for achieving these urgent goals was *propaganda*. Carefully designed propaganda messages engulfed the nation in news stories, pictures, films, phonograph records, speeches, books, sermons, posters, wireless signals, rumors, billboard advertisements, and handbills. Top-level policy makers decided the stakes were so high and the ends were so important that they justified almost any means. Citizens had to hate the enemy, love their country, and maximize commitment to the war effort. They could not be depended upon to do so on their own. The mass media of communication available at the time became the principal tools of persuading them to do so.

Following the war, a number of persons who had been importantly involved in the manufacturing of propaganda were ridden with guilt about the gross deceptions they had practiced. Outrageous lies were told by one side about the other, and when placed before the populations of the time via the mass media, they were often believed. Such large-scale persuasion of entire populations with the use of mass media had never been seen before, and it was conducted in a skillful and highly coordinated manner. Also, those were apparently more innocent times; even the word "propaganda" was not understood by the ordinary citizen. After the war, when former propagandists published a rash of sensational exposés about their wartime deceptions, the general public became more sophisticated.

But to illustrate briefly the material the propagandists found effective and the responses to their stimuli that they were seeking, the following is quoted from one widely read postwar exposé:

> The Atrocity Story was one big factor in English propaganda. Most . . . were greedily swallowed by an unsuspecting public. They would have been less ready to accept the stories of German frightfulness if they had witnessed the birth of the most lugubrious atrocity story at the headquarters of the British Intelligence Department in the Spring of 1917.
>
> Brigadier General J. V. Charteris . . . was comparing two pictures captured from the Germans. The first was a vivid reproduction of a harrowing scene, showing the dead bodies of German soldiers being hauled away for burial behind the lines. The second picture depicted dead horses on their way to the factory where German ingenuity extracted soap and oil from the carcasses. The inspiration to change the captions of the two pictures came to General Charteris like a flash.
>
> . . . the General dexterously used the shears and pasted the inscription "German Cadavers on Their Way to the Soap Factory" under the dead German soldiers. Within twenty-four hours the picture was in the mail-pouch for Shanghai.
>
> General Charteris dispatched the picture to China to revolt public opinion against the Germans. The reverence of the Chinese for the dead amounts to worship. The profanation of the dead ascribed to the Germans was one of the factors responsible for the Chinese declaration of war against the central powers.[21]

Whether this particular propagandist was correct in his assessment of the impact of this falsified newspaper picture need not concern us. The example and the claimed effect give a classic illustration of the kind of theory of mass communication upon which such propaganda efforts were premised. It was a relatively simple theory and it was consistent with the image of mass society that was the intellectual heritage from the nineteenth century. It assumed that cleverly designed stimuli would reach every individual member of the mass society via the media, that each person would perceive it in the same general manner, and that this would provoke a more or less uniform response from all.

Media Messages as Magic Bullets   In the aftermath of the war, there emerged a quite general belief in the great power of mass communication. The media were thought to be able to shape public opinion and to sway the masses toward almost any point of view desired by the communicator. An American political scientist who tried to analyze objectively the impact of wartime propaganda and the role of the media in the mass society came to these conclusions:

But when all allowances have been made, and all extravagant estimates pared to the bone, the fact remains that propaganda is one of the most powerful instrumentalities in the modern world. It has arisen to its present eminence in response to a complex of changed circumstances which have altered the nature of society. Small primitive tribes can weld their heterogeneous members into a fighting whole by the beat of the tom-tom and the tempestuous rhythm of the dance. It is in orgies of physical exuberance that young men are brought to the boiling point of war, and that old and young, men and women, are caught in the suction of tribal purpose.

In the Great Society it is no longer possible to fuse the waywardness of individuals in the furnace of the war dance; a newer and subtler instrument must weld thousands and even millions of human beings into one amalgamated mass of hate and will and hope. A new flame must burn out the canker of dissent and temper the steel of bellicose enthusiasm. The name of this new hammer and anvil of social solidarity is propaganda.[22]

The basic theory of mass communication that is implied by such conclusions is not quite as simple as it might appear. To be sure, it is relatively straightforward S-R theory, but it is also one that presumes a particular set of unspoken assumptions concerning not only the social organization of society but the psychological structure of the human beings who are being stimulated and who are responding to the mass communicated message. It is important to understand the full range of these implicit assumptions because *it has been through their systematic replacement or modification* that more modern theories of the mass communication process have been developed. As new concepts concerning the nature of the human being as an individual and the nature of society became available, these were used to modify the basic theory of mass communication by introducing different sets of *intervening variables* between the stimulus side of the S-R equation and the response side.

This first set of beliefs about the nature and power of mass communications was never actually formulated at the time into a systematic statement by any communication scholar. But in retrospect it has come to be called the "magic bullet theory." In more contemporary times it has also been called by other colorful names, such as the "hypodermic needle theory" and the "transmission belt theory." The basic idea behind these names is that media messages are received in a uniform way by every member of the audience and that immediate and direct responses are triggered by such stimuli.

In view of today's more elaborate perspectives on the mass communication process (which we will discuss later), the magic bullet theory may seem naive and simple. Yet there was more to its assumptions than what such writers as Katz and Lazarsfeld have suggested, namely, "the omnipotent media, on the one hand, sending forth the message, and the atomized masses, on the other, waiting to receive it—*and nothing in between* [italics added]." [23] There were very definite assumptions about what was going on in between. These assumptions may not have been explicitly formulated at the time, but they were drawn from fairly elaborate theories of human nature, as well as the nature of the social order (which we have already examined). It was these theories that guided the thinking of those who saw the media as powerful.

The Magic Bullet Theory as a Corollary of Underlying Postulates

What were the assumptions from which the magic bullet theory was derived? Actually, those assumptions were drawn from a combination of the comparative and the neuro-biological paradigms mentioned in Chapter 1. Even so, these were in a less sophisticated form than they are today. For example, during the time of World War I, *instinct* psychology was at its peak. It was not until the end of the 1920s that the facts of human individual modifiability and variability began to be demonstrable with the use of new mental tests and other research techniques. As a consequence, the image of *homo sapiens* represented by the writings of William MacDougal and his contemporaries was called into serious question. Prior to that time, it was assumed that a given individual's behavior was governed to a considerable extent by inherited biological mechanisms of some complexity that intervened between the stimuli and the responses. Because of this, basic human nature was thought to be fairly *uniform* from one human being to another. People inherited (according to the theories) more or less the same elaborate set of built-in biological mechanisms, which supplied them with motivations and energies to respond to given stimuli in given ways. Much was made of the nonrational or emotional nature of such mechanisms, particularly among theorists of psychoanalytic bent. But even these were, in the final analysis, inherited forces (e.g., libido), which each person received at birth in more or less uniform degrees. The psychology of individual differences had not progressed to the point where a consuming interest in learning would develop among academic psychologists as a means of accounting for such differences.

Given a view of a uniform basic human nature, with a stress upon nonrational processes, plus a view of the social order as mass society, the magic bullet theory, based on instinctive S-R mechanisms and the belief that the media were powerful devices, seemed entirely valid: It stated that powerful stimuli were uniformly brought to the attention of the individual members of the mass. These stimuli tapped inner urges, emotions, or other processes over which the individual had little voluntary control. Because of the inherited nature of these mechanisms, each person responded more or less uniformly. Furthermore, there were few strong social ties to disrupt the influence of these mechanisms because the individual was psychologically isolated from strong social ties and informal social control. The result was that the members of the mass could be swayed and influenced by those in possession of the media, especially with the use of emotional appeals.

Such a theory was completely consistent with general theory in both sociology and psychology as it had been developed up to that time. In addition, there was the example of the tremendous impact of wartime propaganda. This *seemed* to offer valid proof that the media *were* powerful in precisely the manner so dramatically described by Lasswell when he concluded that they were the "new hammer and anvil of social solidarity." [24] There was also the seemingly indisputable facts from the mass advertising of the time that the media were capable of persuading people to buy goods in degrees and variety hitherto undreamed of. This added to the conviction of great power and it reinforced the seeming validity of the magic bullet theory. [25]

There is no doubt that World War I propaganda was effective. However, this does not mean that only one theory is capable of accounting for those effects. If scholars of the day had been in possession of the results of research and thought on mass communication which have accumulated since that time, they might have chosen very different explanations to account for the fact that the population of the United States entered the war with enthusiasm, entertained a series of unrealistic beliefs about the enemy, and so forth, and that the media played a part in shaping their behavior and beliefs.

But theories of human nature, both in terms of social order and personal organization, did not remain static. In the United States, both psychology and sociology had become more firmly established and were increasingly escaping the domination of the thoughtways of their European origins. Both fields became heavily concerned with empirical research. As a result, their theories were forced to be more closely checked against reality. In consequence, many earlier ideas were abandoned and many new ideas were advanced. Inevitably, these new theoretical directions had their impact on those who were attempting to understand the effects of mass communication. The magic bullet theory had been built upon assumptions that were no longer regarded as tenable by general theorists, and consequently the theory had to be rather reluctantly abandoned by students of the mass media. In the meantime, there was very little to take its place.

However, even as newer general paradigms were being devised to describe human nature and the nature of the social order more adequately, the field of mass communication itself was acquiring an *empirical* base. During the late 1920s and early 1930s, scholars developed an interest in the media as objects of research. They were beginning to turn from mere speculation about their effects to systematic studies of the impact of particular communication content upon particular kinds of people. As an increasing variety of research tools became available, their ideas about mass communication could be more adequately checked against findings. Thus, the field of mass communication began to accumulate a body of data from which concepts and propositions could be inductively formulated. As the following chapter indicates, more contemporary views of the media place greater stress on social and cultural factors that limit their operation and power.

NOTES

1. Bernard Berelson, "The State of Communication Research," *Public Opinion Quarterly* 23, no. 1 (Spring 1959): 1–17.
2. Auguste Comte, *The Positive Philosophy,* trans. Harriet Martineau (London: George Bell and Sons, 1915), 2:289. First published in France between 1830 and 1842.
3. Ibid., p. 292.
4. Ibid., p. 293.
5. Ibid.
6. Herbert Spencer, *The Principles of Sociology* (New York: D. Appleton, 1898), pp. 452–62. First published in England in 1876.
7. Ferdinand Tönnies, *Community and Society (Gemeinschaft und Gesellschaft),* trans. and ed. Charles P. Loomis (East Lansing: Michigan State University Press, 1957), p. 47. First published in German in 1887.
8. Ibid., p. 65.
9. Emile Durkheim, *The Division of Labor in Society,* trans. George Simpson (New York: Free Press of Glencoe, 1964). First published in France in 1893.
10. Ibid., pp. 62–63.
11. Ibid., p. 129.
12. Ibid., p. 130.
13. Ibid., p. 131.
14. Ibid., p. 137.
15. Ibid., p. 206.
16. Ibid., p. 353.
17. Ibid., p. 361.
18. See, for example, the well-known treatment of the "mass" by Herbert Blumer, which is still regarded as the classic modern statement of the concept: Herbert

Blumer, "Elementary Collective Behavior," in *New Outline of the Principles of Sociology*, ed. Alfred McClung Lee (New York: Barnes and Noble, 1939), pp. 185–89.

19. Leonard Broom and Philip Selznick, *Sociology* (2nd ed.; Evanston, Ill.: Row, Peterson, 1958), p. 38. The quotation within the passage is from Kimball Young, *Sociology* (New York: American Book, 1949), p. 24.

20. Tönnies, *Community and Society*, p. 47.

21. George Sylvester Viereck, *Spreading Germs of Hate* (New York: Horace Liveright, 1930), pp. 153–54.

22. Harold D. Lasswell, *Propaganda Technique in the World War* (New York: Alfred A. Knopf, 1927), pp. 220–21.

23. Elihu Katz and Paul Lazarsfeld, *Personal Influence* (Glencoe, Ill.: Free Press, 1954), p. 20.

24. Lasswell, *Propaganda Technique*, p. 221.

25. Katz and Lazarsfeld point out that both those who feared the media as potentially insidious devices if controlled by evil men and those who hailed them as beneficial means to improve democracy were assuming a similar great degree of media power. See Katz and Lazarsfeld, *Personal Influence*, pp. 15–17.

Although the mass communication research and theory, both of the recent past and of the contemporary period, has stressed almost uniformly "effects" as the major object of explanation, the present volume has repeatedly suggested that there

8

mass media as social systems

are other, and possibly equally important, aspects of the media that deserve theoretical and empirical attention. One of the most challenging of such issues is their ability to *survive* and for long periods of time provide their audiences with content that powerful elites have regularly condemned as being in bad taste or even downright dangerous. A continuous dialogue has been carried on between the representatives of the mass media and self-appointed representatives of "high culture." This issue of "elite culture" versus "mass culture" has on some occasions stirred debate in the highest political, educational, religious, and legal circles of the nation. A long series of court battles has been fought over books, magazines, and other forms of print that their publishers claim are "artistic" but public prosecutors maintain are "pornographic." The freedom of speech principle versus statutory prohibitions of lewd, lascivious, or salacious portrayals provide ample grounds for lively discussion. The Supreme Court's 1972 decision to allow local communities to determine their own standards of what is and is not pornographic has intensified this debate. Even more controversial for social scientists and others concerned with mass media effects was the 1971 Report of President Johnson's Commission on Pornography and Obscenity, which suggested that there may be *more* desirable and *fewer* undesirable effects of "pornography" than is commonly believed.[1] When it was finally published, this congressionally sponsored report was summarily rejected by President Nixon and many congressional and religious leaders despite its scientific documentation. Such observations indicate that both the conflict and structural-functional paradigms can provide perspectives for understanding the persistence of the media in their presentation of mass culture content.

BACKGROUND OF THE PROBLEM

Long before the mass media were invented, Plato may have provided the opening round in the controversy over the social costs and benefits of mass culture. In his commentary on the training of the children who were to become the leaders of his ideal Republic, he saw the mass culture of his day as posing a threat to the minds of the young:

> Then shall we simply allow our children to listen to any stories that anyone happens to make up, and so receive into their minds ideas often the very opposite of those we shall think they ought to have when they are grown up?
> No, certainly not [replies Glaucon].
> It seems, then, our first business will be to supervise the making of fables and legends, rejecting all which are unsatisfactory; and we shall induce nurses

and mothers to tell their children only those which we have approved. . . . Most of the stories now in use must be discarded.[2]

This theme—popular entertainment is harmful to the minds of the young—has been a consistent one from the beginnings of mass communication. It has been claimed from time to time that such charges can be validated by scientific evidence, but repeatedly this evidence has turned out to be difficult to interpret and therefore controversial.[3] Social scientists insist that any important conclusions about the effects of the media be supported by solid evidence. Because of such insistence upon data rather than emotion, they sometimes find themselves in the awkward position of seeming to defend the media when actually they are simply refusing to accept the inadequately supported claims of critics.

Nevertheless, the insistence that conclusions be based on adequate evidence has never deterred the literary critic from charging the media with a deep responsibility for society's problems. Most nineteenth-century American writers at some point in their careers took time to criticize and condemn the newspaper for superficiality and distortion. The following excerpts from the pens of well-known and influential literary figures are samples of the climate of opinion prevailing among the literati during the time when the mass newspaper was diffusing through the American society:

Henry David Thoreau (written just prior to 1850):
The penny-post is, commonly, an institution through which you seriously offer a man that penny for his thoughts which is so safely offered in jest. And I am sure that I have never read any memorable news in a newspaper. If we read of one man robbed, or murdered, or killed by accident, or one house burned, or one vessel wrecked, or one steamboat blown up, or one cow run over on the Western Railroad, or one mad dog killed, or one lot of grasshoppers in the winter—we never need read of another. If you are acquainted with the principle, what do you care for a myriad instances and applications? To a philosopher all news, as it is called, is gossip, and they who read it and edit it are old women over their tea.[4]

Samuel Clemens (written in 1873):
That awful power, the public opinion of this nation, is formed and molded by a horde of ignorant self-complacent simpletons who failed at ditching and shoemaking and fetched up in journalism on their way to the poorhouse.[5]

Stephen Crane (written about 1895):
A newspaper is a collection of half-injustices
Which, bawled by boys from mile to mile,
Spreads its curious opinion
To a million merciful and sneering men,

While families cuddle the joys of the fireside
When spurred by tale of lone agony.

A newspaper is a court
Where everyone is kindly and unfairly tried
By a squalor of honest men.

A newspaper is a market
Where wisdom sells it freedom
And melons are crowned by the crowd.

A newspaper is a game
Where his error scores the player victory,
While another's skill wins death.

A newspaper is a symbol;
It is a feckless life's chronicle,
A collection of loud tales
Concentrating eternal stupidities,
That in remote ages lived unhaltered,
Roaming through a fenceless world.[6]

One remarkable aspect of these statements is that you could simply substitute the word "television" for "newspapers" and obtain a rather parallel version of the hostility and attacks primarily directed at television by critics today.

THE BASICS OF FUNCTIONAL ANALYSIS

The *tenacity* and *stability* of the mass media generally in the face of such a long history of criticism by powerful voices needs explanation. The problem at first seems deceptively simple: the media appeal to the masses and the masses want the kind of content they get and so the media continue to give it to them.

Many social scientists, such as Skornia,[7] have exposed the inadequacy of this explanation by noting the old chicken-and-egg problem. It is difficult at best to know if the public taste determines the media fare or if the media fare determines public taste. The answer probably lies somewhere in between with public taste being both a cause and effect of media fare. The relationship between public taste and media fare thus becomes a circular one which, in terms of the chicken-egg analogy, is an ongoing process of chickens producing eggs and eggs producing chickens.

A promising approach to understanding the relationship between mass media content and public taste, and for accounting in part for the remarkable continuity of the (low) cultural level of media content is provided by the *structural functional* paradigm discussed briefly in Chapter 1. Such an analysis begins by viewing the media as *social systems* that operate within a specific external system—the set of social and cultural conditions that is the American society itself. In certain respects, this rise of interest in the analysis of social phenomena as occurring within the boundaries of social systems represents a renewal of interest in the theoretical strategies of the past, such as those of Spencer, Tönnies, and Durkheim discussed in Chapter 6.

The structural functional analysis of social systems (or "functional analysis" for short) concerns itself with the *patterns of action* exhibited by individuals or subgroups who relate themselves to one another within such systems. A social system is, for this reason, an *abstraction*—but one not too far removed from the observable and empirically verifiable behaviors of the persons who are doing the acting. The social system, then, is a complex of stable, repetitive, and patterned action that is in part a man-ifestation of the culture shared by the actors, and in part a manifestation of the psychological orientations of the actors (which are in turn derived from that culture). The *cultural system,* the *social system,* and the *personality systems* (of the individual actors), therefore, are different kinds of abstrac-tions made from the same basic data, namely, the overt and symbolic behaviors of individual human beings. They are equally legitimate abstractions, each providing in its own right a basis for various kinds of explanations and predictions. Generally speaking, it may be difficult or nearly impossible to analyze or understand fully one such abstraction without some reference to the others.

But, granted that the term "social system" is a legitimate scientific abstraction, how does this general conceptual strategy help in under-standing the mass media of communication? To answer this question, we need to set forth in greater detail exactly what is meant by the term social system, and what type of analysis it provides. To aid in providing such an explanation we turn briefly to several ideas that are important aspects of the study of social systems. One of the most important of these ideas is the concept of the "function" of some particular *repetitive phenomenon* (set of actions) within such a system. For it was with questions about a particular repetitive phenomenon (the continuous production and distribution of media content in "low" cultural taste) that the present chapter began. The fact that such content has long survived the jibes of influential critics was said to require explanation. One form of explanation will be provided by noting the *function* of such a repetitive phenomenon within some stable system of action. The term "function" in the present context means little more than "consequence." To illustrate briefly, we might hypothesize that the repetitive practice of wearing wedding rings on the part of a given married couple has the function (consequence) of reminding them as well as others that the two are bound together by the obligations and ties that matrimony implies. This practice thereby contributes indirectly to maintaining the permanence of the marriage—the stability of that particular social system. The practice is in a sense "explained" by noting its contribution to the context within which it occurs. A comparison of a number of such systems with and without this particular item (but in other respects matched) would test the assertion.

In the above example, the social system is a relatively simple one. There are only two "components," and each of these happen to be the behavior pattern of an individual. Their patterns of action are derived both from the individual psychological makeup of the partners and from the cultural norms concerning marriage prevailing in their community, social class, and society. It is a miniature system whose stability is dependent upon satisfaction of its "needs." For example, such a system requires that the partners perform roles that meet the expectations each has of the other and the expectations the community has of married couples. This can be thought of as a "need" for adequate role performance, without which the stability of the system would be endangered. Other "needs," related to economic matters and emotional satisfactions, could be cited.

More complex illustrations of social systems can easily be pointed to, where the "components" of the system are not the actions of individual persons but subsystems. A department store, for example, is a complex social system consisting of the actions of managerial personnel, buyers, salespersons, the clerical staff, customers, transportation workers, a janitorial team, and security employees. Each of these components is a smaller system of action within the broader system of the store itself, and it in turn is a complex system of action carried out within the context of the external social conditions of the community. In spite of the complexity, any given set of repetitive actions might be analyzed in terms of their contribution to maintaining or undermining the system's stability. Granting to employees the right to buy merchandise at cost could have the function (consequence) of maintaining their morale and loyalty, and thus would contribute fairly directly to the maintenance of the system. Rigid insistence on the observance of petty rules, such as docking the pay of an employee who on rare occasions was late for work, might be disruptive of morale and loyalty, and by contributing to labor turnover it could be *dysfunctional*. Instead of contributing to the maintenance of the system, it could cause disruptions and instability. Such inductively derived conclusions would be subject to testing for validity, of course, but the functional analysis would have generated the hypothesis to be tested (an important role of theory).

STRUCTURE AND FUNCTION IN MEDIA SYSTEMS

A "functional analysis," then, focuses on some specific phenomenon occurring within a social system. It then attempts to show how this phenomenon has consequences that contribute to the stability and permanence of the system as a whole. The phenomenon may, of course, have a negative influence, and if so, it would be said to have "dysfunctions" rather than "functions." The analysis is a strategy for inducing or locating hypotheses that can be tested empirically by comparative studies or other appropriate research methods.

The analysis of social systems is extremely difficult. No infallible rules specify precisely how to locate and define the exact boundaries of a given social system, particularly if it is relatively complex. As yet, no completely agreed upon criteria exist for establishing linkages between the components of a system, and no standard formulas can uncover the precise contribution that a given repetitive form of action makes to the stability of a system. A functional analysis of the contribution of some item to the stability of a system, then, is a procedure that is somewhat less than rigorous. But in spite of this source of potential criticism, this strategy has proved useful in our attempts to understand complex social phenomena, such as the mass media.

Low-Taste Content as a Repetitive Phenomenon

How can this type of analysis be applied to the mass media? First, we can identify that portion of the content of the mass media that is in "low" cultural taste or provides gratifications to the mass audience in such a manner that it is widely held to be potentially debasing as the "relatively persistent trait or disposition"[8] of the mass media we seek to explain. It would be difficult in practice to construct a *set of categories* under which to analyze the content of the media so that material of "low" cultural taste can be identified readily. It would be difficult, but actually it would not be impossible. Excessive violence, the portrayal of criminal techniques, horror and monster themes, open pornography, suggestive music, and dreary formula melodramas are typical categories of content that arouse the ire of critics. Considerable disagreement would probably occur as to the exact content that should be included in any given category. There would also be debates over the number of categories used. Nevertheless, it is theoretically possible to identify the content of any given medium that is *most* objected to by the largest number of critics. We will assume that given sufficient time and resources, and using survey techniques, preference scales, attitude measuring instruments, and other research procedures now available that the content of any given medium could be divided roughly into something like the following three categories:

low-taste content: This would be media content widely distributed and attended to by the mass audience, but which has consistently aroused the ire of critics. Examples would be crime dramas on television that emphasize violence, openly pornographic motion pictures, daytime serials, confession magazines, crime comics, suggestive music, or other content that has been widely held to contribute to a lowering of taste, disruption of morals, or stimulation toward socially unacceptable conduct. (Whether or not such charges are true.)

nondebated content: This would be media content, widely distributed and attended to, about which media critics have said very little. It is not an issue in the debate over the impact of the media on the masses. Examples would be television weather reports, some news content, music that is neither symphonic nor popular, magazines devoted to specialized interests, motion pictures using "wholesome" themes, and many others. Such content is not believed either to elevate or lower taste, and it is not seen as a threat to moral standards.

high-taste content: This would be media content sometimes widely distributed but not necessarily widely attended to. It is content that media critics feel is in better taste, morally uplifting, educational, or in some way inspiring. Examples would be serious music, sophisticated drama, political discussions, art films, or magazines devoted to political commentary. Such content is championed by critics as the opposite of the low-taste material, which they see as distinctly objectionable.

Of course, the *first* of the above categories is the one to which we wish to direct most of our attention. It is the repetitive phenomenon whose contribution to the media (as a social system) needs analysis. Nevertheless, it would also be possible to study the other two categories with somewhat parallel perspectives, but this will receive relatively little attention in the present discussion.

The Components and Boundaries of the System

We need now to begin to identify the components and boundaries of the social system within which low-taste content occurs so that eventually the contribution it makes to the system can be inductively hypothesized.

Rather than develop a purely descriptive scheme that will apply only to a single medium, it will be more fruitful to attempt to develop a *general* conceptual scheme into which any or all media could be placed, with suitable minor modifications in details. Such a general scheme will emphasize the similarities between media, particularly in terms of relationships between the components in the system.

Audiences　　The first major component of the social system of mass communication is the *audience*. This is an exceedingly complex component. The audience is stratified, differentiated, and interrelated in the many ways that social scientists have studied for years. Some of the major variables that play a part in determining how this component will operate within the system are the major needs and interests of audience members, the various social categories represented in an audience, and the nature of the social relationships between audience members. These variables point to behavioral mechanisms that determine the patterns of attention, interpretation, and response of an audience with respect to content of a given type.

Research Organizations　　The rough typology of content suggested earlier in this chapter is in some degree related to the characteristics of this audience. Organizations devoted to *research,* to measuring the preferences of media audiences, or to various forms of market research provide information to those responsible for selecting the categories of content that will be distributed to the audience. There is a link, then, between the audience as a component in the system and the market research-rating service organizations as a second component. In purely theoretical terms, both components are role systems themselves and are thus actually subsystems. This is in a sense a one-way link. For very minor (or usually no) personal reward, audience members selected for study provide data about themselves to such an agency, but very little flows back. This linkage between components is by comparison relatively simple.

Distributors　　The content itself, of whatever type, flows from some *distributor* to the audience. The role system of the distributor component varies in detail from one medium to another. In addition, several somewhat distinct subsystems exist within this general component. First, there are local outlets, which are likely to be in the most immediate contact with the audience. The local newspaper, the local theater, the local broadcasting station play the most immediate part in placing messages before their respective audiences. But inseparably tied to them are other subsystems of this general component. Newspaper syndicates, broadcasting networks, or chains of movie theaters pass content on to their local outlets. The link between these two subsystems is a two-way one. The local outlet provides money, and the larger distributor supplies content. Or the linkage may be that the local outlet provides a service, and the distributor (who is paid elsewhere) provides money.

The relationship between audience and distributor seems at first to be mostly a one-way link. The distributor provides entertainment content (and often advertising), but the audience provides little back in a direct sense. However, it does provide its *attention*. In fact, it is precisely the attention of the audience that distributors are attempting to solicit. They sell this "commodity" directly to their financial backer or sponsor. In addition, the audience supplies information to the research component and this is indirectly supplied to distributors in the form of feedback so that they may gauge the amount of attention they are eliciting. The linkages between components grow more complex as we seek the boundaries of the system.

Producers and Their Sponsors To the audience, the research, and the distributing components, we may add the role system of the *producer* of content. This component's primary link is with the *financial backer* (or *sponsor*) component and with the distributor, from whom money is obtained and for whom various forms of entertainment content are manufactured. A host of subsystems are included in this producer component, depending upon the particular medium. Examples are actors, directors, television producers, technicians, foreign correspondents, wire-service editors, film producers, labor union leaders, publishers, copyeditors, clerical staff, and many, many more.

Advertising Agencies Linking the sponsor, distributor, producer, and research organization are the *advertising agencies*. Paid primarily by the sponsor, this component provides (in return) certain ideas and services. For the most part, it provides the distributor with advertising messages. It may have links with the research component as well.

Subsystems of Control Over this complex set of interrelated components, there are other subsystems that exert *control*. The legislative bodies, at both the state and national level, which enact regulative statutes concerning the media, constitute an important part of such a control component. Another important part of this role subsystem is the official regulative agencies, which implement the policies that have been legislated. The link between the legislative body (control component) and the audience is, of course, one of votes and public opinion, to which the component is presumably sensitive and dependent. Information lines between audience, legislative bodies, and regulatory agencies are more or less open.

To the regulatory components whose role definitions are found in legal statute can be added the private voluntary associations that develop "codes" and to some degree serve as a control over the distributors. Such distributors provide them with money, and they in turn provide surveillance and other services.

The External Conditions

The regulatory subsystems draw definitions of permissible and nonpermissible content from the general set of *external conditions* within which this extremely complicated system operates. Surrounding the entire structure as an external condition are our society's general norms concerning morality, and the expressions that these find in formal law. Similar, although less likely to be incorporated into law, are our general cultural norms and beliefs regarding what will be likely to entertain or otherwise gratify Americans. Thus, we seldom see traditional Chinese opera but frequently see western horse opera. We seldom hear the strains of Hindu temple music but frequently hear the "strains" and other noises of the latest singer whom teen-agers admire. If our interests run to more serious fare, we are likely to hear the music of a relatively small list of European or American composers who created their works within a span of about three centuries. Or we are likely to view ballet, opera, drama, and so on, of a fairly limited number of artists whose products are defined by our society as classics or as innovative new approaches.

Each of the several media will fit into this general model of a social system in slightly different ways. A complete description of each of the media separately would be tedious. Indeed, each could well occupy the contents of an entire book. Two decades ago, Opotowsky attempted just such a detailed analysis of the television industry, although he did not use the social system concept.[9]

To add to the complexity of this conceptual scheme, it must be remembered that although each medium constitutes a somewhat separate social system in itself, the media are also related *to one another* in systematic ways. Thus, we may speak of the entire set of communication media, including those which have not been specifically analyzed in the present volume, as the mass communication system of the United States.

The structure of this mass communication system has been heavily influenced by the general social, political, economic, and cultural conditions that were current during the period when our mass media were

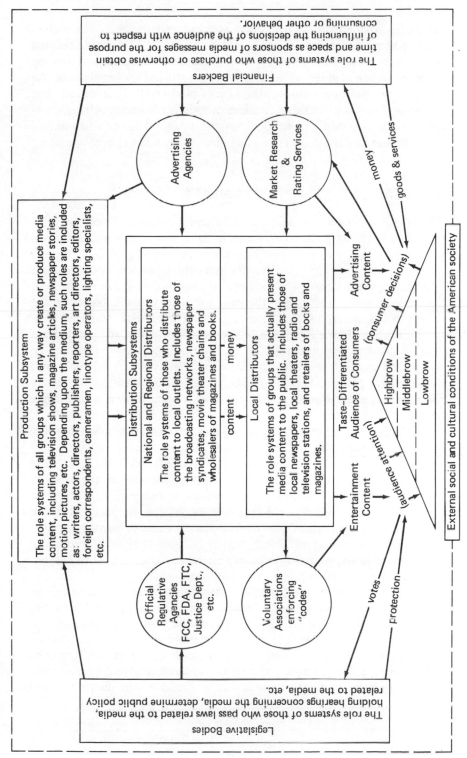

Figure 5. Schematic representation of the mass media as a social system.

developing and remain as important sociocultural forces in the society within which they operate. Because of their importance for understanding our mass media as they are today, these conditions were analyzed in some detail in earlier chapters. Our free enterprise beliefs, our views of the legitimacy of the profit motive, the virtues of controlled capitalism, and our general values concerning freedom of speech constitute further *external conditions* (in addition to those related to moral limits and cultural tastes) within which the American mass communication system operates.

MAINTAINING SYSTEM STABILITY

Within the system itself, the principal *internal condition* is, of course, a financial one. Most of the components in the system are occupational role structures, which motivate their incumbent personnel primarily through money. To obtain money, they are all ultimately dependent upon the most central component of all—the audience. Unless its decisions to give attention, to purchase, to vote, and the like, are made in favorable ways, the system would undergo severe strain and would eventually collapse.

Almost any dramatic change in the behavior of the audience would cause the most severe disruption in the system for any given medium. In an earlier chapter, the swift acquisition of television sets by the movie audience was plotted (Figure 4). The consequences of attention loss to the motion picture theater as a mass medium was shown to be severe (Figure 2).

Such disruptions are infrequent, but they do occur. The key to heading off dramatic changes in audience behavior, of course, is to provide entertainment content that will satisfy and motivate the largest possible number of audience members to carry out their roles in accord with the needs of the system. Such content will, in other words, *maintain the stability of the system.* The ideal, from the standpoint of the system, is content that will capture audience members' attention, persuade them to purchase goods, and at the same time be sufficiently within the bounds of moral norms and standards of taste so that unfavorable actions by the regulatory components are not provoked.

The entertainment content that seems most capable of eliciting the attention of the largest number of audience members is the more dramatic, low-taste content. Since the most central media system goal is economic profit, sex and violence or any other attention-getting and attention-maintaining content is functional in the sense that even though it may be of low-taste, it maximizes the size of the audience exposed to advertisements. In general, the larger the audience, the more the distributor and producer can charge for advertising. For example, ads in prime-time television periods cost substantially more than those aired during relatively low-audience-size periods, such as early in the morning.

The assumption made by many media personnel and advertisers that low-taste content appeals primarily to the relatively uneducated, who still constitute a majority of the potential audience, may be false. In an early study Wilensky found that educated people said that they preferred and exposed themselves to high-taste content more often than did the relatively uneducated. But when observations were made of what the educated and uneducated actually did, there was little difference between their levels of exposure to low-taste media content.[10]

There is a great deal of evidence to show that the relatively uneducated spend more time than the educated being exposed to the mass media.[11] It may be misleading to conclude that they do so only because the uneducated relish low-taste content. The relatively uneducated majority also have relatively low incomes, which probably means they have less choice than their more educated and wealthier counterparts in how they spend their nonworking hours. The mass media may be more appealing to the relatively uneducated and poor in large part because the media are relatively inexpensive forms of leisure. Moreover, as Baker and Ball point out, it is probably superficial to think that the only reason people in general spend time with the media is because of the inherent appeal of their content.[12] Any number of need-fulfillments and gratifications, over and above those related to entertainment or staying informed, are provided by the media. Babysitting and companionship (even when it is electronic companionship) are examples.

When all is said and done, however, it is still true that low-taste content sells—and sells big. This fact establishes it as the key element in the social system of the media. It keeps the entire complex together by maintaining the financial stability of the system. Critics who provoke public attention by denouncing media content or by proclaiming that a causal connection exists between media content and socially undesirable behavior may temporarily receive some recognition. They may also achieve some temporary disturbance in the system, or if they are persistent enough, they may ultimately even displace some specific form of low-taste content from a given medium altogether. Examples from the past are quiz shows that were found to be "rigged," and popular disc jockeys who were receiving "payola" (a fee for repeatedly playing a song to make it popular). In such cases the audience may be temporarily disaffected. However, low-taste content comes in such a variety of forms that the temporary or even permanent absence of one minor form does not alter the major picture. Critics have been complaining about newspaper concentration on crime news for a century, yet there has been no noticeable abatement in the reporting of such stories. Critics of the soap opera may have breathed a sigh of relief several years ago when these programs at last disappeared from radio. Their joy must have been short-lived when such daytime serials turned out to be quite popular with television viewers, so popular in fact that soap operas now appear during prime evening hours. Analyses of the level of violent television content show that it goes down slightly after federal government investigations on the effects of television violence or widespread campaigns by voluntary associations (e.g., the P. T. A.), only to return shortly after the public outcry has subsided. [13]

When a formula is discovered for eliciting attention and influencing purchasing decisions from any large segment of the audience, it will be abandoned by the media only with great reluctance, if at all. The broadcast ballgame, the war movie, the star comedian, the family situation comedy, the western thriller, the detective story, the adventures of the secret agent, the drama of the courtroom—all are beginning to rank with such time-honored formulas as the sob story, the funnies, the sex-murder account, the sports page, and disclosure of corruption in high places as attention-getting devices that can bring the eye or ear of the consumer nearer to the advertising message.

In short, the social system of the mass media in the United States is becoming more and more deeply established. Some future changes can be expected in the kind of content it will produce to maintain its own stability. At present, however, the function of what we have called low-taste content is to maintain the financial stability of *a deeply institutionalized social system that is tightly integrated with the whole of the American economic institution.* The probability that our system of mass communication in this respect can be drastically altered by the occasional outbursts of critics seems small indeed.

Far more likely than media system change brought about by periodic attacks on low-taste media content is media system change brought about by trends in the economic system such as the emergence of a "post-industrial" society. Because the media system is also a subsystem in the larger economic system, it will have to adapt to such changes if it is to survive. If Bell's forecast that systems in the business of producing, processing, and transmitting information will become increasingly involved in key economic sectors of our society is valid, then we would expect significant changes in the nature of the mass media system. [14] One change would surely be a marked increase in the knowledge and technical information functions of the mass media. We would thus hypothesize that the amount of "nondebated" media content will rise sharply with a corresponding decline in low-taste media content.

But as is usually the case when talking about changes in social systems, such future developments in the nature of the mass media are not likely to be that simple. Recall Durkheim's basic principle that as organisms or systems grow, they are likely to become more differentiated or complex.[15] Taking this assumption and combining it with the enormous technological advances in electronic communications' technology witnessed in recent years, it may be hypothesized that media systems will become more specialized. Some media organizations, for example, might specialize in low-taste content, others in knowledge and technical information, others in news content, and still others in high-taste content. Such technological developments as closed-circuit and cable television already are making such specialization possible. In a later chapter, we will present a brief examination of such technological developments and how they, along with changes in the economic system, may bring about significant changes in the content and structure of mass media systems.

NOTES

1. Pornography Commission Report (Washington, D.C.: Government Printing Office, 1971).
2. *The Republic of Plato*, trans. Francis M. Cornford (London: Oxford University Press, 1954), pp. 68–69.
3. Examples of such claims are Herbert Blumer and Philip Hauser, *Movies, Delinquency and Crime* (New York: Macmillan, 1933), and Frederick C. Wertham, *Seduction of the Innocent* (New York: Rinehart, 1954). The latter is a bitter denunciation of comic books. For more recent examples, see Chapter 10.
4. Henry David Thoreau, *Walden, Or Life in the Woods* (Boston and New York: Houghton Mifflin, 1854), 2:148–49.
5. Samuel Clemens, *Mark Twain's Speeches* (New York: Harper & Brothers, 1923), p. 47.
6. Quoted in Milton Ellis, Louise Pond, and George W. Spohn, *A College Book of American Literature* (New York: American Book, 1939), 1:704.
7. Harry J. Skornia, "Television and the News: A Critical Appraisal," in *Mass Media and Mass Man*, ed. Alan Casty (2nd ed.; New York: Holt, Rinehart & Winston, 1973), pp. 214–24.
8. Carl G. Hempel, "The Logic of Functional Analysis," in *Symposium on Sociological Theory*, ed. Llewellyn Gross (New York: Harper & Brothers, 1959), p. 280.
9. Stan Opotowsky, *T.V.: The Big Picture* (New York: Collier Books, 1962).
10. Harold L. Wilensky, "Mass Society and Mass Culture: Interdependence or Independence?" *American Sociological Review* 29 (April 1964): 173–97.
11. See, for example, Bradley S. Greenberg, "The Content and Context of Vio-

lence in the Mass Media," in *Violence and the Media*, ed. Robert K. Baker and Sandra J. Ball (Washington, D.C.: Government Printing Office, 1969), pp. 423–49.

12. Baker and Ball, *Violence and the Media*, pp. 330–33.
13. Ibid., pp. 151–59.
14. Daniel Bell, *The Coming of Post-Industrial Society* (New York: Basic Books, 1973).
15. Emile Durkheim, *The Division of Labor in Society*, trans. George Simpson (New York: Free Press of Glencoe, 1964).

This chapter presents an overview of how thinking concerning the impact of the media on individuals and groups has undergone progressive change. We saw in Chapter 6 that some mass society theorists attributed to the mass media the

9 encountering the media

power to manipulate the minds and actions of the masses. Discovery of psychological and sociological mechanisms that limit the impact of media messages moved social science thinking away from this mass society perspective. At the center of this change in theoretical interpretation was a fundamental redefinition of the nature of the encounter between media and individuals. The idea that people encounter the media as a mass of unconnected individuals was rejected. In its place emerged a conception of the media audience as a set of individuals who encounter the media as social beings connected to their social environments.

THE GROWTH OF UNDERSTANDING

This change of interpretation is somewhat analogous to the growth of understanding about the organizational and structural intricacies of mass media systems discussed in Chapter 7. Developments in social science theory and research led to increased insights into the sometimes subtle ways in which audiences are structured and organized. As media structure and organization affects its approach to their audiences, the informal social organizational ties of audience members affect how they approach the media. As we shall see, the perspective that emerged and prevails today is that *individual audience members encounter media messages as members of groups and that they do so with a constructed social reality that reflects their past and present social experiences.*

Another set of interpretations that posited enormous power to the mass media and that was subsequently rejected by most social scientists was Innis's *technological determinism*. Innis contended that the nature of the media technology prevailing in a society at a given point in time greatly influences how the members of that society think and behave.[1] Books and other print media, for example, are said to promote cause-effect thinking in societies where print media dominate, because the technology of print forces a linear form of presentation either across or up or down a page. In more recent times, McLuhan elaborated Innis's thesis, and characterized television as a "cool" medium because its capacity for rich configurations of audiovisual stimuli elicits high but passive audience participation.[2] From the technological determinist's perspective, the most important characteristic of the audience-media encounter is the technological properties of the medium. Thus, McLuhan asserted that "the medium is the message."[3] While some social scientists are attempting to understand the potential impact of the nature of new media technologies on audiences and society, few would accept the proposition that technology *alone* determines how people encounter and respond to the mass media.

Most, for example, would reject McLuhan's claim that the *content* of media messages has no impact on audiences. Essentially, mass media theorists reject the extreme form of technological determinism put forth by McLuhan for two reasons. Social scientists generally reject the idea that any *single factor*—be it technology, the economy, or chromosomes—can be the single cause of social behavior. This distrust of single-factor theories is buttressed by theory and research developments that demonstrate the influence of both psychological and social factors on the individual's or group's encounter with the mass media. This is not to say that Innis's thesis need be rejected out of hand; most media theorists would accept the proposition that the technological characteristics of a mass medium may be one of many factors that should be taken into account.[4]

EMERGING FRAMEWORK FOR ANALYSIS

We turn now to an examination of the three most important prevailing interpretive frameworks on how people encounter the media—the *individual differences* perspective, the *social categories* perspective, and the *social relations* perspective. We will attempt to show the progression of theory and research that led to each perspective's assumptions about the psychological and social variables which intervene in the audience's encounter with the mass media.

The Individual Differences Perspective

When psychological theorists seeking basic understanding of human conduct turned away from explanations of complex behavior based primarily on inherited mechanisms, they sought new explanations built upon very different principles. If nature failed to endow human beings with the automatic ability to guide their behavior, then they surely had to *acquire* it from their environment. Great interest was to develop among psychologists in the process of human learning. By the end of World War I, academic psychology was intellectually prepared for new directions. One new direction was provided by the concept of *conditioning*.

Learning as Source of Individual Differences   From English empiricism, psychologists had inherited a persistent interest in *association* and *habit* as important aspects of learning. As early as 1890, William James had suggested that habits formed through association may have a physiological basis.[5] John Watson introduced a further significant element to modern psychology with his emphasis on behaviorism.[6] But more than anything else, it was the classical conditioning experiments that fired the imagination of the psychologists of the late 1920s and the early 1930s.[7] Thus, there was a renewed interest in habit formation through learning, a new stress upon objective experiments as an aid in the development of theories of learning, and a broad new concept that promised to link the learning process to physiology. The result of these intellectual trends was a great expansion of interest in learning processes and a host of experiments with animal and human subjects. A number of competing theories of learning were formulated.

Personality Differences   Along with this intellectual movement came an associated interest in *motivation*. The study of incentives in laboratory experiments convinced psychologists that some motivational urges can be acquired through learning and that not all individuals can be motivated by precisely the same incentives. Adding to this trend in the increasing recognition of individual motivation and learning *differences* were the findings of students of human personality. Variations in personality traits became increasingly recognized, and the mental testers began to construct sophisticated devices to quantify those differences.[8]

New concepts were also formulated in social psychology to replace the ideas of instinct. In particular, the term *attitude* grew in importance as a means of explaining differing directions of human preference and action. Introduced as a systematic concept in the writings of Thomas and Znaniecki at the end of World War I, this concept became the most basic and central theoretical tool of social psychology.[9] The invention of several rather elaborate and mathematically sophisticated techniques for attitude measurement added to its importance as a research tool and gave additional emphasis to the study of individual differences and their correlates.[10]

As these basic ideas concerning the psychological organization of the human individual were successively clarified, certain fundamental postulates became rather widely held. It was said that human beings *varied* greatly in their personal-psychological organization. These variations in part began with differential biological endowment, but they were due in greater measure to differential learning. Human beings raised under widely differing circumstances were exposed to widely differing points of view. From these learning environments they acquired a set of attitudes, values, and beliefs that constituted their cognitive makeup and set each person somewhat apart from others. Even twins of almost identical biological makeup became rather different in personality structure when raised in different social environments.

Added to this increasing recognition of human psychological modifia
bility and differentiation was the recognition that personality variables
acquired from the social milieu provided a basis for individual differences
in *perception*. The experimental study of human perception had revealed
that values, needs, beliefs, and attitudes played an influential role in determining how stimuli are selected from the environment, and how
meaning is attributed to those stimuli. Thus, one important product of
human learning was the acquisition of stable predispositions or habits
concerning the perception of events. Perception differed systematically
from one person to another according to the nature of individual personality structure.

Selectivity Based on Differences   With these new paradigms in the
background, students of mass communication had to alter their thinking
about the media. It became clear that the audience of a given medium was
not a monolithic collectivity whose members attended uniformly to whatever content was directed toward them. The *principle of selective attention
and perception* was formulated as a fundamental proposition regarding the
way ordinary persons confronted the content of the mass media. Once
psychologists had established the concept of selective perception based
upon individual differences in cognitive characteristics, it was not difficult
to show that different types of people in an audience selected and interpreted mass communication content in widely varying ways.[11]

Although never specifically formulated as a theory, it can be suggested
that selective attention and perception had become intervening psychological mechanisms that greatly modified the magic bullet mass communication theory (pages 158–164). From a multiplicity of available content,
individual members of the audience selectively attended to messages, particularly if they were related to their interests, consistent with their attitudes, congruent with their beliefs, and supportive of their values. Finally, response to such messages was modified by psychological
makeup. This general idea may be called the *individual differences perspective on the mass communication process*. Rather than being *uniform* among
the mass audience, the manner in which audience members are exposed to
media content could now be seen as *varying* from person to person because
of individual differences in psychological structure. This in turn was said
to lead to varying effects.

Differences as Intervening Variables   When communication "effects" are a focus of research attention, the assumption that the media are
in some way "causes" of those effects is a natural one. Even if it is granted
that intervening processes of some sort can modify this relationship, the

underlying cause-effect conceptualization is not different, only more complicated. The individual differences perspective implies that media messages contain particular stimulus attributes that have differential interaction with personality characteristics of audience members. Since there are individual differences in personality characteristics among such members, it is natural to assume that there will be variations in effect which correspond to these individual differences. Thus, the logical structure of the individual differences view of media effects is a "cause (intervening processes)-effect" structure, just as was the magic bullet theory before it. The intervening processes are the result of learning rather than inheritance, however.

The most obvious contemporary expression of the role of individual differences in the processes of media exposure and effects is the uses and gratifications approach.[12] Uses and gratifications is a general label for an, as yet, unsystematized set of specific theoretical viewpoints tied together by a shared emphasis on an active media audience.[13] These researchers have portrayed the individuals that constitute any mass media audience as active selectors and interpretors of media messages who utilize media messages to gratify their individual needs. Individuals not only selectively expose themselves to media messages, but also selectively avoid media messages.[14] Moreover, audience members, not the mass communicator, are said to determine the usefulness of messages. In a sense, uses and gratifications theorists have elevated the role of individual differences beyond the intervening variable role in modern S-R approaches. Some, for example, contend that the mass media audience is "obstinate" or relatively impervious to mass media effects because the members of the audience actively determine what gratifications of what needs will and will not occur from their exposure to media messages.[15] It is thus not surprising that uses and gratifications researchers have generally shown little interest in conducting studies of mass media effects.

The Social Categories Perspective

Sometimes overlapping the individual differences approach, but stemming from completely different disciplinary sources, is the *social categories perspective*. The latter assumes that there are broad collectivities, aggregates, or social categories, particularly in urban-industrial societies, whose behavior in the face of a given set of stimuli is more or less uniform. Such characteristics as age, sex, income level, educational attainment, rural-urban residence, or religious affiliation provide examples. In fact, knowledge of several simple variables—age, sex, and educational attainment—

provides a reasonably accurate guide to the type of communication content a given individual will or will not select from available media. Comic books are read primarily by the young and less educated; *Ms., Vogue,* and *Cosmopolitan* are read primarily by females; the readers of *Playboy, Field and Stream,* and *Mechanics Illustrated* are predominantly male.

An early research trend in mass media studies made such category membership a central focus. It sought to establish the ways in which such behaviors as newspaper reading, the selection of books, radio listening, and motion picture attendance were related to a variety of simple characteristics by which people could be grouped into aggregates.[16]

Social Location and Behavioral Similarities   The basic assumption of the social categories perspective is a sociological one, namely, that in spite of the heterogeneity of modern society, people with a similar location in the social structure will have similar folkways. These similar modes of orientation and behavior will relate them to such phenomena as the mass media in a fairly uniform manner. The members of a particular category will select more or less the same communication content and will respond to it in roughly equal ways. The social categories approach is a descriptive formula that can serve as a basis for rough prediction and as a guide for research.

Oddly enough, two psychologists, whom you might expect to prefer an individual differences perspective, have suggested that the social categories perspective is a better way to understand the basic process of selective exposure to media message. Sears and Freedman[17] propose that social category differences are more important predictors of media exposure patterns than are individual differences.

Social Differentiation and Subcultures   Actually, the social categories perspective has a more complex theoretical basis than is apparent on the surface. It will be recalled that the sociological theorists of the nineteenth century stressed the increasing degree of *social differentiation* that was taking place in the developing industrial society. In the society with a rudimentary division of labor, Durkheim had suggested, people would be very much alike. But in a society with a complex division of labor, there would be much greater development of what he called "personality" (e.g., "individual differences"). However, people located at similar positions in this social structure would be similar in personality because of similarity of their immediate social environment. Thus, they would be attracted to one another and form categories that were somewhat homogeneous. Earlier, Comte had suggested that people who formed groupings on the basis of similar characteristics would become a "multitude of unconnected corporations, which almost seem not to belong to the same species."[18] In modern terminology we would refer to such "corporations" as "subcultures."

While the individual differences perspective presented a view of the communication process more consistent with findings in general psychology, the social categories perspective was consistent with, and seemingly derived from, general sociological paradigms concerning the nature of the urban-industrial society. Taken altogether, they brought contemporary mass communication theory to a point where both the social differentiation of the early sociological theorists and the individual differences of the personality theorists were taken into account. Both approaches represent modifications of the original magic bullet theory, substituting, on the one hand, latent psychological processes and, on the other, uniformities within social categories as intervening variables between communication stimuli and responses. In 1948 Lasswell summed up precisely these two theoretical orientations, and the situational variables related to them, when he stated:

> A convenient way to describe an act of communication is to answer the following questions:
>
> > *Who*
> > *Says What*
> > *In Which Channel*
> > *To Whom*
> > *With What Effect?*[19]

While these two perspectives on mass communication remain useful and contemporary, there have been further additions to the set of variables intervening between media stimuli and audience response. One additional elaboration represents a somewhat belated recognition of the importance of patterns of interaction *between* audience members.

The Social Relations Perspective

Like many other significant discoveries in science, the role of group relationships in the mass communication process seems to have been discovered almost by accident. Also like many other important ideas, it appears to have been independently discovered at about the same time by more than one researcher. From the standpoint of mass communication research on how people encounter and respond to the media, one study stands out as the context within which the importance of group ties, as a complex of intervening variables between media and audience influence, was discovered. Early in 1940, before the adoption of television as a mass medium, Lazarsfeld, Berelson, and Gaudet developed an elaborate research design to study the impact upon voters of that year's mass-communicated presidential election campaign. At first, they were interested in how the members of given social categories selected material related to the election from the media, and how this material played a part in influencing their voting intentions.[20]

Serendipity in Erie County   Erie County, Ohio, the site of the research, was a rather typical American area that had voted as the nation voted in every prior presidential election in this century. Media campaign materials presented during the contest between Wendell Willkie and Franklin D. Roosevelt constituted the stimulus material. Several representative samples of residents of the area were the subjects. The study used an imaginative procedure that permitted repeated interviewing of a 600-member panel with suitable controls to check for possible effects of the seven independent monthly visits of the interviewers.

Some of the effects under study were participating in the campaign (seeking information about the candidates and the issues), formulating voting decisions, and actually going to the polls. As it turned out, still other kinds of effects could be attributed to the campaign. Some respondents were *activated* by the mass-communicated material; that is, they had latent predispositions to vote in a given direction, but these predispositions needed to be crystallized to the point where they would become manifest. Others among the electorate had pretty much made up their minds early in the campaign and these decisions were *reinforced* by a continuous and partisan selection of additional material from the media. Early vote intentions were reversed in only a small portion of cases. Thus, the campaign had only limited success in converting individuals from one party to another.

The influence of the social categories perspective as a guide to this research was clear. Age, sex, residence, economic status, and education were the key variables. These social category memberships determined "interest" and led to an early or late decision. Acting in concert, this complex of variables influenced not only people's degree and direction of exposure to the mass-communicated campaign material, but also the kinds of effects that such material would have upon them.

As suggested, designing the study around a search for the important intervening social categories was perfectly consistent with the mass society concepts that communication researchers had inherited from European sociological theorists. Little attention was given to the possible role of informal social relationships and such factors as primary group ties because these were presumed to be declining in the emerging Gesellschaft society. Elihu Katz has stated this argument cogently in the following terms:

Until very recently, the image of society in the minds of most students of communication was of atomized individuals, connected with the mass media, but not with one another. Society—the "audience"—was conceived of as aggregates of age, sex, social class, and the like, but little thought was given to the relationships implied thereby to more informal relationships. The point is not that the student of mass communication was unaware that members of the audience have families and friends but that he did not believe that they might affect the outcome of a campaign; informal interpersonal relations, thus, were considered irrelevant to the institutions of modern society.[21]

But when the interviewers talked with the people of Erie County, they kept getting somewhat unanticipated answers to one of their major lines of questioning:

Whenever the respondents were asked to report on their recent exposures to campaign communications of all kinds, *political discussions* [italics added] were mentioned more frequently than exposure to radio or print.[22]

As a matter of fact, on the average day during the election campaign period, about 10 percent more people engaged in some sort of informal exchange of ideas with *other persons* than were exposed to campaign material directly from the mass media. About midway through the series of interviews, the researchers began to probe systematically into this personal influence in an attempt to unravel the role of informal contacts with other people as an important set of variables in determining the effects of the media.

The Two-Step Flow   The end result of this somewhat unanticipated turn of events was the serendipitous recognition that *informal social relationships* play a significant part in modifying the manner in which given individuals will act upon a message that comes to their attention via the mass media. In fact, it was discovered that there were many persons whose firsthand exposure to the media was quite limited. Such people obtained most of their information about the election campaign from other people who *had* gotten it firsthand. Thus, the research began to suggest a movement of information through two basic stages. First, information moved from the media to relatively well informed individuals who frequently attended to mass communication. Second, it moved from those persons through interpersonal channels to individuals who had less direct exposure to the media and who depended upon others for their information. This communication process was termed the "two-step flow of communication."[23]

Those individuals who were more in contact with the media were called "opinion leaders" because it was soon discovered that they were playing an important role in helping to shape the voting intentions of those to whom they were passing on information. They were not only passing on information, of course, but they were also passing on their *interpretations* of communication content. This "personal influence" became immediately recognized as an important intervening process that operated between the mass communication message and the responses made to that message.

Subsequent studies were aimed more directly at studying the mechanisms of interpersonal influence and the part played by social relationships in mediating the movement of information from the media to the masses. In fact, a rich literature has accumulated indicating that informal social relationships operate as important intervening variables between the stimulus and the response in the mass communication process.

It was suggested earlier that the role of informal social relationships in the communication process was independently discovered by more than one researcher at about the same time. Students of rural sociology had long recognized that informal social relationships among farmers played an important part in determining their propensity to adopt a given agricultural innovation. The rural society is one in which the farm family normally has strong social ties with its neighbors. When new ideas come from the outside, the interpretations made by neighbors in such a setting can be of critical importance in determining the likelihood of adoption. The adoption of new farm technology is a process closely related to mass communication. New ideas are first presented to farm operators via communication media of one kind or another. These may be mass media, or they may be other formal channels of communication such as county agents or agricultural experiment station bulletins. The question is whether or not the individual farmer will respond to these communications in ways advocated by the communicators, namely, by adopting the recommended practice. Thus, conceptually speaking, a considerable similarity exists between the case of a farmer being advised to adopt a new form of weed spray via a radio program devoted to farm problems and the case of a person being advised to adopt a new household detergent via a radio commercial designed to sell soap. Both may adopt the innovation in accordance with the communicated suggestion, or they may resist it. The variables that mediate the decision to adopt or not to adopt may be quite similar in each case.[24]

The recognition of the convergence of theory between the students of mass communication and students of rural sociology who were studying the diffusion of farm technology stimulated a surge of interest in the diffusion and adoption process insofar as it was linked to mass communication. Intensive studies were undertaken concerning the nature of opinion leadership, the way it occurred in various contexts, and the part played by interpersonal relationships. In general it has been found that opinion leaders who are influential in the adoption process are in some respects very much like those whom they influence. They tend to conform closely to the norms of their groups, and they tend to be leaders in one area but not necessarily in others.[25] Opinion leadership does not seem to travel down the social structure, but is more likely to be horizontal. It appears to take place primarily between persons of somewhat similar status, although this is not always true. Katz and Lazarsfeld found that position in the "life cycle" was a key variable in determining who would influence whom in areas such as marketing, fashions, and public issues.[26] Young working women, in closer contact with fashion magazines and other media information about such issues, were sought by the less informed for advice about hairstyles, clothing, and the like. Married women with large families, who were well informed from appropriate media sources about household products, were sought as advisers on marketing, trying out new products, and so on. Thus, the age, marital status, and number of children (social categories) of women in traditional roles predisposed them to acquire information about issues related to those roles. These in turn were the criteria used by those needing advice on particular subjects when they turned to an opinion leader (social relationships) for information and influence.

A number of studies have suggested conditions of social structure and social functioning that lead to the emergence and functioning of an opinion leader.[27] Moreover, the conditions that lead to the institutionalization— relatively permanent establishment—of an opinion leader have also been addressed in research.[28]

THE FUTURE OF MASS COMMUNICATION THEORY

One of the most pressing problems in the interdisciplinary study of mass communication is the strengthening of its theoretical base. There has been an unfortunate tendency among students of the media to equate the idea of "theory" with relatively unsophisticated matters such as classification schemes, the preparation of abstract diagrams that purport to symbolize the communication process, or the mere listing of factors that somehow will "make a difference" in the way some communication effect takes place. Criteria of what constitutes a theory in more sophisticated fields are considerably more demanding. In a very real way, the three perspectives on mass communication that have been discussed in the present chapter reflect these limitations. By any formal criteria, they are certainly not theories. They are conceptual frameworks that have been given easy-to-remember names for purposes of convenience. In reality, these conceptualizations did not emerge fullblown from research in precisely the way they have been discussed. They have been pulled together for the purposes of the present chapter and given these names, although they have been implicit or explicit in debates, writing, and research for years.

To some extent the lack of continued dedication to fundamental theoretical problems related to the media may be a product of the history of mass communication as a field of research and study. Until recently, it has been little more than a kind of intellectual way station—unclaimed territory where people from various disciplinary backgrounds have come in, picked up research problems, worked through them for a while, and then dropped them in favor of more pressing interests or pursued their implications back into the mainstream of their own discipline. Perhaps now that the field of communication has developed as a discipline in its own right, with its own research training, formal degree programs, increasing specialization, and a growing conceptual apparatus, it will be able to concentrate more fully on the systematic accumulation of theories of mass communication.

Theories about the mass communication process need to be set forth as systematic sets of propositions that show in straightforward terms just what is supposed to be related to what in terms of *independent* and *dependent* variables. To do this, some difficult definitional work will have to be undertaken so that the exact phenomena to which the concepts in the theories refer can be specified. Relationships between concepts within given propositions will have to be identified by means of some logical *calculus*—some set of recognized rules for reasoning—so that orders of dependency between propositions can be established. If this is done, such theories can be tested empirically. Only then can their validity be adequately assessed.

This does not mean that all mass communication theory must be reduced to algebraic equations. The steps suggested above are possible without resorting to mathematics. Nevertheless, it is one thing to state propositions like this: "Ideas often flow from the media to opinion leaders and from them to less active populations." It is quite another thing to specify precisely what quantitative relationships are meant by such terms as "often" and "less," and to note exact empirical referents for other terms in such a statement, such as "ideas," "flow," "leaders." In other words, we must specify more rigorously the conditions under which these events will occur, in what quantity or with what probability, and with what step-by-step theoretical implications for related media behavior.

We pointed out earlier the equally serious problem that many communication researchers lack an understanding of the basic paradigms of the social and behavioral sciences. Many of the variables and assumptions used in communication research are drawn from these paradigms. The development of communication theory depends on a more complete familiarity of these vital theoretical roots.

This call for raising scientific standards in media theory construction indicates that students of mass communication have a great deal of homework to do before they can increase the sophistication of their theoretical formulations to the level of other disciplines. There is a serious gap between what we *think* we know about how people encounter and respond to the mass media and a rigorous set of theoretical formulations that specify how these events *actually* take place. In other words, there is a need to establish increased confidence that these basic perspectives are true (or else replace them) and thereby increase the degree to which we can discuss cause-effect sequences in mass communication in precise terms. We must, for example, ask such disturbing questions as to whether or not the declines in political party membership and party identification have reduced the import of social categories in shaping media exposure and effects regarding political messages, or whether the dramatic increase in the number of states holding primary elections may have increased the direct role of the media in people's voting decisions.[29]

Until formulations such as those identified in this chapter have been studied, restudied, reformulated, and restudied again, they will remain forever as "pretheories"—interesting and seemingly plausible speculations that appear to be more or less consistent with our limited amount of media research but about which we really are not sure.

NOTES

1. Harold A. Innis, *Empire and Communication* (London: Clarendon Press, 1950).
2. Marshall McLuhan, *Understanding Media* (New York: McGraw-Hill, 1964).
3. Ibid.
4. Couch has criticized sociologists for ignoring the form of audience-media relations that derive, in large part, from the nature of media technology. See Carl Couch, "Theoretical Notes of the Form and Consequences of Mass Communication" (paper presented at the annual meeting of the American Sociological Association, August 1972).
5. William James, *Principles of Psychology* (New York: Henry Holt, 1890); see p. 566.
6. John B. Watson, *Behavior: An Introduction to Comparative Psychology* (New York: Henry Holt, 1914).

7. Although the basic idea of conditioning was understood before the turn of the century, physiologists such as Ivan Pavlov and Vladimir Bekhterev made it popular among American psychologists. An excellent discussion of this historical development is that of Ernest Hilgard and Donald Marquis, *Conditioning and Learning* (New York: Appleton-Century-Crofts, 1940), esp. pp. 1–50.

8. For an outstanding overview of development during this period of thought concerning human personality, see Gordon W. Allport, *Personality: A Psychological Interpretation* (New York: Henry Holt, 1937).

9. W. I. Thomas and Florian Znaniecki, *The Polish Peasant in Europe and America*, 5 vols. (Chicago: University of Chicago Press, 1918–21).

10. For a discussion of the history and present status of attitude and its measurement, see Melvin L. De Fleur and Frank R. Westie, "Attitude as a Scientific Concept," *Social Forces* 42 (October 1963): 17–31.

11. A major section in one of the first textbooks in mass communication consists of a series of reprinted research reports dealing with audience selectivity and its basis. See Wilbur Schramm, ed., *Mass Communications* (Urbana: University of Illinois Press, 1949), pp. 387–429.

12. Jay Blumler and Elihu Katz (eds.), *The Uses of Mass Communications: Current Perspectives on Gratifications Research* (Beverly Hills: CA: Sage, 1974).

13. Jay Blumler, "The Role of Theory in Uses and Gratifications Studies," *Communication Research* 6 No. 1 (1979): 9–36; David Swanson, "Political Communication Research and the Uses and Gratifications Model: A Critique," *Communication Research* 6 No. 1 (1979): 37–53; Elihu Katz, "The Uses of Becker, Blumler, and Swanson," *Communication Research* 6 No. 1 (1979): 74–83.

14. Lee Becker, "Measurement of Gratifications," *Communication Research* 6 No. 1 (1979): 54–73.

15. Raymond Bauer, "The Obstinate Audience," *American Psychologist* 19 (1964): 319–328.

16. The following are representative examples of research reports guided by the social categories theory: Paul F. Lazarsfeld, "Communications Research," *Current Trends in Social Psychology* (Pittsburgh: University of Pittsburgh Press, 1949), pp. 233–48; Wilbur Schramm and David White, "Age, Education, and Economic Status as Factors in Newspaper Reading," in Schramm, *Mass Communications*, pp. 402–12; and H. M. Beville, Jr., "The A B C D's of Radio Audiences," in Schramm, *Mass Communications*, pp. 413–23.

17. D. Sears and J. Freedman, "Selective Exposure to Information: A Critical Review," *Public Opinion Quarterly* 31 (1967): 194–213.

18. Auguste Comte, *The Positive Philosophy*, trans. Harriet Martineau (London: George Bell and Sons, 1915), vol. 2.

19. Harold D. Lasswell, "The Structure and Function of Communication in Society," in *The Communication of Ideas*, ed. Lyman Bryson (New York: Harper & Brothers, 1948), pp. 37–51.

20. Paul F. Lazarsfeld, Bernard Berelson, and Hazel Gaudet, *The People's Choice* (New York: Duell, Sloan & Pearce, 1944).

21. Elihu Katz, "Communications Research and the Image of Society: Convergence of Two Research Traditions," *American Journal of Sociology* 65, no. 5 (1960): 436.
22. Lazarsfeld, Berelson, and Gaudet, *People's Choice*, p. 150.
23. An excellent summary of this process is contained in Elihu Katz, "The Two-Step Flow of Communication: An Up-to-Date Report on an Hypothesis," *Public Opinion Quarterly* 21, no. 1 (Spring 1957): 61–78.
24. For an excellent summary of research on farm adoption, see C. Paul Marsh and A. Lee Coleman, "Group Influences and Agricultural Innovations: Some Tentative Findings and Hypotheses," *American Journal of Sociology* 61, no. 6 (May 1956): 588–94. See also C. M. Coughenour, "The Functioning of Farmer's Characteristics in Relation to Contacts with Media and Practice Adoption," *Rural Society* 25 (September 1960): 263–97; Walter Weiss, "Effects of the Mass Media of Communication," pp. 77–195 in Gardner Lindzey and Elliot Aronson (eds.), *Handbook of Social Psychology* 5, 2nd edition, (Reading, Mass.: Addison-Wesley, 1969).
25. For a review of literature on such issues, see Everett M. Rogers, *Diffusion of Innovations* (New York: Free Press of Glencoe, 1962), esp. pp. 208–47.
26. Elihu Katz and Paul F. Lazarsfeld, *Personal Influence* (Glencoe, Ill.: Free Press, 1954).
27. Melvin L. De Fleur, "The Emergence and Functioning of Opinion Leadership: Some Conditions of Informal Influence Transmission," in *Decisions, Values and Groups*, ed. Norman Washburne (New York: Macmillan, 1962), 2:257–78.
28. For a review of relevant research, see chaps. 5–11 in Ithiel de Sola Pool et al., eds., *Handbook of Communication*.
29. For relevant research, see Jay Blumler and Dennis McQuail, *Television in Politics: Its Uses and Influence* (London: Faber and Faber, 1968); Donald Shaw and Maxwell McCombs, *The Emergence of American Political Issues: The Agenda-Setting Function of the Press* (St. Paul, Minn.: West, 1977); Charles Atkin, "Mass Communication and Persuasion" pp. 285–308 in Michael Roloff and Gerald Miller, *Persuasion: New Directions in Theory and Research* (Beverly Hills, CA: Sage, 1980).

The perspectives discussed in Chapter 8 on how people encounter media content selectively set the stage for an examination of social science theories of the *effects* of exposure to media messages. Despite the dominance

10

theories of the effects of media violence

of the effects question in discussions of the media's role in our society, social scientists have not formulated general theories of mass media effects. Rather, effects theories have been developed around rather specific public concerns, such as the effects of media messages on people's attitudes toward presidential candidates,[1] their feelings about the "enemy,"[2] their willingness to buy war bonds,[3] or their readiness to eat unconventional foods.[4]

We focus our attention in this chapter on specific theories of what has probably been the central effects question of recent decades—the impact of media portrayals of violence on audience behavior. We will outline the central assumptions of five specific theories that have generated most of the research on the effects of media violence. These theories are called *catharsis, aggressive cues, observational learning, reinforcement,* and *cultivation.* We will also illustrate how each theory has grown out of one or more of the perspectives previously discussed on how people encounter the media.

BACKGROUND OF THE PROBLEM

Attempts to understand and identify how audiences are affected, particularly by violent television programming, were intensified in the 1960s and early '70s by a national sense of urgency concerning the causes of real-world violence. The 1960s will probably be remembered by social historians as a decade of violence—a time of urban riots, increasing rates of violent crime, and collective protests against such matters as the Vietnam war, institutionalized racism, and pollution. It was also a decade of assassinations of such major political figures as Martin Luther King, Jr., John Kennedy, and Robert Kennedy. Many concerned and politically powerful observers of the social scene could not resist making what seemed to be a logical connection between the incessant portrayals of media violence on the one hand and the seemingly increasing rates of real-world violence on the other.[5]

There are good reasons why television more than any other mass medium generates public concern. History reveals that public outcries against the harmful effects attributed to violent media content tend to focus on the newest mass medium. In the 1960s this was television, and youthful members of the first TV generation were the most visible participants in the violence of this era. Television requires little in the way of reading or other skills. Thus it is uniquely accessible to persons of all ages and education. Moreover, violence is a pervasive aspect of television programming. Gerbner and his associates in studies of typical weeks of TV content categorized 70 percent of prime-time and 92 percent of children's weekend television entertainment as violent programs.[6]

Government commissions asked social scientists to organize available theoretical and empirical work to see what tentative conclusions could be drawn about the effects of television violence. Social scientists also initiated research that might provide new insights into the relationship between media and real-world violence. The end products of these efforts are presented in the extensive reports of two national commissions dealing with the impact of media violence. These were the Violence and the Media Task Force Report of the National Commission on the Causes and Prevention of Violence,[7] and the Surgeon General's (NIMH) Report on Television and Social Behavior.[8]

THE BASICS OF THE VIOLENCE THEORIES

Our present aim is to summarize briefly the most prominent theories underlying research on the influence of media violence. We will try to show how these theories have grown out of more general perspectives on the ways people encounter and use the mass media. To a lesser extent, we will summarize what the research evidence can tell us about the validity of the catharsis, aggressive cues, observational learning, reinforcement, and cultivation theories.

Catharsis Theory

The central theme of catharsis[9] theory is that people in the normal course of daily life build up frustrations that eventually lead them to engage in aggression. Catharsis is the relief of such frustrations through vicarious participation in others' aggression. Aggressive tendencies, then, are effectively controlled by psychological and social mechanisms involved in vicarious experience. Seymour Feshbach is the most prominent proponent of the catharsis approach. For the catharsis theorist, viewing violent television content provides audiences with vicarious aggressive experiences. This serves as a harmless vehicle for relieving their feelings of hostility or frustration. For example, audience members watching TV characters cast in the role of "superspy" or "private eye" subjectively participate in the TV character's aggression. This lessens their own need to engage overtly in aggressive acts. The basic prediction made by catharsis theory, then, is that exposure to violent television content *decreases the probability of violent behavior* by TV viewers.

Feshbach and Singer contend that televised violence may have a more important catharsis function for lower-class as opposed to middle-class audience members.[10] They reason that the family training or socialization given middle-class children equips them with a fairly good capacity to control their aggressive impulses. In contrast, the family training given lower-class children does not produce well-developed internal control mechanisms, thereby making them more dependent on the external control provided by cathartic TV violence.

Many differences between the catharsis theory and other specific theories of the effects of televised violence are due to their differing commitments to the assumptions of the more general formulations we have called the individual differences, social categories, and social relations perspectives on mass communication. In Chapter 9 it was said that the individual differences perspective is the oldest of the three. Its central proposition is that differences in motivation, learning, personality, attitudes, and the like, result in differences in the media content people select (selective exposure). Differences in perception of media messages (selective perception) lead in turn to differences in how people interpret and respond to mass media stimuli. The social categories perspective, on the other hand, is based on the assumption that people who share a number of similar social characteristics (e.g., age, sex, race) also tend to share similar attitudes, norms, and values. These in turn lead them to respond to media messages in roughly similar ways. The central concern of the social relations perspective is the role of group relationships in influencing people's responses to media messages. Interpersonal influence networks in the form of opinion leaders are said to act as conduits and interpreters of mass media messages for their followers (the two-step flow process of mass communication).

When we examine the relative impact of these perspectives on the orientation and assumptions of catharsis theory, we find that it is rooted in the individual differences perspective. The individual differences most central to catharsis theory are the level of accumulated frustration and hostility individuals are experiencing prior to exposure to violent TV programs. The cathartic effect of televised violence should be greatest for those individuals with the strongest catharsis need, namely, individuals who have built up considerable frustration and hostility.

When Feshbach and Singer[11] incorporated the idea that lower-class persons may have greater catharsis needs than middle-class persons, they based their modification of catharsis theory on an important "social category." The proposition that the effects of violent TV programming will be similar for members of the same social class, but different across social classes, moves catharsis theory beyond a concern with individual differ-

THEORIES OF MASS COMMUNICATION

ences. It becomes a special case of the social categories perspective. Thus, both perspectives are evident in this specific formulation.

Stimulating Effects (Aggressive Cues) Theory

Leonard Berkowitz has been the primary framer of the stimulating effects approach (also referred to as the aggressive cues approach) to the effects of media portrayals of violence.[12] Its major assumption is that exposure to aggressive stimuli will increase a person's level of physiological and emotional arousal, which in turn will increase the probability of aggressive behavior. Seeing a violent boxing match, for example, is said to stimulate emotional arousal leading to aggressive behavior on the part of TV audience members. Violent encounters, weapons, or threats are said to not only physiologically and emotionally arouse audience members but also clue them into aggressive responses. Tannenbaum[13] suggests that the audiovisual media are particularly potent elicitors of physiological arousal that heightens viewers' levels of emotional intensity and thus the likelihood of intense behavioral responses. Arousal is likely to be converted into intense aggressive behavior when people are called upon to perform acts involving aggression or when they misattribute the cause of their arousal to some real-world target rather than a stimulating media presentation.

The stimulus-response (S-R) relationship in the stimulating effects theory is neither simple nor unconditional. An aggressive stimulus (e.g., a violent TV program) does not always elicit an aggressive response, nor will it be likely to elicit the same degree of aggressiveness in all audience members. One factor that is said to heighten both the likelihood of an aggressive response and increase the degree of aggressiveness of responses is frustration at the time of exposure to a violent TV program.

The way in which violence is portrayed in programs is also said to affect the likelihood of audience members behaving aggressively. Most important in this regard is whether or not the violence of media characters is portrayed as justified. When such violence is presented as justified (e.g., on grounds of vengeance or self-defense), it increases the likelihood of aggressive responses. This is so because viewers can adopt such justifications for their own aggressive behavior.[14] Another factor that, according to Berkowitz and his associates, can affect the nature of responses to televised violence is the extent to which the television portrayal is similar to anger-provoking circumstances with which the audience member is currently trying to cope.[15] Similarity can be established by such simple things as a media character having the same name or occupation as a person who is angering the viewer.

A factor said to lower the probability of an aggressive response is inhibition of aggressive tendencies. For example, a television portrayal of a violent interpersonal encounter can elicit a sense of guilt in viewers by directing the viewers' attention to the pain and suffering of the victim of the violent attack. This presumably inhibits their aggressivity by sensitizing them to the pain and suffering that their aggressive responses may cause others.[16]

Stimulating effects theory also has its primary theoretical origins in the individual differences perspective and ultimately in the cognitive paradigm. Individual differences in level of frustration or arousal at the time of exposure are said to affect the probability of aggression following exposure to violent programs. The process of selective perception, so central to the individual differences perspective, may also account for some of the variability in audience members' responses to aggressive stimuli. When the camera focuses on the painful consequences of aggression, for example, it has the effect of guiding viewers' perceptions to emphasize selectively the victim's pain and suffering. As noted, such emphasis seems to inhibit most, but not all, viewers' aggression. An individual difference that might affect the degree of inhibition different viewers feel is the extent of their prior exposure via the media and personal experience to the pain-and-gore consequences of violence. Those having much prior experience would probably not respond with the same degree of emotional arousal and inhibition as those with little prior experience.

Observational Learning Theory

This theory, as developed primarily by Bandura and Walters,[17] rests on the assumption that people can learn aggressive behavior by observing aggression in media portrayals and, under certain conditions, model their behavior after aggressive media characters. Televised or other forms of media violence increase the probability of audience aggression not only by providing opportunities for audiences to learn aggression but also by presenting violent characters who act as behavior models for viewers. The fundamental learning processes by which children come to learn all forms of new behavior are also said to operate when children are sitting in front of a television set watching violent programs.[18] As they might acquire new patterns of conduct from observing their brother's or sister's activities, they can learn new forms of aggressive behavior from observing violent media characters.

Observational learning theorists do not contend that audience members will automatically perform the aggressive acts they have learned.

THEORIES OF MASS COMMUNICATION

Learned violent acts, like a great deal of the behavior learned in class-rooms, is not put into practice unless a situation arises that calls for performance of that learned behavior. The probability of audience members' exhibiting learned violent behavior is enhanced by such factors as an expectation of being rewarded by others for such behavior, similarity between the situation presented in the TV portrayal and the social situation encountered by viewers after exposure, and anticipation of social support from a co-viewer who praises the violent actions of TV characters. [19]

Observational learning theory is a special case of the individual differences perspective, but it also includes aspects of the social categories and social relations perspectives. For example, one form of social relationship considered by observational learning theorists is the extent to which viewers encounter real social situations that are similar to those presented in television programs. Encountering similar interactional situations increases the likelihood of performance of aggressive behavior learned from observation of violent media characters. Viewers frequently involved in interpersonal conflict would, for example, probably see more similarity between TV stories and their own life situations than would people who rarely have to cope with conflict. [20]

The influence of the social categories perspective on observational learning theory can be illustrated by examining interpretations made of the finding that while girls learn as much aggressive behavior from observation of violent TV characters as do boys, they perform fewer acts of learned aggression. Rather than saying that these individual girls exhibit less aggressive behavior than these individual boys, the subjects are treated as representatives of social categories—males and females. The explanation given for less actual aggressive behavior by girls than boys is that the female sex role and subcultural norms against aggressive female behavior operate to reduce the likelihood of girls displaying the aggressive acts they have learned. [21]

Reinforcement Theory

The central assumption of this specific theory of effects is that television portrayals of violence *reinforce whatever established pattern of violent behavior that viewers bring with them to the media situation.* Klapper, [22] the major proponent of reinforcement theory, contends that television and other media violence usually does not produce significant increases or decreases in the probability of audience aggression.

Reinforcement theorists look to such factors as cultural norms and values, social roles, personality characteristics, and family or peer influences as the primary determinants of violent behavior. These and other psychological and social factors are also said to determine the effects of violent media portrayals. For example, viewers' norms and attitudes should guide their perceptions of violent television programs. Those who have developed into rather violent persons with norms and attitudes that support violence as a means to personal and social ends probably "selectively perceive" the violent actions of TV characters in ways that support (reinforce) their norms and attitudes. Relatively nonviolent viewers, on the other hand, would "selectively perceive" the messages of the program so that it conforms to their antiviolence norms and attitudes. Thus, the effect of televised violence would be to reinforce the established norms and attitudes of both the violent and nonviolent viewers, making them no more or no less likely to engage in violent behavior than they would have been if they had not watched television.

A major exception to this rule, according to reinforcement theorists, involves a small minority of viewers who lack personal and social stability. People, particularly young children and adolescents, who lack strong and stable relationships with family, friends, teachers, and so on, may not have developed clear guidelines for their participation in aggression. Moreover, they may not receive sufficient group control over their use of aggression. Violent television programming may fill a void in these people's lives to the extent that they refer to the beliefs and actions of violent TV characters as guides for their own behavior.[23] In such cases, the effect of violent TV programs would go past reinforcement to bring about significant increases in the probability of these viewers' level of aggressive behavior.

Reinforcement theory shares with the other theories of aggression effects deep roots in the individual differences perspective. For example, reinforcement theory explains how people with different characteristics can all be reinforced by the same violent TV program. This is done by incorporating the process of selective perception into their theorizing. But there are fundamental differences between reinforcement and the other aggression effects theories. Most of these differences reflect the more central roles of the social categories and the social relations perspectives in reinforcement theory.

While catharsis and observational learning theorists have generally included one or two social categories in their thinking, they still tend to deemphasize the ways in which individuals are tied to a multiplicity of social categories and groups. Reinforcement theorists, in comparison, tend to view individuals as representatives of social categories. Race, sex, socioeconomic status, and religion are examples of social categories that reinforcement theorists usually take into account. Individuals belonging to the same social categories should share similar norms, attitudes, values, prior experiences, and many other social and personal characteristics. These, as noted, should operate to make them respond very similarly to media portrayals of violence.

The social relations perspective lies at the heart of the reinforcement theorist's rationale for the claim that most viewers will not undergo significant change as a result of exposure to violent television programming. If people's social relationships at home, work, and play are stable and effective, then their aggressive behavior should be governed more by the role expectations and norms of their friends or family members than by the behavior of violent media characters. According to reinforcement theory, violent media programming should have a significant effect upon the probability of aggressive behavior only when social relations are disrupted or are unstable.

Cultivation Theory

Cultivation theory has been developed primarily by Gerbner[24] and his associates. Its basic thesis is that the symbolic world of the media, particularly television, shapes and maintains—i.e., cultivates—audiences' conceptions of the real world (in other words, their constructions of reality). Television, with its presence in the vast majority of American homes, is said to be the common symbolic environment into which most children are born and thus the most pervasive source of exposure to everyday symbolic cultures that Americans share or have in common. The symbolic world of television is shown by content analyses to be a "mean" world where violence is commonplace. Violence is used by most TV characters, usually to gain the upper hand in struggles for power. The young, white males who dominate the TV world as leading characters also dominate others, particularly women, minorities, and old people, via the successful use of violence. According to cultivation theory, this violent white-male-dominated TV world seeps into viewers' consciousness so that they see the real world as being like the TV world.

In contrast to the other theories we have discussed, the major effect that concerns cultivation theorists is not so much violent behavior but emotions, such as fear, anxiety, and alienation among people adopting the symbolic and violent worlds of the media as reflections of reality. To the extent that people believe the real world to be as extremely violent as the media world, they should experience fear and anxiety in such routine activities as walking down the street, and this fear should create a state of alienation from others.

In a recent elaboration of cultivation theory, Gerbner and his associates[25] have incorporated the concepts of "mainstreaming" and "resonance." Mainstreaming refers to a kind of homogenization within groups whose light viewers, because of other influences, have divergent perceptions of the world, but whose heavy viewers are influenced by exposure to television to hold a more common and shared ("mainstream") view of the real world. Resonance refers to an increased salience effect in which people who live in unusually violent circumstances resonate to the even more violent TV world so that their conception of the real world as violent is amplified or intensified by TV exposure.

Although its proponents have never explicitly set forth the origins of cultivation theory, it can obviously be traced back to the symbolic interactionism paradigm and the communication processes by which shared constructions of reality are achieved. Cultivation theory also incorporates aspects of both the individual differences and the social categories perspectives. The two major individual differences of interest to cultivation theorists are differences between individuals that affect the degree of media exposure and differences in experience that affect individuals' perceptions of the real world and the symbolic media world. Social category differences in sex, race, social class, residence, and other social factors enter the picture because people who share similar social category characteristics are also likely to share similar experiences and conceptions of the real world, and thus are likely to be similarly affected by exposure to the media world.

Summary

This brief review suggests that psychology has had more impact than sociology on the way specific theories of the effects of televised audience have been conceptualized and studied. The dominance of the cognitive paradigm is evidenced by the relatively heavy influence of individual differences perspective. As noted in Chapter 8 the concepts and assumptions of the individual differences perspective (e.g., variations in needs, interests, or feelings affect perception) reflect the traditional psychological emphasis on the individual. The traditional sociological view that individuals are tied into a complex web of categories, associations and symbolic interaction which play a part in determining the effects of violent TV programs, is contained in the social categories and social relations perspecthe catharsis, stimulating effects and observational learning theories. Reinforcement theory probably comes closest to being derived from a fairly even mixture of both traditional general psychological and sociological theory. Cultivation theory rests clearly on symbolic interactionism and the social categories perspective.

POLICY IMPLICATIONS

Each of the five specific theories of the effects of media portrayals of violence has policy implications for either *how much* media violence should be presented or *how* it should be presented. Catharsis theory has some very interesting implications. If catharsis theory is correct, television networks could argue that by including violent portrayals in their broadcasts, they are performing a public service. Logically, under this view, moves to reduce the amount of violent programming should be resisted on the grounds that this would limit opportunities for catharsis. This in turn would increase the probability of audience aggression.

The stimulating effect theorist, in contrast, regards televised violence as a source of aggressive cues that probably *increase* aggressive behavior. In terms of policy implications, the aggressive cues theorist is led to recommend extreme care in the *way* violence is presented in the mass media. If this theory is correct, writers, producers, and directors should carefully design portrayals of violence so that factors which tend to reduce the probability of aggressive responses are incorporated into the script.[26] Such program design, theoretically, would reduce tendencies toward violence among susceptible members of the audience.

The observational learning theorist usually recommends similar policies. Media portrayals of violence should be based upon an informed understanding of principles of learning so that even if audiences learn violent acts, they may not actually perform those learned acts. Violent media characters, for example, should not be rewarded for their violence.

The major policy implication of reinforcement theory is that attempts to reduce the incidence of real-world violence by reducing the level of violence in media portrayals or changing the way it is presented are bound to fail. These theorists direct policy concern to the learning processes that occur in families or peer groups; the theorists regard what takes place in media encounters as a far less important source of real-world violence.

Cultivation theory suggests that policy makers should recognize the unique transmission of symbolic culture role of the media that requires their serious consideration of the global messages that are sent about the prevalence and the utility of violence. Serious consideration is warranted, according to the cultivation theorist, because people will incorporate the media world of violence into their shared constructions of reality, which can result in widespread fear and alienation. The clear policy implication is fundamental change of media entertainment content to reduce the prevalence of violence.

The consistently high level of violence in television and other media presentations is probably a rather simple consequence of the profitability of such programming. One need not assume that it is a product of deliberation by media personnel about which effects theory is correct. In view of the considerable public concern over violence in the media, however, it seems appropriate to conclude this chapter with an overview of what the research literature can and cannot tell us about the validity of these specific theories. Policy implications, after all, are only as good as the theories in which they are based.

SUMMARY OF THE RESEARCH

For the most part, research on catharsis, stimulating effects, and observational learning hypotheses has been focused on the "short-term" effects of violent[27] television programming. Such research usually involves exposing subjects to anywhere from a few minutes to a few hours of TV programs followed by observations of the subjects' behavior for, at most, several hours after exposure. Most studies conducted to test catharsis, stimulating effects, or observational learning hypotheses have been carried out in research laboratories and have employed experimental research designs. In their simplest form, these experimental designs involve comparing two groups of subjects who are alike in all respects except one—the kind of programs they see. One group sees nonviolent programs and is called the "control" group. The other group sees violent programs and is called the "experimental" group. Because the only difference between the control and experimental groups is presumably the programs they were exposed to, any differences in their behavior following exposure is said to be a result of differences in the programs they saw. The type of program— violent or nonviolent—is called the "independent" variable because it should be the cause of any differences observed in the "dependent" variable—level of aggressive behavior after exposure. The aggressive acts used as dependent variables include such behaviors as verbal or written expressions of hostility, hitting a large inflatable "Bobo doll," and administering electric shocks to other people.

Without going into further detail about how these various studies were conducted, we can briefly summarize the general conclusions that can be drawn from their findings. We will look first at how such research evidence bears upon the validity of catharsis theory. Actually, we find little support for its central prediction, namely, that subjects exposed to violent programming (experimental group) will be *less* aggressive than subjects exposed to nonviolent programs (control group). In most instances, the subjects exposed to violent programs were *more* aggressive following exposure than the subjects who saw nonviolent programs. In fact, this outcome

THEORIES OF MASS COMMUNICATION

is consistent with the prediction made in both stimulating effects and observational learning theories.

While such findings from laboratory research on the short-term effects of violent television programs provide general support for the stimulating effects and observational learning theories, they do not really establish their validity. Validity requires more than correct prediction. It also requires demonstrating that the process outlined in the theory is the *actual* chain of events set off by exposure to violent programs culminating in aggressive behavior on the part of subjects. A number of studies involving far more complex experimental procedures than those outlined above have been carried out by both observational learning and stimulating effects researchers. It would take a separate volume to give thorough examination to the details of such research and its findings.[27] For our purposes, suffice it to say that most of the data tend to support both the observation learning process and the stimulating effects process described in the first part of this chapter.

Proponents of reinforcement and cultivation theories tend to downplay the importance of such laboratory research findings.[28] For example, they express doubt that laboratory research findings can be generalized to predict the effects of viewing actual violent TV programs in the natural setting of the home. The primary bases for their misgivings are that the artificial laboratory setting may elicit artificial behavior, the aggressive behavior studied in the lab (e.g., electric shocks or hitting Bobo dolls) bears little relationship to real-life aggressive acts (e.g., murder and assault), and cumulative effects of long-term exposure on people's conceptions of social reality are not studiable in the laboratory. There is no easy answer to these charges.

Reinforcement and cultivation theorists are more likely to utilize field or survey research techniques in which selected samples of people respond to a researcher's questions by filling a questionnaire or by being interviewed.[29] One of the many ways in which these responses can be analyzed is to see if membership in relevant social categories is correlated with the way people respond to various questions. For example, researchers may ask questions designed to measure respondents' preferences for violent television programs. Then statistical tests are employed to see if differences in preferences are correlated with social category differences in age, sex, education, race, and so on. Other questions frequently included in surveys are designed to measure social relations variables, such as stability of family life or degree of integration into the community. Still other common survey questions assess respondents' attitudes and norms about violence, their frequency of participation in violent behavior, or their fears and anxieties about violence.

The reinforcement theorist is particularly interested in finding out if various social categories, social relations, or individual differences in attitudes and the like show stronger correlations with differences in frequency of violent behavior than do differences in degree of exposure to violent TV programming. The survey research literature does not contain conclusive evidence on this point. Some findings support, but others do not support, the hypothesis that violent TV programming reinforces preestablished patterns of violent behavior.[30] The cultivation theorist seeks to find out if individuals' and certain social categories' conceptions of social realities and fears and anxieties about real-world violence are strongly correlated with their degree of exposure to the media world of violence. Again, the research findings are mixed: Some find such cultivation effects, and others[31] do not.[32]

There is a fundamental difficulty in utilizing correlational evidence obtained from a single survey to assess the validity of reinforcement, cultivation, or any other specific theory of effects. Put simply, the problem is that correlations do not really inform us about the underlying mechanisms of cause-effect relationships. For example, suppose that researchers did find that the most violent people are also the most frequent viewers of TV violence. They would then face the familiar "chicken and egg" problem of not knowing which is the cause and which is the effect.

Questions of cause and effect become very complicated when trying to unravel the effects of the media. Their resolution is most likely to come from research that examines the long-term effects of exposure to violent television content. The problem of determining cause-effect relationships might be resolved by the kind of experimental procedures described earlier. But the previously noted debate about whether findings obtained from research laboratories can or cannot be generalized to real-life conditions still undermines confidence in the broad applicability of emerging conclusions. Moreover, the experimental literature on short-term effects may not be very informative about the cumulative effects of years of exposure to violence in the media. Both problems are resolved when a long-term field experimental design is employed. Instead of observing subjects in artificial laboratory conditions, they are observed in their natural settings. The researcher makes arrangements with the subjects, their parents, or their supervisors to have some subjects view only violent programs (the experimental group) and other subjects view only nonviolent programs (the control group). Over a period of weeks or months, or even longer, trained observers record how much aggressive behavior is exhibited by each subject. Such procedures allow researchers to observe a wide variety of normal and realistic aggressive acts exhibited by their subjects without any prodding from the observer. When the field experiment terminates, researchers can determine if the experimental group's subjects participated in more, less, or about the same level of aggressive behavior as the control group's subjects. They can also compare the short-term effects of a day's exposure with the long-term effects of more extensive exposure.

While long-term field experiments are clearly desirable, they are extremely difficult to conduct. The major difficulty stems from the need to ensure that the only significant difference between the experiences and conditions that experimental subjects face and those encountered by the control group's subjects is the media content they are exposed to (e.g., violent or nonviolent). Another obvious difficulty is making sure that the observers are in a position to observe all the subjects and all their aggressive activity.

Despite these considerable difficulties, a few effects researchers have conducted field experiments in recent years.[32] For a number of reasons, including methodological problems, these studies have not provided incontrovertible evidence regarding the validity of catharsis, stimulating effects, observational learning, or cultivation theory. There is reason to hope, however, that methodological problems will be resolved, and that future field experiments might provide the kind of evidence required to determine both the short-term and the long-term effects of viewing violent television programming. Until that time, debates about the validity of these specific theories of the effects of violence in the media will continue.

NOTES

1. Paul F. Lazarsfeld, Bernard Berelson, and Hazel Gaudet, *The People's Choice* (New York: Columbia University Press, 1948).
2. For a view of such studies, see Carl I. Hovland, Irving L. Janis, and H. H. Kelley, *Communication and Persuasion* (New Haven: Yale University Press, 1953).
3. Robert K. Merton, *Mass Persuasion: The Social Psychology of a War Bond Drive* (New York: Harper & Brothers, 1946).
4. Hovland et al., *Communication and Persuasion*.
5. It is questionable that the level of violence in the 1960s was actually much higher than in prior periods of American history. See Hugh Graham and Ted Gurr, *Violence in America* (Washington, D.C.: Government Printing Office, 1969).
6. George Gerbner, Larry Gross, Michael Morgan, and Nancy Signorielli, "The Mainstreaming of America: Violence Profile No. 11," *Journal of Communication* 30 (1980): 10–29.
7. Baker and Ball, *Violence and the Media*.

8. *Television and Growing Up: The Impact of Televised Violence, Report to the Surgeon General, United States Public Health Service, from the Surgeon General's Scientific Advisory Committee on Television and Social Behavior* (Washington, D.C.: Government Printing Office, 1972); *Television and Social Behavior, Reports and Papers:* vol. 1, *Media Content and Control,* ed. George A. Comstock and Eli A. Rubinstein; vol. 2, *Television and Social Learning,* ed. John P. Murray, Eli A. Rubinstein, and George A. Comstock; vol. 3, *Television and Adolescent Aggressiveness,* ed. George A. Comstock and Eli A. Rubinstein; vol. 4, *Television in Day-to-Day Life: Patterns of Use,* ed. Eli A. Rubinstein, George A. Comstock, and John P. Murray; vol. 5, *Television's Effects: Further Explorations,* ed. George A. Comstock, Eli A. Rubinstein, and John P. Murray.

9. Seymour Feshbach, "The Stimulating vs. Cathartic Effects of a Vicarious Aggressive Experience," *Journal of Abnormal and Social Psychology* 63 (1961): 381–85.

10. Seymour Feshbach and Robert Singer, *Television and Aggression* (San Francisco: Jossey-Bass, 1971).

11. Ibid.

12. Leonard Berkowitz, *Aggression: A Social Psychological Analysis* (New York: McGraw-Hill, 1962).

13. Percy Tannenbaum, ed., *The Entertainment Functions of Television* (Hillsdale, N.J.: Lawrence Erlbaum Associates, 1980), pp. 107–31.

14. J. Hoyt, "Vengeance and Self-Defense as Justification for Filmed Aggression" (Master's thesis, University of Wisconsin, 1967).

15. Leonard Berkowitz and Russell Geen, "Stimulus Qualities of the Target of Aggression: A Further Study," *Journal of Personality and Social Psychology* 5, no. 3 (1976): 364–68.

16. For reviews of the relevant literature, see Russell Geen and Leonard Berkowitz, "Some Conditions Facilitating the Occurrence of Aggression After the Observation of Violence," *Journal of Personality* 35 (1967): 666–76; and Richard Goransen, "A Review of the Recent Literature," in Baker and Ball, *Violence and the Media,* pp. 395–413.

17. Albert Bandura and Richard Walters, *Social Learning and Personality Development* (New York: Holt, Rinehart and Winston, 1963).

18. Albert Bandura, *Social Learning Theory* (Englewood Cliffs, N.J.: Prentice-Hall, 1977).

19. David Hicks, "Effects of Co-observer Sanctions and Adult Presence on Imitative Aggression," *Child Development* 39 (1968): 303–9.

20. See Goranson, "Review of Recent Literature," for a review of relevant studies.

21. Ibid.

22. Joseph Klapper, *The Effects of Mass Communication* (New York: Free Press, 1960).

23. Joseph Klapper, *Statement before the National Commission on the Causes and Prevention of Violence* (Washington, D.C.: Government Printing Office, 1969).

24. George Gerbner and Larry Gross, "The Violent Face of Television and Its Lessons," in Edward Palmer and Aimee Dorr (eds.): *Children and the Faces of*

THEORIES OF MASS COMMUNICATION

Television: Teaching, Violence, Selling (New York: Academic Press, 1980).

25. George Gerbner, Larry Gross, Michael Morgan, and Nancy Signorielli, "The Mainstreaming of America: Violence Profile No. 11," *Journal of Communication* 30 (1980): 10–29.

26. See Goranson, "Review of Recent Literature."

27. There are exceptions. See, for example, David Hicks, "Imitation and Retention of Film-mediated Aggressive Peer and Adult Models," *Journal of Personality and Social Psychology* 2, no. 1 (1965): 97–100.

28. See Walter Weiss, "Effects of the Mass Media of Communication," in *The Handbook of Social Psychology*, ed. G. Lindzey and E. Aronson (2nd ed.; Reading, Mass.: Addison-Wesley, 1969), pp. 77–195; and George Comstock, S. Katzman, N. McCombs, and Donald Roberts, *Television and Human Behavior* (New York: Columbia University Press, 1978).

29. See Ruth Hartley, *The Impact of Viewing Aggression: Studies and Problems of Extrapolation* (New York: Columbia Broadcasting System, 1964).

30. For illustrations of such studies, see Comstock, Katzman, McCombs, and Roberts, *Television and Human Behavior.*

31. Ibid.

32. M. Hughes, "The Fruits of Cultivation Analysis: A Reexamination of Some Effects of Television Watching." *Public Opinion Quarterly* 44 (1980): pp. 287–302; and Paul M. Hirsch, "On Not Learning From One's Own Mistakes: A Reanalysis of Gerbner et al.'s Findings on Cultivation Analysis Part II," *Communication Research* (1981), vol. 8, no. 1, pp. 3–37.

33. For example, Feshbach and Singer, *Television and Aggression*; and Aletha Stein and Lynette Friedrich, "Television Content and Young Children's Behavior," in *Television and Social Behavior*, ed. J. P. Murray, E. A. Rubenstein, and G. A. Comstock (Washington, D.C.: Government Printing Office, 1971), vol. 2.

In the previous chapter we saw how
the general theoretical perspectives
on mass communication underlie
theories of the effects of televised
violence. In this chapter we show
how these same theoretical
perspectives—individual differences,

11

basic models of
persuasion via the
mass media

social categories, and social relationships—have affected the development of models for describing how persuasion effects are achieved via mass communication.

The development of theoretical perspectives on the way in which mass-communicated messages influence audiences have led to numerous attempts to capitalize on these conceptualizations for the purpose of *deliberately* manipulating people's action. The mass efforts of the advertising world to influence purchasing are one obvious example. Perhaps equally obvious are public service campaigns that attempt to persuade people to engage in a variety of socially approved behaviors. Again obvious is the case of political persuasion, where the voting act is the object of continuing efforts to manipulate behavior with mass communication content.

The relationship between contemporary perspectives on mass communication and conceptualizations of how persuasion can be achieved is not a straightforward one. Creating effective advertising has always been more of an art than an activity based upon scientifically formulated theories. The same is true of other forms of persuasion. Nevertheless, analyses of contemporary persuasion campaigns reveal certain regularities, certain significant similarities, in their *apparent underlying assumptions* about how the persuasion process works. These assumptions can be formalized into two rather broad "models" of the persuasion process that are described below.

In attempting to describe the nature of these formulations, two things will be clear. First, these models of the persuasion process (which is simply another way of talking about a "theory" of how it works) are *extensions* and *utilizations* of the theoretical perspectives on mass communication reviewed in Chapter 8. Second, these models are *roughly formulated* at the present time.

Roloff and Miller[1] noted a substantial decline in persuasion theory and research during the 1970s. Prior to that decade, major theoretical advances in persuasion theory came as a result of concerted efforts to solve pressing persuasion problems, such as social scientists' attempts to contribute to the war effort in World War II by figuring out how to use the mass media more effectively to persuade people to contribute to the national efforts and goals. It is thus surprising that in times of seemingly pressing persuasion problems, such as altering people's ideas on energy use, crime prevention, and so forth, that there is not a marked upsurge of social science activity to advance our understanding of persuasion processes.[2] Practical decision makers in industry, politics, religion, science, and health care have not shown any tendency to decrease their utilization of the mass media for persuasion purposes, however. To the contrary, persuasion uses of the media are rampant in our society, ranging all the way from the conduct of political campaigns to religious revivals to attempts to persuade people to stop smoking or engaging in other health-destructive behaviors. Thus, we agree with Roloff and Miller's sentiments that the importance of building better theories of persuasion persists, in spite of what may be a temporary decline in social science interest.

In spite of the lessening research interest in the problem, two rather general strategies for using communication to achieve persuasion have emerged from earlier decades of research and theory testing. These two strategies are widely used in the day-to-day tasks of advertising, solicitation, and campaigning.

The first, the *psychodynamic* approach, is rooted in the cognitive paradigm, or in some cases, the psychoanalytic paradigm. The second, the *socio-cultural* strategy, has its origins in both the structural functional and symbolic interactionism paradigms. We will refer to these approaches or strategies as models of the persuasion process and show how they are related to their underlying general paradigms via the individual differences, social categories, and social relationships perspectives discussed in Chapter 9.

THE PSYCHODYNAMIC MODEL

The psychodynamic model of the persuasion process is based almost exclusively on the cognitive paradigm and the individual differences perspective on mass communication. Although one of the earliest to be recognized, the individual differences perspective continues to be widely used. This is revealed by the impact it has had on the advertising and public relations world where it remains very popular. It has also provided the principal set of assumptions underlying sociopsychological research on persuasion by behavioral scientists.

The essence of this application of the individual differences perspective is that an effective message is said to be one that has properties capable of *altering the psychological functioning* of individuals in such a way that they will respond overtly (toward the item that is the object of persuasion) with modes of behavior desired or suggested by the communicator. In other words, it has been assumed that the key to effective persuasion lies in modifying the internal psychological structure of the individual so that the psychodynamic relationship between latent internal processes (motivation, attitudes, etc.) and manifest overt behavior will lead to acts intended by the persuader.[3]

There have been many specific forms or variants of this general approach to persuasion, depending upon the particular psychological phenomenon under manipulation, and upon the presumed dynamic relationships thought to prevail between the psychological process and the overt behavior patterns it supposedly activates. For example, extensive use has been made of persuasive messages aimed at individual *attitudes* under the assumption that there is a close relationship between attitudinal structure and the way people behave in overt social situations.[4] A common example would be the mass communication campaign aimed at reducing ethnic discrimination (overt behavior) by attempting to reduce ethnic prejudice (emotional attitude purported to lead to discrimination). Another example would be an attempt to promote the purchase of a patent medicine (overt action) by instilling a *fear* of poor health or continued suffering (psychological state or process). The general idea could be illustrated with examples ranging from blood-donation drives and charity appeals to antilitter campaigns and political oratory. Among the many other psychological concepts that have been used as intervening variables are sexual urges, status drives, desires for social approval, anxieties, opinions, vanity, and a host of others. In simple graphic terms, the *psychodynamic model* of the persuasion process would be as follows:

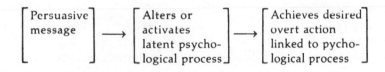

State of the Research Evidence

An extensive social-psychological literature has accumulated with respect to many variables thought to be potentially useful as modifiers of overt action.[5] Psychological theories of motivation, perception, learning, and even psychoanalysis have suggested ways in which attitudes, opinions, fears, self-conceptions, perceptions of source credibility, reinforcement, and many other variables are related to persuasion.

Some studies among the accumulated literature on such topics have been so widely quoted and reprinted that the rather tentative nature of the original conclusions is in danger of being forgotten. But wide quotation or reprinting is not equivalent to wide replication. Further evidence is needed to support the psychodynamic model of persuasion. Systematic and valid assertions are needed to predict which variables under what exact circumstances can be used to manipulate what specific people toward what definite patterns of action when messages incorporating those variables are brought to their attention. Not only is the evidence as yet incomplete concerning the utility of this approach to persuasion, but those who employ this strategy sometimes make unrealistic assumptions. For example, some experimentalists have been willing to assume that if their communication was demonstrably able to change attitudes or opinions, then patterns of overt behavior would be correspondingly changed. Such an assumption is unwarranted. Festinger has reviewed relevant literature on this problem.[6] Fishbein and Ajzen[7] have responded to this problem by shifting attention to modification of behavioral intentions rather than modification of attitudes.

But the fact that the validity of the psychodynamic model of the persuasion process has as yet not been fully verified does not mean that it is incorrect. It seems to work some of the time. For example, during an eclipse of the sun, the population of a midwestern town was repeatedly warned by local media to avoid viewing the eclipse directly or through dark glasses. Fear-threat appeals that described possible severe eye damage were used to persuade people to obtain a recommended viewing apparatus or avoid exposure altogether by viewing the event on television. A study conducted immediately following the eclipse indicated that there was a positive relationship between the amount of fear aroused and degree of overt compliance.[8]

In contrast, an earlier experimental study of somewhat parallel fear-threat messages regarding dental health among groups of high school students showed the reverse. Illustrated lectures showing damage to teeth as a result of improper dental hygiene were presented to several groups of subjects. An inverse relationship between fear-threat compliance was found. Those who received the strongest fear-threat showed the least compliance with the preventive program advocated by the communicator. Those experiencing the least fear-threat showed the most compliance. The results of this well-controlled and frequently quoted study were exactly the opposite of those from the study of the eclipse.[9] Such seemingly opposite findings in the case of two variants of a fear-threat health campaign indicate emphatically the need to sort out the conditions under which a given psychodynamic variable will lead to a particular action and when it will "boomerang" and suppress it.

The same can be said of the individual differences perspective in general. There are many kinds of "effects" that a message can touch off other than overt adoption of some action advocated in a persuasive communication. For example, the way in which children learn new ideas and practices from the media through a process of *observational learning* was discussed in the previous chapter. What children or adults learn may be totally unrelated to the intent of communicators. People may take up new habits, adopt new fads, change their musical tastes, or bolster their loyalty to a

220

political party without complying in any sense to a persuasive message deliberately designed to manipulate them.[10] While the individual differences perspective suggests that variations in their personality structures will play an important part in determining the manner in which this happens, it would be incorrect to say that a fully articulated theory is now available explaining the role of such factors. At the same time, an impressive array of research findings shows how *some* individual characteristics do play *some* part in determining the kind of effect that a given message content will have on a particular person. These studies along with many others have been reviewed by Klapper.[11] He points up the need to consider many other variables besides individual personality characteristics in developing theories of the effects of the media, and the dangers inherent in constructing simple cause-effect types of theory. This is a point of view with which we heartily agree. This chapter treats several theories in cause-effect terms because it is attempting to show the *development* of mass communication theory over time as well as its broad scope.

In 1948 Bernard Berelson attempted to summarize the status of the field of mass communication as it then existed. He noted that the older magic bullet theory of the all-powerful media had largely been abandoned, and he identified five central factors that seemed to be the focus of research at the time:

> Now, in the 1940's, a body of empirical research is accumulating which provides some refined knowledge on the effect of communication on public opinion and promises a good deal more in the next years.
> But what has such research contributed to the problem? . . . The proper answer to the general question, the answer which constitutes a useful formulation for research purposes, is this: Some kind of *communication* on some kinds of *issues*, brought to the attention of some kinds of *people* under some kinds of *conditions*, have some kinds of *effects*.[12]

This set of propositions may have been far short of being a tightly formulated theory of mass communication, but it clearly rested upon the kinds of assumptions we have called the individual differences perspective. Faced with the need to predict the probable impact of a given communication on a given issue, and in cases where the "conditions" of communication (radio, print, etc.) are understood or controlled, the major variables not manipulatable by the communicator are the "kinds of people" (i.e., individual differences among persons). In other words, communicators able to select their messages and issues, and by and large structure the conditions of communication as they wished, still had no direct control over their audiences' prejudices, predispositions, amount of prior information, and so forth. Thus, the independent variables (messages on a given issue presented under known conditions) are modified in their impact on the dependent variables (effects) by the action of intervening variables (i.e., individual differences in relevant psychological variables).

The Berelson formulation quoted above did extend somewhat the elementary form of the individual differences perspective by calling specific attention to the fact that variations in the *stimulus material* and variations in the *social setting* or other related conditions, as well as in the psychological structures of members of the audience, could be expected to have an impact upon the kinds of effects produced. In spite of its simplicity, it served as a guide for new directions in research. It was a general statement of the salient categories of factors and variables which, along with individual differences, must be considered in trying to understand the communication process.[13]

The Value Theory Alternative

A far more specific psychodynamic formulation based on individual differences is Rokeach's theory of value change.[14] The value-change procedure is quite different from previous attempts to change people's attitudes. Rather than present information about the harmful or beneficial consequences of a particular activity or object, a technique of *comparative feedback* is used: Individuals take a value test and are given factual information about their own values as compared to the values of other people. Individuals who discover that they have ranked certain values in a manner that contradicts their conceptions of themselves as moral and competent persons will experience self-dissatisfaction. It is this self-dissatisfaction, not others' fear tactics or rational appeals, that sets the value-change process into motion and leads to modification of personal value hierarchies.[15] In other words, change emanates from self-education as opposed to external forces. For example, when individuals' conceptions of themselves as people who are strong believers in equalitarian democratic ideals are contradicted by finding out after taking a values test that they actually place little importance on the value Equality, they are likely to experience self-dissatisfaction. One way to remove this self-dissatisfaction is to increase the importance of Equality in their personal value hierarchy. Thus, the feedback of comparative value information that causes self-dissatisfaction also points the way to regain a positive self-concept by appropriate value change.

In Rokeach's procedure, the internal psychological factor that is al-

THEORIES OF MASS COMMUNICATION

tered is the relative importance people place on a particular value. According to this theory, values underlie attitudes and behavior; therefore, change in a person's values should lead to changes in related attitudes and behavior. In a laboratory experiment, Sanders and Atwood[16] have demonstrated the potency of this theoretical procedure when employing a mass media channel. What is more important, Ball-Rokeach, Rokeach, and Grube have recently concluded a successful test of value theory in a field experiment in which people voluntarily exposed themselves to a television program constructed for the research purpose and aired on commercial TV channels.[17] These researchers observed long-term value, attitude, and behavior change that may be attributable to exposure to the half-hour television program.

There are, of course, numerous instances in which the mass communicator's persuasion goal requires value change. Public affairs programming intended to persuade audiences to increase the priority of ecological concerns, for example, clearly seeks to accomplish basic value change. Yet basic research on values shows that value-change effects are extremely unlikely unless the communicator has a valid guide as to how to construct and present persuasion messages. The Rokeach procedure suggests that communicators seeking to increase something like an audience's priority for behavior in accord with ecological concerns should first provide its members with information leading them to conclusions about the amount of importance they personally place on values related to ecology (like "A World of Beauty") as compared to specific categories of other people. For example, if a communication shows that people who place relatively low importance on values related to ecology are litterers, water contaminators, and air polluters, some portion of the audience, on coming to believe that they personally have a *similar* hierarchy of values, may experience self-dissatisfaction. Those who want to entertain conceptions of themselves as ecologically responsible would, according to the theory, feel very dissatisfied with the fact that their value hierarchy paralleled those of ecologically irresponsible people. Those experiencing the self-dissatisfaction should then be significantly more likely to increase the importance of ecologically linked values within their own value hierarchy. Presumably, such value change would produce an increase in the frequency or likelihood of desired forms of behavior.

THE SOCIOCULTURAL MODEL

While the individual differences perspective led to the formulation of the "psychodynamic model" of the persuasion process in attempts to use the theory for practical purposes, this model has by no means been the only one that has been tried. A somewhat more complicated alternative stems from a combination of the social categories and social relationships perspectives discussed in Chapter 8. For the lack of a better term, we will refer to this as the *sociocultural model* of the persuasion process.

Little systematic theory has emerged from the experimental literature on persuasion regarding the use of sociocultural variables as a basis for appeals in persuasive communication. Social and cultural variables have been widely recognized by communication researchers and other social scientists as playing an important part in determining the way in which people adopt new ideas and things. But the way in which such variables can be deliberately incorporated into messages to facilitate persuasion has not received much attention. In fact, existing theories of persuasion, and of the adoption of innovations see group, interaction, and cultural variables mainly in terms of *obstacles* to achieving persuasion or adoption. [18] The reason for this may have been the almost overwhelming preoccupation with the psychodynamic model that has already been discussed. [19]

Much basic research in behavioral science indicates that what we are terming "sociocultural variables" are important sources from which individuals gain definitions of appropriate behavior in a group context. They are, as we will indicate in greater detail, important sources from which the individual derives *interpretations of reality* as well as being significant forms of *social control*. [20] In Chapter 1 we showed how the social sciences from anthropology to sociology have developed basic paradigms concerning such issues. In addition, classic laboratory experiments such as those of Asch and Sherif show how even in the simplest and most artificial setting, the influence of *norms* plays a powerful role in guiding, defining, and modifying the behavior of individuals, somewhat independently of the state of their internal predispositions. [21] Sociological studies have supported this generalization. The work of Lohman and Reitzes, [22] Minard, [23] Newcomb, [24] De Fleur and Westie, [25] Gorden, [26] Merton and Kitt, [27] Mead, [28] Kohn, [29] and Newcomb et al. [30] indicate the way in which such variables as *organizational membership, work roles, reference groups, cultural norms,* and *primary group norms* can play a part in shaping and channeling overt action in ways that are to some extent uninfluenced by internal psychological predispositions. At the least, it must be recognized that the behavior patterns of a given individual can seldom be accurately interpreted on the basis of individual psychological variables *alone*. Individuals almost always act within a social context that they take into account when making decisions about their behavior. To explain, predict, or manipulate such behavior, reference must be made to the social norms, role systems,

THEORIES OF MASS COMMUNICATION

social controls, and hierarchies of social ranking that surround action, in order that it can be effectively understood.

The sociocultural processes present in a given individual's situation of action, then, are important determiners of the directions that such action will take, or indeed, whether action will occur at all. These actions can even be contrary to individual predisposition, although certainly this is not the general case. The more frequently occurring situation would be one in which sociocultural variables modify the way that psychological processes give rise to overt action.

The sociological model of the persuasion process suggested from these considerations is based upon the assumption that mass-communicated messages can be used to provide individuals with new and seemingly group-supported interpretations—social constructions of reality— regarding some phenomenon toward which they are acting. By so doing, it may be possible to mediate the conduct of individuals as they derive definitions of appropriate behavior and belief from suggested interpretations communicated to them. Even in cases where individual predispositions run contrary to the suggested action, it may be possible to obtain compliance by suggesting a set of social and cultural constraints to which they feel compelled to conform. An even simpler situation would be one in which individuals have not yet formulated strong psychological predispositions one way or the other toward the object of persuasion. In such a case they would hold few group-derived definitions of appropriate action toward it. Under such circumstances, suggested definitions would pose little social or psychological conflict in following the modes of action prescribed by the communicator. Represented schematically, such a model of the persuasion process looks something like this:

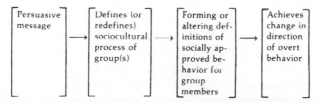

The Interplay between Group and Media Roles in Social Definitions

But what are the means by which groups provide the individual with "sanctioned" or "approved" modes of conduct toward objects, events, or issues that are brought to the individual's attention? This apparently takes place in many ways. Such concepts as *norms, roles, social control,* and *social ranking* are some of the elements in the "definitions of situations" that are culturally provided for individuals acting in social settings. These group-derived definitions of situations specify modes of orientation toward a wide variety of objects and events toward which responses must habitually be made. These modes of orientation constitute an important part of the institutionalized patterns of social organization of human groups. With respect to innovations, or new ideas, beliefs, or things of any kind, groups and societies vary widely in the degree to which stable, institutionalized rules exist "ready-made" for prescribing actions of the individual toward new phenomena.[31] Margaret Mead has described societies having rigid and deeply institutionalized cultures that provide the individual with a ready-made "reality" against which to interpret *any* new phenomena.[32] Other societies are at the other extreme, where individuals are on their own to construct modes of reaction to new events on the basis of their own internal processes. The American society apparently lies somewhere between these two extremes. Individuals are members of groups that are of significance to them, but at the same time the social organization patterns of such groups are sufficiently complex, contradictory, and heterogeneous so that modes of reaction to new issues are not uniformly prescribed.

We may suggest, then, that anthropological, psychiatric, social-psychological, and sociological evidence indicates clearly that one of the main functions of groups is to provide shared definitions for members by means of which they can interpret and act with respect to realities to which they as individuals have only limited direct access at best.[33] Realities are defined and interpreted within social frameworks. This generalization has often been called the *reality principle*, and the interactional process by means of which such definitions are achieved has been referred to as *consensual validation*.

These two concepts have bearing on the present conceptualization in that it is suggested the *persuasive messages presented via the mass media may provide the appearance of consensus regarding orientation and action with respect to a given object or goal of persuasion.* That is, such messages can present definitions to audiences in such a way that listeners are led to believe that these are the socially sanctioned modes of orientation their groups hold toward given objects or situations. The communicator thus provides social constructions of reality, shortcutting the process of consensual validation, particularly with respect to objects or practices concerning which groups do not yet have fully institutionalized cultural interpretations, or in the case where such interpretations are not contrary to the goals of the persuasion.[34]

In specific terms it can be suggested that the communicator can stress the way in which a specific *role* is defined (so as to include the use of the

THEORIES OF MASS COMMUNICATION

object of persuasion). Such messages can demonstrate how adoption of the communicator's goal is *normative* in the group within which this role lies. The communicator can show how the nonadopter is a *deviant* and a *nonconformist* (in the negative sense). The way in which negative *social sanctions* are brought to bear upon such deviants and nonconformists may be clarified. The fact that only persons of *low rank* would behave otherwise can be explained. At the same time, the manner in which *social rewards* and *social approval* are given to the adopter of the communicator's goals may be stressed. Finally, the manner in which adoption achieves *group integration*, and how such behavior is consistent with *group-approved values*, can be brought out.

Illustrative Example of the Sociocultural Model in Use

To illustrate in concrete terms the actual use of the sociocultural model as a strategy for persuasion, we may examine the tactics used by certain charity drives, commonly called United Appeals, Community Funds, and so forth. Such persuasive campaigns make use of both the psychodynamic and the sociocultural models of the persuasive process. As will be seen, they not only use mass communication as part of their tactics but other types of messages as well.

For the sake of emphasis, we will assume a hypothetical group of individuals who are not particularly sympathetic to this form of campaign, preferring to make their donations privately and specifically to their favorite charity. As we shall see, in spite of their contrary internal predisposition, they have little chance of resisting. In other words, it is very likely that they will be persuaded to make a donation when the persuasive campaign reaches them.

The first step in the campaign of the typical United Appeal solicitation is an announcement (via the mass media) that the community has a specific quota that must be met by the drive. Thus, a group *goal* is defined with the suggestion that this has widespread approval in the community. This goal has been arbitrarily formulated by the organizers of the drive, of course; it does not necessarily flow from grass-roots sentiment on the part of the community members. Nevertheless, it is very likely to go unchallenged. Goals have a rather compelling quality in themselves if it is believed that they have group support (consensus). Such an impression can be created by getting socially eminent persons in the community to participate in the announcement of the quota. Such persons are eager to confirm their high rank publicly by participating. The mass media will always obligingly give full coverage to such an event and thereby confer status upon it.

Another significant step is to announce to the community that the "fair share" for citizens is some specified percent of their earnings. This concept will also be given ample coverage by the media. The idea of a "fair share' is sociologically meaningful. It is compelling to the individual because it seems to be an approved and shared *norm*. Who wants to be identified as "unfair," and thus *deviant* from approved values? If individuals are led to believe that others are in fact giving according to this norm, they will at least feel some pressure toward conformity.

At the heart of the persuasion campaign is the task of creating *role systems* that are linked to the fund drive within work and neighborhood groups in the community. In stores, factories, schools, and as many other organizations as possible, a "chairperson" for the drive is appointed with attendant publicity. Leaders of such organizations feel compelled to cooperate in this because of the need to maintain appearances that the organization operates in the interest of the public. The chairperson usually appoints collectors for various divisions of the organization if it is at all large. The rank-and-file member of the group must play a *counter-role* to the roles of these collectors within their work setting. When asked personally by another worker, it is difficult to refuse a donation.

A tactic sometimes used in this sociocultural strategy is to prepare and distribute to members an IBM card with their name on it and with a place to mark how much they are "pledging" (to be collected later). Persons who choose not to pledge anything must sometimes signify their deviancy by signing the card to indicate refusal, or personally tell the group collector that they will not make a donation.

If our hapless individuals, who really wanted to give their funds to another worthy cause, have not been persuaded by these strategies, they will be confronted with an even more compelling situation when they get home. The organizers of the campaign appoint "voluntary collectors" who will call on residents in their immediate area and request a donation. Here we have the role of *neighbor* and that of *good citizen* (which includes charity) locked into a reciprocal system in miniature. It is socially embarrassing to refuse a neighbor a reasonable and socially approved request for a modest donation. Potential negative sanctions underlie such refusal, to say nothing of a degradation of status. Who want to be known to neighbors as a tightwad who would refuse to donate a modest sum to an important charitable cause? Therefore, our friends at this point reach into their pockets for some folding money, and possibly grit their teeth a little while they smilingly conform. However, for capitulation to social pressure they will be given positive enforcement. They will get a little button to wear in their lapels, or at least a card to place in their windows, that will help indicate to others the nature of the approved norms.

228

With the skillful use of the media, therefore, plus the use of goals, social norms, roles, social controls, and ranking in real ways, such campaigns can be very successful. The variables utilized give potential donors an unmistakable "definition of the situation" and place them within a set of sociocultural constraints that are nearly impossible to ignore. While this rather complex illustration of sociocultural strategy does not use mass communications exclusively, they occupy a central place in the activities of the persuaders.[35] In other adaptations of this strategy, the entire persuasive effort might be handled by the media alone. If there is any doubt that this strategy is widely used, the reader is invited to spend an evening before the TV set viewing commercials within the perspective of this sociocultural strategy. The smiling and happy people who act out their little dramas concerning beer, laxatives, deodorants, and denture paste are offering a most fascinating variety of "definitions of the situation." It is made abundantly clear that to be caught with the wrong beer, a detectable body odor, inactive bowels, or loose dentures places one far outside the pale of social respectability.

There are undoubtedly numerous other ways in which persuasion processes could be conceptualized. The psychodynamic and sociocultural strategies, however, seem to capture two widely used models of persuasion via mass communication.

NOTES

1. Michael Roloff and Gerald Miller, *Persuasion: New Directions in Theory and Research* (Beverly Hills, Calif.: Sage, 1980).
2. For reviews of the most recent research, see Peter Clarke, ed., *New Models for Communication Research* (Beverly Hills, Calif.: Sage, 1973); Alice Eagly and S. Himmelfarb, "Attitudes and Opinions," in L. Porter and M. Rozenweig, eds., *Annual Review of Psychology 29*, (Palo Alto, Calif.: Annual Reviews Inc., 1978); H. Hunt, ed., *Advances in Consumer Research 5* (Ann Arbor, Mich.: Association for Consumer Research, 1977); and R. Petty, Thomas Ostrom, and Timothy Brock, eds., *Cognitive Response in Persuasion: A Text in Attitude Change* (Hillsdale, N.J.: Lawrence Erlbaum, in press).
3. This was the central thesis of Vance Packard in his controversial book *The Hidden Persuaders*. He suggested that modern advertisers, using psychoanalytic mechanism as intervening variables, were achieving powerful effects in persuading people to purchase consumer products. See Vance Packard, *The Hidden Persuaders* (New York: David McKay, 1957). It was also the guiding principle underlying the work of Carl Hovland and his students in an impressive number of publications.

4. This assumption has been called into serious question in studies of the relationship between attitudes and action. See Melvin L. De Fleur and Frank R. Westie, "Verbal and Overt Acts," *American Sociological Review* 23, no. 6 (December 1958): 667–73.

5. Carl Hovland, Irving Janis, and Harold Kelley, *Communication and Persuasion* (New Haven: Yale University Press, 1954); Gerald Miller and Michael Burgoon, "Persuasion Research: Review and Commentary," in *Communication Yearbook II,* ed. B. Rubin (New Brunswick, N.J.: International Communication Association, 1978).

6. Leon Festinger, "Behavioral Support for Opinion Change," *Public Opinion Quarterly* 28, no. 3 (Fall 1964): 404–17.

7. Martin Fishbein and I. Ajzen, *Belief, Attitude, Intention and Behavior* (Reading, Mass.: Addison-Wesley, 1975).

8. Sidney Kraus, Elaine El-Assal, and Melvin L. De Fleur, "Fear-Threat Appeals in Mass Communication: An Apparent Contradiction," *Speech Monographs* 33, no. 1 (March 1966): 23–29.

9. Irving Janis and Seyman Feshback, "The Effects of Fear-Arousing Communications," *Journal of Abnormal and Social Psychology* 48 (1953): 78–132.

10. See Jay Blumler and Elihu Katz, eds., *The Uses of Mass Communications: Current Perspectives on Gratifications Research* (Beverly Hills, Calif.: Sage, 1974).

11. Joseph T. Klapper, *The Effects of Mass Communication* (Glencoe, Ill.: Free Press, 1960).

12. Bernard Berelson, "Communications and Public Opinions," in *Mass Communications,* ed. Wilbur Schramm (Urbana: University of Illinois Press, 1949), p. 500.

13. For a more recent summary, see Michael Burgoon and Erwin Bettinghaus, "Persuasive Message Strategies," in Roloff and Miller, *Persuasion: New Directions in Theory and Research.*

14. Milton Rokeach, *The Nature of Human Values* (New York: Free Press, 1973).

15. For an extensive review of the relevant literature, see Milton Rokeach "Value Theory and Research: Review and Commentary" in *Communication Yearbook II,* ed. Dan Nimmo (New Brunswick, N.J.: Transaction Books, 1979).

16. Keith Sanders and L. Atwood, "Value Change Initiated by the Mass Media," in *Understanding Human Values: Individual and Societal,* ed. Milton Rokeach (New York: Free Press, 1979).

17. Sandra Ball-Rokeach, Milton Rokeach, and Joel Grube, *Influencing Political Beliefs and Behavior Through Television* (forthcoming).

18. An example of such analyses would be Herbert H. Hyman and Paul B. Sheatsley, "Some Reasons Why Information Campaigns Fail," *Public Opinion Quarterly* 11 (Fall 1947): 412–23.

19. To illustrate, one chapter of Hovland's widely read book on *Communication and Persuasion* is entitled "Group Membership and Resistance to Influence."

20. See Kurt Lewin, "Group Decision and Social Change," in *Readings in Social Psychology,* ed. Eleanor Maccoby et al. (New York: Henry Holt, 1958); Peter Berger and Thomas Luckman, *The Social Construction of Reality* (Garden City,

N.Y.: Anchor Books, 1967); Carolyn Sherif, "Social Values, Attitudes, and The Involvement of the Self," in *1979 Nebraska Symposium on Motivation,* ed. Monte Page (Lincoln: University of Nebraska Press, 1980).

21. See Solomon E. Asch, "Effects of Group Pressure upon the Modification and Distortion of Judgments," in Maccoby et al., *Readings in Social Psychology,* pp. 174–83.

22. Joseph Lohman and Dietrich Reitzes, "Deliberately Organized Groups and Racial Behavior," *American Sociological Review* 19 (June 1954): 342–44.

23. R. D. Minard, "Race Relations in the Pocahontas Coal Fields," *Journal of Social Issues* 8, no. 1 (1952): 29–44.

24. Theodore M. Newcomb, "Attitude Development as a Function of Reference Groups: The Bennington Study," in Maccoby et al., *Readings in Social Psychology,* pp. 265–75.

25. De Fleur and Westie, "Verbal Attitudes."

26. Raymond L. Gorden, "Interaction between Attitude and the Definition of the Situation in the Expression of Opinions," *American Sociological Review* 17 (1952): 50–58.

27. Robert Merton and A. Kitt, "Contributions to the Theory of Reference Group Behavior," in *Continuities in Social Research: Studies in the Scope and Method of the American Soldier,* ed. Robert Merton and Paul Lazarsfeld (Glencoe, Ill.: Free Press, 1950).

28. Margaret Mead, "Public Opinion Mechanisms among Primitive People," *Public Opinion Quarterly* 1, no. 3 (July 1937): 5–16.

29. Melvin Kohn, *Class and Conformity* (Homewood, Ill.: Dorsey, 1969).

30. Theodore Newcomb, Kathryn Koenig, Richard Flacks, and Donald Warwick, *Persistence and Change* (New York: Wiley, 1967).

31. Daniel Lerner and Wilbur Schramm, eds., *Communication and Change in Developing Countries* (Honolulu: East-West Center Press, 1967).

32. Mead, "Public Opinion Mechanisms among Primitive People."

33. Thomatsu Shibutani, *Improvised News* (Indianapolis: Bobbs-Merrill, 1967).

34. For example, see Gaye Tuchman, *Making News: A Study in Construction of Reality* (New York: Free Press, 1978).

35. For another example, see Sandra Ball-Rokeach and Irving Tallman, "Social Movements as Moral Confrontations: With Special Reference to Civil Rights," in Rokeach, *Understanding Human Values: Individual and Societal.*

The foregoing chapters discussed a variety of theoretical paradigms, issues, approaches, and perspectives on mass communication. Chapter 1 presented broad paradigms from which specific media theories are drawn.

12

toward an integrated model of mass media effects

Several chapters examined the patterns of growth of the media and their functioning in society. Another chapter discussed the nature of human communication. In several places we reviewed the way in which people are exposed to media messages, and in other places dealt with the effects of mass media content on behavior. The present chapter returns once again to the issue of effects in an attempt to place it in a broader context.

We have seen that there are theories of specific effects, such as those dealing with the impact of media portrayals of violence. We have also seen that there are theoretical formulations concerning persuasion, such as the psychodynamic and sociocultural models. What we lack is a *general* theory of the effects of mass communication on individuals and society. Such a theory should provide an explanatory framework for a broad range of media effects including audience cognitions, feelings, and overt behavior.

The present chapter sketches the outlines of an integrated theory. This includes identifying major factors and variables that must be part of such a theory as well as identifying many of the relationships that prevail between these components. While this effort requires presentation of some new material, much that has already been presented in previous chapters can now be pulled together.

At this point in time, our skeleton integrated theory must remain rather tentative and vague in places because the underlying specific formulations from which it is drawn are in many cases themselves tentative and vague. Even so, its outlines can be perceived; and it is important to grope toward such a higher level of abstraction in order to understand where our research and analyses appear to be leading us.

SPECIFIC THEORIES AS STARTING POINTS

How does one start to develop an "integrated" theory? In any scientific field, efforts toward integration begin with specific formulations that deal with defined aspects of a process. These more specific theories are grouped together into some logical and empirically valid configuration. More abstract propositions and statements of relationship among components in the configuration are then induced.

Turning to mass communication, what are these more specific theories and what do they tell us? Starting with basics, we know from the discussion in Chapter 6 that a prerequisite of effective mass communication is a mode of message sending that reduces incongruence in meanings to a minimum so that the message reaching the audience is pretty much the same as that intended and sent by the mass communicator. Moreover, the perspectives discussed in Chapter 9 on how audiences encounter the media pull together a substantial body of theory and research to demonstrate the basic psychological and social factors that prevent the media from having arbitrary control over their audiences. This body of theory and research, moreover, presents a strong challenge to the theoretical notions about mass society discussed earlier (Chapter 7). Rather than assume the loose uncon-nectedness of people that would necessarily prevail in a mass society, it was shown that members of the media audience relate themselves to one another in groups and are engaged in stable social relations. These associ-ations not only produce and maintain social constructions of reality that individuals share to varying degrees but also operate to insulate individuals from easy media manipulation. These several theoretical issues must con-tinue to be taken into account.

Chapter 8 showed that the media are social systems that operate ac-cording to specific goals, values, organizational styles, and technological capabilities. Earlier, in Chapters 2 through 4, our examination of the historical development of each of the contemporary American media il-lustrated how they evolved as sytems with specific forms shaped by con-flicts and other events in their surrounding sociocultural context. These earlier chapters also provide concrete illustrations of the fundamental sociological proposition that the current media are linked to the larger society in systematic ways. These systematic links must be established before any of the emerging media technologies discussed in Chapter 5 can become a part of the media system.

In other words, the media do not exist in a vacuum. The behavior of a given medium is not only governed by the dictates of its own internal system but is also affected and limited by the characteristics and context of the societal system within which it operates. Media content must be com-patible with the sociocultural context as a whole in order for it to be comprehensible and desirable to an audience large enough for the medium to achieve its economic goals. Furthermore, media personnel are products of their society with learning experiences affecting every aspect of their communication behavior.

In as brief a form as possible we can now summarize what has been said up to this point in our overview of previous chapters:

> Mass media not only lack arbitrary influence powers, but their personnel lack the freedom to engage in arbitrary communication behavior. Both the media and their audiences are integral parts of their society. The surrounding socio-cultural context provides controls and constraints not only on the nature of media messages but also on the nature of their effects on audiences.

These broad propositons must be a part of any attempt to construct an integrated general perspective on mass media effects. For the most part, however, these propositions describe *limitations* on effects. As previous chapters have shown, the majority of scientific evidence gathered from laboratory and survey approaches to the study of media effects finds the media to have little *direct* influence on people, or only limited power under restricted circumstances. On the other hand, theorists such as Harold Innis, Charles Cooley, and Daniel Lerner, plus a host of others from the past and the present, make a convincing case that the coming of new media to a society makes a tremendous difference in the lives of people and in the social process.

We are caught, then, in a dilemma. A trustworthy method—science—says the media have few effects. Another trustworthy method —careful study by insightful historians and other analysts of the broader picture—say that they have sweeping effects. Is this a flat contradiction, or have these two approaches operated on different levels of abstraction? We feel the latter is the case. Most scientific work in laboratory or survey settings is conducted in the here and now; it looks for immediate signs that specific persons have been altered by specific messages. In reality, things probably do not work that way. Specific theories resulting from a scientific approach (individual differences, social relations, theories of response to violence, and the like) show many limitations on media power. Yet, here we are about to develop a theory that shows the media have a number of rather powerful effects on people. We are also saying that this theory can be obtained in part from the same specific theories that mainly pose limitations on effects.

To unravel this dilemma, we need first to return to some of the classical analyses formulated by sociologists observing the growth of urban-industrial society. These theoretical paradigms identify the changing organizational features of society that lead one logically to the assumption of broad patterns of media influence. These paradigms are a product of many classic analyses that range from Durkheim's structural complexity theories[1] through Tönnies's Gemeinschaft-Gesellschaft typology[2] to Marx's dialectical mechanisms for change.[3] While these various theories of societal evolution were formulated before the mass media were well developed, they nonetheless pointed to the fundamental reason why the mass media were to become essential to the operation of modern societies. This fundamental reason is captured in the postulate that *as informal relationships characteristic of more traditional nonindustrial societies come into decline, unfulfilled needs for information rise accordingly.* Extending this reasoning, it follows that people become dependent on mass media channels when informal channels bringing information to their immediate groups begin to be disrupted. We noted earlier that these informal channels become more difficult to maintain when a society shifts from mechanical to organic solidarity, from Gemeinschaft to Gesellschaft, or from communal to associate (bureaucratic) relationships. As a result of such shifts, social differentiation increases, societal structure becomes more complex, and people have less and less contact with the social system *as a whole*. In other words, without the media, people in modern societies could not be well informed about events beyond their own position in the structure. All these analyses of growing societal complexity lay the theoretical foundation for concluding that the mass media of modern societies play significant roles in people's lives.

In order to understand why the media do play certain roles and do not play others in the lives of individuals in a modern society, we need to construct a map of the major connections that exist in the society between the media and other social systems. In the same way that travelers driving into an unfamiliar city must first identify the primary freeways or arterials before they can develop a plan for getting to a particular street, we must first identify the pattern of interconnections between the media and other crucial social systems before we can understand the ways in which individuals and groups are connected to the media. The conceptual vehicle that we employ is *interdependence*.

THE INTERDEPENDENCE OF THE MEDIA AND OTHER SOCIAL SYSTEMS

How do modern governments communicate to their citizens, and how do corporations communicate to their potential customers? They cannot rely solely or even primarily on interpersonal communication to inform, activate, or persuade the millions of individuals and thousands of organizations and groups that they must somehow reach. Political, economic, and other large systems in modern societies thus come to depend upon the mass media for these communication links. In other words, the media control information and communication resources that political, economic, and other systems need in order to function effectively in modern complex societies.

But, as we know, the mass media are not all powerful. The media depend upon resources controlled by the political, economic, and other social systems, resources that the media need in order to function effectively. We can describe these relationships of mutual need between the media and other social systems with the concept of interdependence. Relationships between the media, on the one hand, and other large social systems, on the other, are interdependent because neither could attain its

THEORIES OF MASS COMMUNICATION

respective goals without being able to use the other's resources. Interdependence is the social glue binding the media to the other social systems of modern society.

We can illustrate such interdependence by briefly examining the relationships between the media and the political, economic, and other systems in American society. What, for example, are the goals of the economic or the political system that most clearly require the use of media resources, and what media goals most clearly require the use of the political and economic systems' resources?

Media and Economic Relations

The goals of the economic system that are contingent upon media information resources include (1) inculcation and reinforcement of free enterprise values; (2) establishing and maintaining linkages between the producer or seller and the consumer that inform the consumer about what products are available and that stimulate consumers to purchase those products; (3) controlling and winning internal conflicts, such as between management and unions, or conflicts that develop with external organizations, such as regulatory agencies. The well-being of the economic institution would be seriously threatened if, for some reason, the media attacked basic values that justify the free enterprise system. The economic system could not operate effectively if the media did not provide massive advertising links between producers, distributors, and consumers. The media in American society are also essential tools in economic conflict. Corporations need public support, and decision-maker cooperation can be activated by convincing people via media messages of the validity of the corporation's position in struggles with federal agencies, environmentalists, tax authorities, and so forth.

On the other hand, the goals of the media are contingent upon the resources of the economic system. Such goals include (1) profit from advertising revenue; (2) technological development to reduce costs and compete effectively by having the most advanced products; (3) expansion via access to banking and finance services; as well as access to international trade.

We can see that the media and the economic system depend upon each other's resources to attain rather basic goals of survival and prosperity. Such interdependence not only gives rise to stable relations that are essential to a smooth-running free enterprise consumer society but, as we shall see later in this chapter, these relations also shape the economic roles of the media for individuals in our society.

Media and Political System Relations

The goals of the political system that are contingent upon the resources of the media include (1) inculcation and reinforcement of political values and norms, such as freedom, equality, obedience to the law, and voting; (2) maintenance of order and social integration as, for example, by creating value consensus or generating processes of public opinion formation and resolution; (3) organization and mobilization of the citizenry to carry out essential activities, such as waging war or conducting an election; (4) controlling and winning conflicts that develop within political domains, such as "Watergate," or that develop between the political system and other social systems, such as between politics and religion with regard to the separation of church and state. The media goals of profit, technological development, and expansion are contingent on political system resources that include (1) judicial, executive, and legislative protection and facilitation, such as First Amendment guarantees, licensing, and anti-trust laws; (2) formal and informal information resources required to cover the news, as, for example, in access to press conferences and off-the-record comments; (3) revenue that comes from political advertising, tax writeoffs, or subsidies. The Fourth Estate (or people's watchdog on government) role of the media may create conflict between the media and various parts of the political system. These periodic conflicts do not alter the more basic fact that neither the media system nor the political system could survive and prosper without the fundamental cooperation of the other. This cooperation is based upon their interdependence.

Media and Other Social System Relations

The interdependencies between the media and the political and economic sectors of our society are central to our understanding of the role of the media in American society and in the lives of individual Americans. We should, however, briefly illustrate the media's interdependent relations with such other social systems as the family, religion, education, and the military. In general, these relations are more lopsided or asymmetric, because more of the goals of the family, religious, educational and military systems are contingent on the information resources of the media than the other way around. The goals of the family system, for example, that are contingent on media resources include (1) inculcation and reinforcement of such values as family security; (2) recreational and leisure; (3) coping with everyday problems of child rearing and marriage, as well as coping with financial and health crises. In contrast, only the media profit goal implicates family system resources; namely, the resource of family members to decide to be or not to be consumers of media products. Similarly, several goals of the religious system are, at least in part, contingent on media resources; inculcation and reinforcement of religious values, transmitting the religious message to the masses, and successfully competing with other religious or nonreligious philosophies. The media, however, depend only to some extent upon the religious system to attain profit from religious organizations' purchase of space or air time.

Like family and religious systems, the goals of the educational system that are contingent on media resources include value inculcation and reinforcement and waging successful conflicts or struggles for scarce resources. They also include the unique goal of knowledge transmission as, for example, in media public affairs and "educational" programming. Media goals contingent on the resources of the educational system are limited to such specific pragmatic concerns as access to expert information and being able to hire personnel trained in the educational system. Finally, the goals of the military system that are contingent on media resources include value inculcation and reinforcement; waging and winning conflicts; and specific organizational goals such as recruitment, mobilization, and intelligence. The goals of the media contingent on military system resources are limited to access to insider or expert information.

IMPLICATIONS FOR INDIVIDUALS

The web of interdependencies between the media and the social systems we have discussed is a critical background factor for understanding why social analysts regard the media as a central feature of modern society. This web of interdependencies is also a critical background factor for understanding why and how individuals use, and are thus likely to be affected by, the media. We can summarize this point with the proposition that the dependencies that individuals *can have* on the media are determined, in large part, by this web of interdependent relations between the media and other social systems. How, for example, can we account for the following observations: Individual Americans depend upon media resources to attain the individual goals of being an informed citizen; making voting decisions; learning about new developments in recreation; medicine, and fashions; relaxation and entertainment; coping with economic problems and making consumption decisions; and a multitude of other goals. Should we say that it has something to do with the personality of Americans in general or of some subgroup of Americans? The answer is clearly no. It is rather the media's interdependent relations with other social systems that determine the media's societal roles and therefore determine the ways in which Americans *can* use the media. Individuals cannot control or determine the kinds of media messages disseminated any more than they, as individuals, can control the kinds of messages that are not disseminated. As individuals, we encounter the media as an ongoing system that has established relations with other systems. These, in turn, largely determine what messages will and will not be disseminated. This is why we say that the media's interdependent relations with other social systems shape the nature and scope of how individuals can depend on the media.

Of course, as we learned in Chapter 9, what individuals actually do with the media, as opposed to the range of possible uses, is affected by their individual and social characterizations. Because of the peculiar media-political system relation in America, for example, all Americans could depend on the media for a variety of political information that would not be available in other societies (such as the USSR), where the media-political system relation is different. But some individual Americans are more interested than others in political affairs, and so this individual difference affects how much people actually take advantage of or develop dependencies upon the media for political information.

MEDIA SYSTEM DEPENDENCY AND MEDIA EFFECTS

As we have seen from our discussion of interdependence, it is not necessary to subscribe to either the more naive assumptions of mass society theories or unsophisticated accusations that there are media conspiracies to conclude that the media influence many important aspects of our lives. Rather, we assume that the ultimate basis of media influence lies in the nature of the interdependencies between the media and other social systems and how these interdependencies shape audience relationships with the media. Indeed, we propose that the nature of the tripartite audience-media-society relationship most directly determines many of the effects the media have on people and society.

The degree of audience members' dependence on media information is a key variable in understanding when and why media messages alter their beliefs, feelings, or behavior. We have suggested that audience dependency on media information is a ubiquitous condition in modern society. One finds it in settings ranging from specific goals, (e.g., finding the best buys at the supermarket) to more general or pervasive goals (e.g., obtaining information that will help maintain a sense of connectedness and familiarity with the social world outside one's neighborhood). We can classify the numerous ways in which audience members are dependent on the media system to satisfy their information goals into the need to understand one's social world, the need to act meaningfully and effectively in that world, the need for play, sheer expressive satisfaction, or for escape from daily problems and tensions. The greater the need, and consequently the stronger the dependency, in such matters, the greater the likelihood that the information supplied will alter various forms of audience cognitions, feelings, and behavior.

As societies develop more complex and intense interdependencies with the media, and as the quality of media technology improves, the media provide more and more unique information-delivery services for members of the audience. In the American society, for example, the media are presumed to provide several unique services. They operate as a Fourth Estate delivering information about the actions of government; they serve as the primary signaling system in case of emergencies; they constitute the principal source of the ordinary citizen's conceptions of national and world events; they provide enormous amounts of entertainment information for fantasy-escape.

Some of the media's information-delivery services are more essential than others for individual well-being. Providing national sports coverage to residents of small towns is probably a less central service than providing them with information about national economic or political decisions that strongly affect their lives. It can be hypothesized that the greater the number and centrality of the specific information-delivery services provided by a medium, the greater the audience dependency on that medium.

The second condition in which dependency is heightened occurs when a relatively high degree of change and conflict is present in a society. Forces operating to maintain the structural stability of a society always coexist with forces geared toward conflict and change. The relative distribution of forces for stability or for change varies over time and place. Societies undergoing modernization, for example, experience high levels of conflict leading to rapid change until societal adaptations are made that reduce conflict and promote structural stability. Social conflict and social change usually involve challenges to established institutions, beliefs, or practices. When such challenges are effective, established social arrangements become, to one degree or another, inadequate as frameworks within which members of a society can cope with the situation. People's dependence on media information resources is intensified during such periods. This is a joint consequence of the reduced adequacy of their established social arrangements and the media's capacity to acquire and transmit information that facilitates reconstruction of arrangements. We can hypothesize, therefore, that in societies with developed media systems, audience dependency on media information increases as the level of structural instability (societal conflict and change) increases.

These basic propositions of dependency theory can be summarized as follows: The potential for mass media messages to achieve a broad range of cognitive, affective, and behavioral effects will be increased when media systems provide many unique and central information-delivery services. That potential will be further increased when there is a high degree of structural instability in the society due to conflict and change. We need to add, however, the idea that altering audience cognitive, affective, and behavioral conditions can feed back in turn to alter both society and the media. This is what was meant by a tripartite relationship between media, audience, and society. The general relationships implied in these propositions are presented in diagrammatic form in Figure 6.

What kinds of effects are we alluding to? They are effects that are not easily detected in laboratory experiments or in before-after studies of people who have been exposed to specific messages. We are referring to the enlargement of people's belief systems that new media bring; to the formation of attitudes toward a constant flow of new topics; to subtle shifts of individual and collective sentiment that may not be seen in the actions of individuals; and to a number of other society-wide changes. We believe that these changes come about mainly because of the persistent, sometimes intense, audience dependencies on media system information resources.

Cognitive Effects

Cognitive effects are distinct from effects on overt behavior, but the two are clearly related. This section makes a reference to people's feelings of ambiguity, their attitudes, beliefs, and values.

Ambiguity   The creation and resolution of *ambiguity* serves as the first example of a cognitive alteration effect that is particularly likely to receive the attention of investigators working from a dependency model. Ambiguity is a problem of either insufficient or conflicting information.[4] Ambiguity can occur because people lack enough information to understand the meaning of an event or because they lack adequate information to determine which of several possible interpretations of an event is the correct one. Research evidence shows that when unexpected events occur, such as natural disasters or the assassination of a political leader, many people first become aware of them through mass media information channels.[5] When the initial information gathered and delivered by the media is

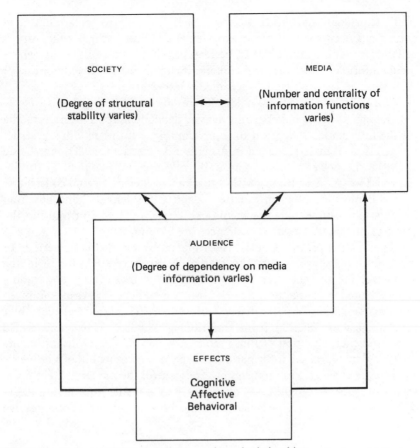

Figure 6. Society, media, and audience: reciprocal relationships.

incomplete, feelings of ambiguity are created whereby audience members know that an event has occurred, but do not know what it means or how to interpret it. More information will probably be sought in attempts to resolve such ambiguity. In many instances, the only source for that information is the mass media. The ambiguity resulting from incomplete or conflicting media reports will probably be resolved by more complete information subsequently delivered by media to their audiences. In such cases, the media's role in ambiguity creation and resolution is relatively easy to see.

What is perhaps harder to see, but what may have more sociopolitical significance, is the extent to which people are dependent on the media for continuous or ongoing ambiguity resolution. People living in times of rapid social change, in settings marked by relative instability or social conflict, or confronted with specific situations in which something unexpected has occurred will often experience ambiguity. Such ambiguity is usually stressful. Ambiguity can be resolved in a matter of seconds where media information delivery is adequate; it can persist for days, months, or even years in the absence of such media information.

Thus, *dependency* on the media for resolution of ambiguity is easy to understand. When people become heavily dependent upon the mass media for the information they need to resolve ambiguity, the defining or structuring effect of mass-mediated information is considerable. The media do not have the power to determine uniformly the exact content of the interpretations of "definitions of the situation" that every person constructs. But by controlling what information is and is not delivered and how that information is presented, the media can play a large role in limiting the range of interpretations that audiences are able to make.

Examination of the essential roles played by the media in periods of modernization suggests that the media clearly have such a role in the reconstruction of social reality.[6] Persons living in societies undergoing change from traditional to industrial forms experience pervasive ambiguity. This ambiguity is particularly acute during the period between their psychological unhitching from traditional customs, values, and world views and their adoption of more modern versions. The utility of having relatively standardized information packaged and transmitted via media by those agencies seeking to promote and control the modernization process has long been recognized. Control over such media information delivery is essential precisely because of the need to control how people resolve ambiguity.

Attitude Formation   Another cognitive effect that can be particularly common when audiences rely heavily upon media information resources to keep up with their changing world is *attitude formation*. During any year or decade in recent history, numerous instances of media-initiated attitude formation can be found. Publics have formed new attitudes about such events as speed limits, environmental problems, energy crises, specific wars, religious cults, and political corruption. New attitudes are continually being formed as various persons gain the public eye. Modern society presents a constant parade of new political figures, religious leaders, sports personalities, scientists, and artists. There is also a seemingly endless variety of social movements toward which orientations must be worked out. Even physical objects become the focus of attitude formation. These can include new household gadgets, clothing, birth-control devices, car safety mechanisms, and innovations in communication technology. The media push a never-ending flow of such events, issues, objects, and persons into public attention. People work out their feelings toward them as they confront this flow.

The media are not monolithic in their influence on such attitudes. The selectivity processes emphasized in earlier perspectives undoubtedly play a role in the attitude formation process. Likewise, local community opinion leaders selectively channel people's attention to events and influence the content or intensity of the attitude formed. Nevertheless, these psychological and social processes probably play more of a role in determining the *specific* content and intensity of the attitudes formed than they do in determining which events, people, or objects are likely to become candidates for attitude formation.

Agenda-Setting Another cognitive effect centers around the media's role in *agenda-setting*. Neither individuals nor their opinion leaders control the selection activities of the media that sort among potential topics for presentation or among available sets of information about those topics. Moreover, even though the media deliver information on a broad range of topics, people have neither the time nor the energy to form attitudes and beliefs about everything. They must select some more limited set of topics and issues about which to concern themselves. It is out of this set of necessities that the effect of agenda-setting takes place.[7] We need to understand two major features of this process. First, why is there a considerable similarity in the agenda of concern regarding certain topics among members of the media audience? Second, in spite of such instances of similarity, why do members of the public who attend to the media show numerous differences in their agendas of concern regarding media-presented topics?

This seeming dilemma between tendencies toward both uniformity and differences in personal agendas can be resolved quite simply. Not all persons respond uniformly to media-presented information on a given topic; this has been understood by social scientists since the early formation of the individual differences perspective. People select material from the media in somewhat predictable ways that are related to their personality characteristics, problems, and needs. This does not mean that media audiences show no uniformities, however. We noted earlier that the social categories perspective permitted predictions to be made about differences in media habits because a given set of people were located at a similar point in the social structure (e.g., older, white, farmers in the Midwest vs. younger, black, industrial workers in urban areas).

From the individual differences and social categories perspectives come hypotheses concerning the agenda-setting effects of the media. To be certain, specific individuals will set their personal agendas in relation to their unique background of prior socialization, experience, and personality structure. However, the society produces broad strata of people with sufficient uniformity of social circumstances that they share many problems and concerns in greater or lesser degree in spite of individual differences. In our society, for example, many people are wage earners with limited monetary resources to obtain their mass-produced necessities. In this sense they are *alike* regardless of their personality differences; they share a concern over such matters as rising prices, taxes, unemployment, and other economic matters that can quickly alter their standard of living. These override their individual differences. Thus, when the media present information of importance on economic matters, these topics can be expected to be placed high on their agendas of concern.

Where individual differences play an important role in agenda-setting is with respect to topics that are less tied to such social locations. Animal lovers of any social category will be likely to attend to and respond strongly to media-delivered stories of mistreatment of animals. People of all walks of life who enjoy fishing are likely to include in their agendas new policies of the Fish and Game Department.

Agenda-setting, in other words, is an interactional process. Topics are sorted by the media for presentation to the public. Information about those topics is selectively assembled and selectively disseminated. The public then sorts out their interest and concern with this information as a function of both their individual differences in personal makeup and their location in societal strata and categories. Out of this system of variables and factors emerges a list of topics to which varying numbers of people give differential assignments of importance. That list is the agenda of the media audience as a whole.

Enlargement   Still another cognitive effect that occurs in a media-dependent society is the expansion of people's systems of *beliefs*. As we pointed out in Chapter 1, Charles H. Cooley long ago used the term "enlargement" to refer to the idea that people's knowledge and belief systems expand because they learn about other people, places, and things from the mass media.[8] This idea can be more specifically explained by examining what Altman and Taylor call the "breadth" dimension of belief structure.[9] Beliefs are organized into categories. These categories, pertaining to religion, family, politics, and so forth, reflect the major areas of a person's social activity. The breadth dimension refers to the number of categories in a belief system and how many beliefs are found in each category. Belief systems can be broadened (enlarged) by either increasing the number of categories or the number of beliefs in a given category. For example, the vast amount of new information about ecological matters disseminated by the media in recent years has surely fostered the enlargement of people's beliefs about everything from automobiles to Baggies, from babies to compacters, and so on. These can be incorporated into existing opinions, attitudes, and values concerning free enterprise, recreation, work, religion, and the family. By their constant surveillance and presentation of aspects of the changing social and physical world we live in, the media broaden their audiences' belief categories and enlarge their belief systems.

Values The final cognitive effect that needs consideration is the media's impact on *values*. Values may be defined as very basic beliefs that people hold about either "desirable end states of existence" (e.g., salvation, equality, freedom) or "preferred modes of conduct" (e.g., honest, forgiving, capable).[10] Only under rare conditions would we expect mass media information to be able singlehandedly to alter such basic beliefs.[11] Mass-mediated information can, however, play an important part in creating the conditions for *value clarification*. One way that the media facilitate value clarification is by presenting information that precipitates *value conflict* within audience members. For example, the recent civil rights and ecology movements not only received broad media coverage but also involved fundamental value conflicts. Civil rights movements posed a conflict between individual freedom (e.g., property rights) and equality (e.g., human rights). Ecology movements bring economic values into conflict with aesthetic and survival values.

Most people did not, however, have the interest, inclination, or information necessary to see these issues as value conflicts. Mass-mediated information, in the form of reports of statements made by movement leaders or in the form of interpretations of the movement's motives and actions, usually includes identification of the underlying value conflicts. Once the value conflicts inherent in such movements are posed and clarified by the media, audience members are moved to articulate their own value positions.[12] This articulation can be painful because it can force a choice between mutually incompatible goals and the means for obtaining them. For action to take place, however, choices must be made. In the process of trying to decide which is more important in a particular case, general value priorities become clarified. Thus, the media indirectly have had a cognitive impact on members of their audiences.

Affective Effects

Affective processes are those we generally refer to in terms of various categories of feelings and emotions. Human beings like and dislike; they fear, hate, love, and are amused by various features of their environment. In a society that has developed a considerable dependency on its media for information, affective change in people can be anticipated when the media deliver such information. The impact of media messages on an audience's feelings and emotional responses is one of the least explored kinds of effects. Nevertheless, a limited body of writing on the matter makes some suggestions.

Desensitization   It has been hypothesized that prolonged exposure to violent media content has a "numbing" or *desensitization* effect.[13] Such effects may promote insensitivity or the lack of a desire to help others when violent encounters are witnessed in real life. Along a similar line, Hyman has pointed out that social scientists have not paid attention to the effects of violent media content on audience *sentiments*.[14] There is some evidence to suggest that the level of physiological arousal caused by exposure to audiovisual portrayals of violence does decline over time. But such evidence is no substitute for the kind of direct research on emotional responses that Hyman is calling for.

Fear and Anxiety   Fear, anxiety, and trigger-happiness are illustrations of affective effects that could be researched. For example, prolonged exposure to news messages or even TV dramas that portray cities as violence-ridden jungles may increase people's fear or anxiety about living in or even traveling to the city.[15] In a state of anticipation of the worst, city residents or visitors may be emotionally triggered to respond violently to others' actions. These effects may be particularly likely for residents of nonmetropolitan areas who depend largely on the media for information about what's going on in the cities, and who have little firsthand experience with city life.

Actually, almost all media effects could be examined in terms of their affective dimension. For example, the affective element of attitude formation can have serious social consequences. In periods of intense social conflict the police may form a number of attitudes from media characterizations about groups with which they have to deal. If media-derived attitudes contain affective elements such as *anger, hostility,* and *frustration,* it may retard the ability of the police to keep their cool when the encounter actually comes. Exactly this pattern developed in 1968 in Chicago during the disruptions of the Democratic National Convention.

Morale and Alienation   Morale and alienation serve as the final examples of the kinds of alterations in audience affect that can result from media messages. Klapp has proposed that in societies in which the mass media play central communication roles, the nature of media information has substantial effects on people's morale and level of alienation.[16] The reason why can be found in the pioneering writings of Emile Durkheim.[17] The sense of collective well-being and "we feeling" that promotes morale and combats alienation is a fragile product of successful social relations that cannot be developed or maintained without effective communication systems. A key element in that effective communication is the presence of regular and positive information about the groups and categories to which people belong, such as their society, community, profession, or ethnic group. People who rely on mass media systems as a primary source of information about their groups and categories can thus experience changes in morale and level of alienation when there are notable changes in the quantity or quality of the information delivered by the media about those collectives. According to this line of reasoning, any number of groups including women, blacks, Native Americans, or even Americans generally would be expected to undergo increased or decreased morale and changes in level of alienation as the nature of media messages about them underwent change.

Behavioral Effects

Overt action is, of course, the kind of effect that interests most people. Changes in attitude, belief, and affective states are interesting as well, but it is the degree to which they influence overt action that makes them important. Of the numerous effects of media messages on behavior that could be considered, we have chosen to discuss *activation* and *deactivation*.[18]

Activation   Activation refers to instances in which audience members do something that they would not otherwise have done as a consequence of receiving media messages. As already suggested, activation may be the end product of elaborate cognitive or affective effects. For example, people may engage in *issue formation* or *issue resolution* as a consequence of attitudes they have formed and feelings they have developed. Take as an illustration, people whose primary contact with the contemporary women's movement is via the media. They may initially react to movement leaders' allegations of "sexism" with ambiguity, perhaps not even knowing what the term means. The problem of resolving ambiguity and the stress that accompanies it gain a high place on their cognitive agenda. Resolution of ambiguity leads to the formation of new attitudes and feelings about sexual equality and the women's movement. The culmination of this chain of effects is a felt need to act. Once established, the need to act is transformed into overt action by public expression of these new attitudes and feelings, thereby participating in issue formation. Subsequent media information, such as an announcement of a protest in support of a proposal made by a women's group, may further activate people to join the protest, while others may be activated to organize a counterprotest. These overt actions become part of the issue resolution process.

So much attention has been given to the undesirable behavioral consequences of television content that it might be well to mention briefly one socially desirable behavioral effect. Stein and Friedrich's research suggests that TV viewers may be activated to engage in both prosocial and antisocial behavior.[19] Subjects in their research who viewed a popular children's show ("Mr. Rogers") increased their level of cooperative activity over several weeks of exposure. Those subjects exposed to violent content, on the other hand, increased their level of aggressive activity. Thus the research showed that both *cooperation* and *aggression* may be activated, depending on the nature of the television message received.

Research conducted in the 1940s suggests that media messages may activate altruistic economic behavior. Merton examined how a radio marathon featuring a well-known singer of that era (Kate Smith) activated large numbers of people to buy war bonds.[20] Processes by which media messages are used to activate charitable contributions were examined in Chapter 11.

Deactivation In many instances, such as voting and consumption, deactivation, or what people would have otherwise done but which they *don't* do as a consequence of media messages, can be as important as what they are activated to do. Yet deactivation effects have not received as much research attention. *Not* voting and *not* consuming provide two examples of deactivation effects that could be examined. As shown in our discussion of interdependency, most people are heavily dependent on the media for information about state and national political contests and about the state of the economy. Political campaigns have not only become longer but have also depended more and more on the media to communicate to voters. Such campaigns may not change many established attitudes toward the contestants. They might, however, elicit affective responses, such as overwhelming boredom, disgust, or the cognitive assessment that it makes no difference who wins. These inner states can culminate in nonvoting or the deactivtion of people's intention to vote.

In like manner, when media messages help to create an affective state of fear about one's own and the nation's economic future or the belief that a depression is unavoidable, people may *not* buy stocks, new cars, certain foods, or a multitude of other products that they would have otherwise bought. This would actually have the effect of deepening a recession by too much deactivation of consumption behavior.

THE INTEGRATED MODEL OF MEDIA EFFECTS

Having outlined the assumptions of the dependency theory of media-audience relations and some of the alteration effects it aids in understanding, we are now ready to address the problem of bringing this theory together with the previously discussed perspectives on factors that inhibit media influence.

The basic elements of an integrated theory of mass media effects are presented in Figure 7. This diagram presents an almost overwhelmingly complex set of factors and variables. Yet it is within such a complex system that mass communication effects are generated. We can summarize the relationships symbolized in the diagram in the following terms:

A flow of events emerges from a society in which social systems have ongoing, interdependent relations with the media. Every society has its established material and symbolic culture. The dynamic processes of culture include forces toward stability, such as consensus, control, and adaptation, as well as forces for conflict and change. The structure of a society includes informal and formal aggregates and groups, as well as hierarchically organized social positions.

The established interdependencies of social systems and the media, as well as the culture and social structure of a society, set important limitations and boundaries on the media system and have considerable impact on its characteristics, information-delivery services, and operating procedures. The societal system as a whole also has an enormous impact on persons; it gives rise to influences on persons that inhibit arbitrary media power, such as individual differences, membership in social categories, and participation in social relations. The societal system also operates to create needs within persons; namely, the needs to understand, act in, and play in one's world. Finally, the interdependencies of the society's social systems and its media shape how people can and do develop dependencies on the media to satisfy these needs, thereby setting the media effects process into motion.

Media systems cover the flow of events emanating from the society and from persons acting within that society. Operating procedures arise from the characteristics of the media system itself. These characteristics include its goals, resources, organization, and interdependent relations with other social systems. These in turn determine the number and the centrality of

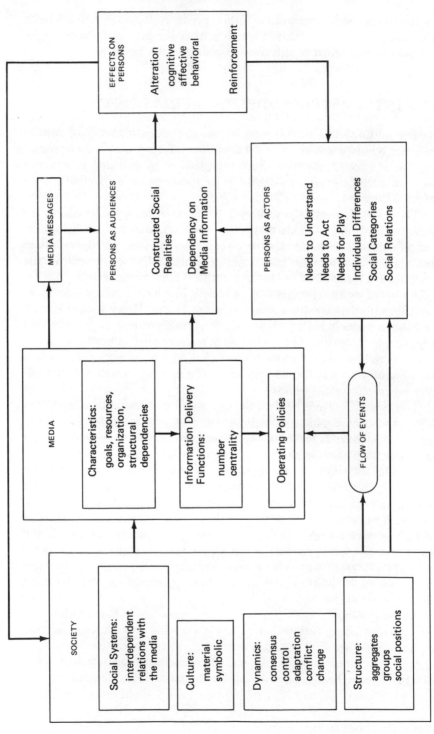

Figure 7. Mass media effects on individuals: an integrated model.

its information-delivery services. The major product of media activity with regard to the flow of events is the delivery of selected information pertaining to a limited range of topics. This constitutes media messages about the flow of events and the information available to the audience.

The key to this integrated framework is that persons as members of media audiences encounter media messages with both constructed social realities and numerous dependencies on media information resources. The social realities people hold are the product of the processes by which the society enculturates and socializes persons and structures their social action. The dependencies people have on media information are products of the nature of the interdependencies of the media and other social systems, which determine the number and centrality of the unique information functions that the media system serves for individuals and for society, as well as by the individual's needs, which are shaped by the societal culture, societal dynamics, and the individual's location in the social structure.

When media messages are not linked to audience dependencies, and when people's social realities are entirely adequate before and during message reception, media messages will have little or no alteration effects. They may reinforce existing beliefs or behavioral forms. In contrast, when people do not have social realities that provide adequate frameworks for understanding, acting, or escaping, and when audiences are dependent in these ways on media information received, such messages will have a number of alteration effects. Media messages, in this instance, may be expected to alter audience behavior in terms of cognitive, affective, and/or overt activity. Thus, both the relative adequacy of the audience's social realities and the relative degree of audience dependency on media information resources must be taken into account to explain and predict the effects of media messages.

Finally, the effects of media messages flow back to influence people's needs or psychological and social characteristics. In some cases, they flow back to alter the nature of the society itself. Behavioral alteration effects, for example, in some rare instance may take the form of massive protest that not only gets people involved in producing a new series of events to be covered by the media but may also increase the level of societal conflict or create new social groups. This series of events, in turn, can force changes in the nature of the relationships between social systems and the media system, such as the passing of new laws designed to change the media's operating policies.

CONCLUSION

The rather complex model presented in Figure 7, then, allows for a continuous process of interaction among the society, the media system, and the people who compose media audiences. It is also a feedback model in the sense that the effects of media messages on the audience about ongoing events may themselves set into motion another chain of events. Most important, this model avoids a seemingly untenable all-or-none position: The media have no significant impact on people and society, or the media have an unbounded capacity to manipulate people and society. It allows us to specify in a limited way when and why media messages will or will not have significant effects upon how audiences think, feel, and behave.

Other social scientists will undoubtedly wish to make additions to, revise, or even reject totally this integrated model of mass media effects. Nevertheless, we believe that it is a more theoretically sophisticated and sounder framework than has heretofore been available. There is little doubt that it is *very complicated*. For that we offer no apology! The process of mass communication is itself dreadfully complicated. Little wonder that numerous oversimplified approaches to describing it have failed to portray the effects it can have on people individually and collectively.

The present theory is obviously developed at a level of abstraction that would make a simple all-or-none test with empirical data impossible.[21] This is a characteristic of every integrated theory. One must go to the specific theories for empirical testing and not to the abstract integrations induced for them.

The overall implications are that the study of mass communication—one of our newest academic disciplines—has already advanced to a point where such an integration can be attempted. The present formulation may prove hopelessly premature. Yet, if this model acts only to provoke others to denounce it and to formulate a better theory, the result will be advances in mass media theory and research. Under such circumstances, we will be satisfied. When all is said and done, the common purpose of social science examinations of the media and their relationship to people, whether of yesterday, today, or tomorrow, is ultimately to understand mass communication's impact on how we think, feel, and behave.

NOTES

1. Emile Durkheim, *The Division of Labor in Society,* trans. George Simpson (New York: Free Press of Glencoe, 1964).
2. Ferdinand.Tönnies, *Community and Service,* trans. and ed. Charles Loomis (East Lansing, Mich.: State University Press, 1957).
3. Karl Marx, *Economic and Philosophic Manuscripts of 1844* (Moscow: Foreign Languages Publishing House, 1961).
4. S. J. Ball-Rokeach, "From Pervasive Ambiguity to a Definition of the Situation," *Sociometry* 36, no. 3 (September 1973): 378–89.

THEORIES OF MASS COMMUNICATION

5. See, for example, Paul B. Sheatsley and Jacob J. Feldman, "The Assassination of President Kennedy," in R. Evans, *Readings in Collective Behavior* (Chicago: Rand McNally, 1969), pp. 259–83.
6. Daniel Lerner, *The Passing of Traditional Society* (New York: Free Press, 1959).
7. For a discussion of the various ways in which the term agenda-setting has been used, see Jack McLeod, Lee Becker, and James Byrnes, "Another Look at the Agenda-Setting Function of the Press," *Communication Research* 1 (April 1974): 131–66.
8. Charles Cooley, *Social Organizations* (New York: Scribner's, 1909).
9. Irwin Altman and Dalmas A. Taylor, *Social Penetration* (New York: Holt, Rinehart & Winston, 1973), pp. 15–20.
10. Milton Rokeach, *The Nature of Human Values* (New York: Free Press, 1973).
11. See Sandra Ball-Rokeach, Milton Rokeach, and Joel Grube, *Influencing Political Beliefs and Behavior Through Television* (forthcoming), for an example of such rare conditions.
12. See Sandra Ball-Rokeach and Irving Tallman, "Social Movements as Moral Confrontations with Special Reference To Civil Rights," in *Understanding Human Values: Individual and Societal*, ed. M. Rokeach (New York: Free Press, 1979).
13. For example, see Frederich Wertham, *Seduction of the Innocent* (New York: Holt, Rinehart & Winston, 1954); and A. Rosenthal, *Thirty-eight Witnesses* (New York: McGraw-Hill, 1964).
14. Herbert Hyman, "Mass Communication and Socialization," *Public Opinion Quarterly* 37, no. 4 (Winter 1973): 524–40.
15. George Gerbner, Larry Gross, Michael Morgan, and Nancy Signorielli, "The Mainstreaming of America: Violence Profile No. 11," *Journal of Communication* 30 (Summer 1980): 10–29.
16. Orrin Klapp, *Currents of Unrest* (New York: Holt, Rinehart and Winston, 1972).
17. Durkheim, *Division of Labor in Society.*
18. For an earlier discussion of activation effects, see Otto N. Larsen, "Social Effects of Mass Communication," in *Handbook of Modern Sociology,* ed. Robert E. L. Faris (Chicago: Rand McNally, 1964), p. 348.
19. Aletha Stein and Lynette Friedrich, "Television Content and Young Children's Behavior," in *Television and Social Behavior* (Washington, D.C.: Government Printing Office, 1971), 2:202–317.
20. Robert Merton, *Mass Persuasion: The Social Psychology of a War Bond Drive* (New York: Harper, 1946).
21. See S. Ball-Rokeach, Rokeach, and Grube, *Influencing Political Beliefs and Behavior Through Television,* for the first direct empirical test of portions of this theory.

index

De Forrest, Lee, 78
De Landa, Diego, 5, 26n
Della Porta, Giovanni, 48, 66n, 70, 99n
Dennis, Everette, 26n
Dependency theory, 236–251
Dependent variables, 195
Dialectic process, 19
Diffusion pattern: of the mass press, 39–41, (illus.) 41; of motion pictures, 64, 65, (illus.) 64; of radio, 90, 91, (illus.) 91; of television, 95, (illus.) 98
Division of labor, 149, 153–155
Dodd, Stuart C., 43n
Drucker, Peter, 113n
Durkheim, Émile, 15, 153–156, 164n, 170, 181, 182n, 189, 235, 254n, 255n
Dysfunction, 17

Eagley, Alice, 229n
Eastman, George, 55, 56
Eder, Josef M., 66n
Edison, Thomas Alva, 56, 57
Effects of mass communication: activation, 249, 250; affective, 247, 248; agenda-setting, 245, 246; attitude formation, 244, 245; behavioral, 249–251; cognitive, 242–244; deactivation, 250, 251; desensitization, 248; enlargement, 246, 247; fear and anxiety, 248; general theory of, 232–254; integrated theory of, 232–254; morale and alienation, 248, 249; summary, theory of, 234; values, 247
El-Assal, Elaine, 230n
Ellis, Milton, 181n
Emery, Edwin, 26n, 42n
Engels, Frederick, 19, 26n
Evolutionary perspective: in development of broadcasting, 68; in development of mass media, 29; in development of motion pictures, 45; of society, 17–18
Eysenck, H.J., 27n

Federal Communications Act of 1934, 86
Federal Communications Commission (FCC), 86, 103

Feedback: and accuracy in communication, 133; defined, 133; in role-taking, 133
Feldman, Jacob J., 255n
Feshbach, Seymour, 201, 214n, 215n, 230n
Fessenden, Reginald, 77
Festinger, Leon, 27n, 230
Field, Cyrus W., 74
Fishbein, Martin, 220, 230n
Freedman, J., 197n
Freud, Sigmund, 27n
Friedrich, Lynette, 255n
Function: concept of, in study of social systems, 170; of society, 16
Functional alternatives: to the newspaper, 41
Functional analysis: of mass media, 172–173; of social systems, 170–172

Garrison, Garnet R., 99n
Gaudet, Hazel, 190, 197n, 213n
Gemeinschaft, 150–153
Gerbner, George, 200, 207, 208, 213n, 214n, 255n
Gernsheim, Alison, 66n
Gernsheim, Helmut, 66n
Gesellschaft, 150–153
Gestures: conversation of, 120–121; as symbols, 120; vocal, 120–121
Gillmor, D., 112n
Gilula, M.F., 27n
Goldmark, Peter, 110, 112n
Goldsmith, Alfred N., 99n
Goransen, Richard, 214n
Gordon, Raymond B., 231n
Graham, Hugh, 213n
Green, Russell, 214n
Greenberg, Bradley S., 181n
Griffith, Richard, 66n
Gross, Larry, 214n
Grube, Joel, 223, 255n
Gurr, Ted, 213n

Habermas, Jürgen, 26n
Habit: as aspect of learning, 185
Hartley, Ruth, 215n
Hauser, Philip, 181n
Hayakawa, S.I., 141n
Hegel, G.W., 19
Hempel, Carl G., 181n

Meaning: as configuration of traces,
127–128; connotative, 117–118;
denotative, 117; established, 135;
extended, 135; incongruence in, 233;
and labeling, 128–129; and language,
136–137; non-verbal, 130; as
response to gestures, 120–121;
stabilization, 135; substitution, 135
Mechanical solidarity, 153–155
Media: as social systems, 234;
technologies, 234; types of, 134
Media content: categories of, 173
Media systems, new: potential impact
of, 108–112; and social system,
236–239
Mediated dialogue, 111–112
Meltzer, Bernard N., 21, 27n
Menninger, K., 27n
Merton, Robert K., 15; structural
functionalism, 16; 26n, 224, 231n
Metasymbols: cultural beliefs as, 138;
defined, 131; as patterned meaning,
131
Miller, Gerald, 217, 229n, 230n
Minard, R.D., 231n
Morris, Charles W., 141n
Morse, Samuel F.B., 53, 74
Motivation: and personality
differences, 186
Murray, John P., 214n

Neurobiological approach, 27
Newcomb, Theodore M., 231n
New York Sun, The, 33–35
Nickelodeon, 59–60

O'Brien, Rita Cruise, 112n
Observational learning, 220
Obsolescence: of mass media, 41; of
motion pictures, 65–66; of radio, 92
Opinion leaders, 192–193
Opotowsky, Stan, 181n
Organic conception of society, 146;
analogy, 149–150
Organic solidarity, 153–155
Overspecialization, 147–148

Packard, Vance, 229n
Paradigm: definition of, 14;
evolutionary, 146; vs. mass
communication theory, 144–146

Parataxic mode, 128
Paris, John, 50
Parker, Edwin, 104, 109, 112n
Parsons, Talcott, 15
Pavlov, Ivan P., 27n
Pemberton, H. Earl, 43n
Penfield, Wilder, 141
Penny press, 8
Peptides, 127; peptide revolution, 127
Perception: defined, 129–130; as
shaped by language, 136; stages in,
130; principle of selective attention
and, 187
Personal influence: and two-step flow
of communication, 192–193
Personality differences: and individual
differences perspective, 186
Persuasion: basic models of, 217–229;
and individual differences, 221;
motivating factors in, 218–220;
psychodynamic model of, 218–220;
and social constructions of reality,
223–228; sociocultural model of,
223–229; underlying assumptions of,
217
Petty, R., 229n
Plateau, Joseph, 50, 51
Postulate(s): definition of, 14; and
Magic Bullet theory, 162–164; of
societal information needs, 235
Preecs, Bart, 113n
Premedia, 4
Private ownership, concept of, 78–79,
86
Propaganda, 159–162; and
Gemeinschaft, 159; and social
solidarity, 163; World War I, 163
Protataxic mode, 128
Psychological isolation, 155–156

Quigley, Martin, 66n

Rachlin, H., 27n
Radcliffe-Brown, A.R., 15, 26n
Radio Act of 1912, 83, 85–86
Radio Act of 1927, 86
Radiotelephone, 77
Reality principle, 216
Recall, selective: basis of, 126–127
Reinforcement, 191